Robert F. Kennedy and the 1968 Indiana Primary

Robert F. Kennedy

and the 1968 Indiana Primary

Ray E. Boomhower

Indiana University Press
Bloomington and Indianapolis

Portions of this book previously appeared in the spring 1997 and winter 1999 issues of the Indiana Historical Society publication *Traces of Indiana and Midwestern History.*

This book is a publication of

Indiana University Press
601 North Morton Street
Bloomington, IN 47404-3797 USA

http://iupress.indiana.edu

Telephone orders 800-842-6796
Fax orders 812-855-7931
Orders by e-mail iuporder@indiana.edu

The paper used in this publication meets the minimum requirements of American National Standard for Information Sciences—Permanence of Paper for Printed Library Materials, ANSI Z39.48-1984.

Manufactured in the United States of America

Library of Congress Cataloging-in-Publication Data

Boomhower, Ray E., date
    Robert F. Kennedy and the 1968 Indiana primary / Ray E. Boomhower.
        p. cm.
    Includes bibliographical references and index.
    ISBN-13: 978-0-253-35089-3 (cloth)
    1. Kennedy, Robert F., 1925–1968. 2. Kennedy, Robert F., 1925–1968—
Oratory. 3. Presidential candidates—United States—Biography. 4. Political
campaigns—Indiana—History—20th century. 5. Primaries—Indiana—History—
20th century. 6. Indiana—Politics and government—20th century. 7. United
States—Politics and government—1963–1969. 8. Speeches, addresses, etc., American.
9. Legislators—United States—Biography. 10. United States. Congress. Senate—
Biography. I. Title.
E840.8.K4B66 2008
973.922—dc22   2007031882

1 2 3 4 5 13 12 11 10 09 08

973.922
Boo

For the two most important women in my life: my wife, Megan, and my late mother, Joyce Holdren

Let's dedicate ourselves to what the Greeks wrote so many years ago: to tame the savageness of man and make gentle the life of this world.

Let us dedicate ourselves to that, and say a prayer for our country and for our people.

ROBERT F. KENNEDY, APRIL 4, 1968, INDIANAPOLIS

Contents

Acknowledgments

Memory, according to the Greek tragedian Aeschylus, is both the handmaid and the mother of the Muses. For writers of nonfiction, memories are a vital part of our work, leading sometimes to truth, but often down blind alleys. A memory can also inspire what we spend our time researching and writing about, as was the case with this book on Robert F. Kennedy's campaign in Indiana during the 1968 presidential primary season. Growing up in Mishawaka, Indiana, at this time, I remember our living room in my family's home on West Battell Street as being dominated by a large television–record player combo. My two brothers and I used the television every Saturday to faithfully watch a cartoon rabbit attempt to trick a cartoon hunter, while my mother used the turntable to listen to Johnny Cash records. Cash's mournful lament of "I fell into a burning ring of fire / I went down, down, down / And the flames went higher" remains a haunting memory from my youth.

On one Saturday in early June 1968, however, the television networks abandoned the usual mindless cartoons to broadcast the funeral of a U.S. senator from New York. I could not help but sit, transfixed at the age of nine, by this public display of grief for a man I had seen photographs of in our local newspaper, the *South Bend Tribune*. Death had been a stranger to my family up to that point, and the anguish displayed on the faces of the crowd that gathered to mourn Robert Kennedy at St. Patrick's Cathedral in New York was too much for my young mind. I vaguely knew the details of the senator's assassination: someone with a strange-sounding name had shot him just after Kennedy declared victory in some election in California. I could not believe that someone so young and vibrant could be snatched away like that in the blink of an eye. My mother, Joyce, walked into the room. I told her that I hoped someone—anyone—would kill the person responsible for this horror.

Perhaps my mother remembered the death of another young politician—President John F. Kennedy—and the subsequent shooting of the alleged assassin, Lee Harvey Oswald, by Dallas nightclub owner Jack Ruby. Perhaps she had watched on television as Ruby rushed up to Oswald as authorities were taking him from police headquarters to the nearby county jail on November 24, 1963. All I know for sure is that my mother reproached me for my remark, noting that Robert Kennedy had been known as a compassionate man who, because of the tragedy in his own family, abhorred such violence and had worked to heal, not harm.

My mother's words that day have stayed with me and may have been the impetus behind my research and writing about Kennedy's famous speech in Indianapolis following the killing of civil rights leader Martin Luther King Jr. Indulging me in this pursuit was J. Kent Calder, the original managing editor of the Indiana Historical Society's popular history magazine, *Traces of Indiana and Midwestern History*. The magazine's assistant editor, Megan McKee, proved so adept at turning my dross into gold I could not help but marry her. Over the past eighteen years, she has been a keen critic when needed, as well as a source of solace when the words would not come. I owe her everything.

Works of this sort could not be written without the dedication and support of archivists and librarians. I received helpful guidance from such dedicated professionals as Ruth E. Dorrel, archivist at Franklin College's B. F. Hamilton Library, and John Straw, director of the Archives and Special Collections Research Center at Ball State University's Bracken Library. This book would not have been possible without the generous support of a research grant from the John F. Kennedy Presidential Library in Boston, Massachusetts. Sharon Kelly at the library provided able assistance with both the grant process and my search of collections while I was in Boston.

At the Indiana Historical Society's William Henry Smith Memorial Library, Susan Sutton did her usual fine job of helping to find suitable photographs for the book. My thanks as well to David Turk for his photos of the memorial A *Landmark for Peace* in Indianapolis and to Susan Darnell for her able transcription of many of the interviews I conducted for the book.

Nick Cullather, Indiana University Associate Professor of History, and Marjorie Hershey, Indiana University Professor of Political Science, both provided helpful suggestions for improving the book. Former Indiana University Press editor Lee Ann Sandweiss shepherded my proposal for the Kennedy book through the press's editorial review process, and Linda Oblack provided helpful guidance the rest of the way.

Robert F. Kennedy and the 1968 Indiana Primary

1 2 3 4 5 6 7

A Landmark for Peace

The Indianapolis parks and recreation department is responsible for adminis-
tering approximately two hundred properties stretching over more than eleven
thousand acres in the central Indiana city. One of these properties, the Dr.
Martin Luther King Jr. Park at 1702 North Broadway Street on the city's near
north side, has within its fourteen acres the usual recreational components for
an urban park—a basketball court, playground, softball field, picnic shelters,
and an outdoor pool. As Center Township residents while away the hours at
play, their eyes are no doubt sometimes drawn to one of the park's most in-
triguing features, a sculpture titled *A Landmark for Peace* created by Indiana
artist Greg Perry and placed in the park in 1995.[1]

The memorial, which is located at the park's south end and includes in its
construction guns melted down in a gun-amnesty program, features two
curved panels facing one another. Near the top of each panel is a figure of a
man with an arm and hand outstretched toward, but failing to touch, the

other. The men depicted in the sculpture—neither of whom is alive to help bridge the racial gap that still exists today—are the slain civil rights leader Martin Luther King Jr. and the former junior U.S. senator from the state of New York Robert F. Kennedy. By chance and the vagaries of a political campaign, the two are forever bound together in the park, and in Indiana and American history as well.

The predominantly African American crowd that gathered at Seventeenth and Broadway streets for an outdoor rally on a cold and windy evening on April 4, 1968, appeared to be in a festive mood. And why not? Those milling about the Broadway Christian Center's outdoor basketball court—an audience estimated at anywhere between one thousand and three thousand people—would be among the first in the Hoosier State to hear from Robert Kennedy, who had announced his run for the Democratic Party's presidential nomination on March 16. With his late entry into the race, Kennedy had decided to take his case directly to the people. "Our strategy is to change the rules of nominating a president," noted Adam Walinsky, Kennedy's chief speechwriter. "We're going to do it a new way. In the streets."[2]

Kennedy had selected Indiana as his first test before Democratic voters. In the state's May 7 primary he would face two challengers, Indiana governor Roger D. Branigin, running as a favorite son, and U.S. senator Eugene McCarthy, whose strong showing in the New Hampshire primary against incumbent president Lyndon B. Johnson—along with Kennedy's entrance into the race—had helped convince Johnson to abandon his reelection effort. At the end of a March 31 speech to the nation, in which he announced a halt to the bombing of North Vietnam, Johnson had stunned everyone by stating: "I shall not seek, and I will not accept, the nomination of my party for another term as your President."[3]

Those who waited for long hours huddled against the cold to hear Kennedy speak would long remember what they heard. As volunteers registered voters at nearby tables, a band played, and spectators waved banners and signs touting Kennedy's candidacy, two sixteen-year-old North Central High School students, Mary Evans and Altha Cravey, milled about with the rest of the audience, who were, as one participant described it, "packed in like sardines."[4] Like many young people during that political season, Evans and Cravey had become transfixed by the antiwar candidacy of McCarthy, the Minnesota senator who had decided to take on Johnson to protest America's involvement in Vietnam. Inspired by their growing disgust with the war and McCarthy's commitment to ending the conflict, the local students had volunteered to work for the senator's campaign in Indiana. Despite their allegiance to McCarthy, both, because of their keen interest in politics and public policy, wanted to hear what Kennedy had to say. Neither had heard the news that Dr. King had been killed.

There were some in the throng, however, who had grown tired of the choices offered by America's two political parties and were looking for more radical change. A number of black activists had learned of King's death and were gathering support in the African American community for violent action. William Crawford, at this writing an Indiana state representative from Indianapolis, was then a member of a Black Power organization known as the Radical Action Program. He and his friends were, he recalled in 1994, very close to resorting to violence as a way to register their grief and rage at the loss of the civil rights leader. One estimate had close to two hundred militants sprinkled throughout the crowd. Those responsible for local arrangements for the speech, including respected Black Power leader Charles "Snooky" Hendricks, grew so fearful that Kennedy's life might be in danger that they recruited people to check the area for possible assassins. "There was a lot of anger and frustration that Dr. King, whose message was one of nonviolence and working within the system, was the victim of that kind of racism," Crawford remembered.[5]

The potential for a disturbance also had some Indianapolis power brokers worried. Michael Riley, an Indianapolis attorney and chairman of the Indiana Committee to Elect Robert Kennedy, had received a phone call from Mayor Richard Lugar urging that the rally be canceled for fear that a riot would break out when the crowd learned King had been murdered. City officials had even told Riley they would place fire hoses across the streets leading to the rally site to stop people from attending. Winston Churchill, the city's chief of police, warned the Kennedy campaign staff that he could not guarantee the senator's safety if he decided to go ahead with his speech.[6]

Before traveling to Indianapolis, Kennedy had made two other campaign stops that day, one at the University of Notre Dame in South Bend and the other at Ball State University in Muncie. During a question-and-answer session following the Ball State speech, a young black man had asked the candidate whether he could justify his belief in the good faith of white people toward minorities. Kennedy answered that the majority of people in the country wanted to do "the decent and the right thing."[7] As Kennedy boarded the plane for Indianapolis to formally open his campaign headquarters on East Washington Street and to make an appearance at the outdoor rally in the heart of the city's African American community, Marshall Hanley, one of his key supporters in east-central Indiana's Delaware County, informed him that Dr. King had been gunned down on the balcony of the Lorraine Motel in Memphis, Tennessee. King had traveled to Memphis to support the city's striking black sanitation workers and their attempts to organize a union. After he arrived at Indianapolis's Weir Cook Airport, Kennedy learned that the Nobel Prize–winning activist had died. Thinking back to the answer he had given in Muncie, a distraught Kennedy told a *Newsweek* reporter that it grieved him that he had just attempted to placate the young man only to have him learn later that a white man had shot his race's "spiritual leader."[8]

Kennedy decided to cancel his stop at his campaign headquarters, but to proceed on to Seventeenth and Broadway as planned. He did, however, send his pregnant wife, Ethel, on ahead to the Marott Hotel on North Meridian Street. After making a brief statement on King's death to the press assembled at the airport, Kennedy climbed into a car that would take him to the rally, jotting down some notes on what he might say on the back of an envelope. John Bartlow Martin, an Indianapolis native and close adviser to Kennedy during the Indiana primary campaign, had also returned from dinner to the Marott, where he and Kennedy speechwriter Jeff Greenfield were to work on potential statements on the tragedy for Kennedy to deliver to the press after the rally. Outside the hotel Martin saw a local police inspector parked at the curb. He went up to the car and asked the officer if the candidate should go ahead and address the crowd. "He said, with a fervor I imagine was rare in him, 'I sure hope he does. If he doesn't, there'll be hell to pay,'" Martin remembered.[9]

Arriving at the rally, Kennedy, wearing a black overcoat that had once belonged to his brother John, climbed onto a flatbed truck located in a paved parking lot near the Broadway Christian Center's basketball court. After asking those waving signs and banners to put them down, he announced that King had been killed. The audience, which had been anticipating a raucous political event and for the most part had been unaware of the shooting, responded to the announcement with gasps, shrieks, and cries of "No, no." Tom Keating, a police reporter for the *Indianapolis Star*, had raced to the scene with two policemen. He noted that the crowd reacted to the news almost like "a wounded animal."[10]

Facing the stunned and incredulous audience, some of whom were weeping, Kennedy gave an impassioned, extemporaneous, approximately six-minute speech that has gone down in history as one of the great addresses in the modern era. A New York journalist close to Kennedy observed that the candidate "gave a talk that all his skilled speech writers working together could not have surpassed."[11] John Lewis, a seasoned veteran of the civil rights movement who had helped organize the rally, recalled that when Kennedy spoke the crowd hung on his every word. "It didn't matter that he was white or rich or a Kennedy," said Lewis. "At this moment he was just a human being, just like all of us, and he spoke that way."[12]

To help explain the terrible tragedy, Kennedy recalled the words of Aeschylus, the Greek tragedian whose words from *Agamemnon* had comforted him following the assassination of his brother President John F. Kennedy. Aeschylus, he said, "once wrote: 'Even in our sleep, pain which cannot forget falls drop by drop upon the heart, until, in our own despair, against our will, comes wisdom through the awful grace of God.'" He went on to attempt to calm the crowd's growing anger about King's killing with these words:

"What we need in the United States is not division; what we need in the United States is not hatred; what we need in the United States is not violence or lawlessness; but love and wisdom, and compassion toward one another, and a feeling of justice toward those who still suffer within our country, whether they be white or they be black. . . .

"We can do well in this country. We will have difficult times; we've had difficult times in the past; we will have difficult times in the future. It is not the end of violence; it is not the end of lawlessness; it is not the end of disorder. . . .

"But the vast majority of white people and the vast majority of black people in this country want to live together, want to improve the quality of our life, and want justice for all human beings who abide in our land.

"Let us dedicate ourselves to what the Greeks wrote so many years ago: to tame the savageness of man and to make gentle the life of this world.

"Let us dedicate ourselves to that, and say a prayer for our country and for our people."[13]

Later, when Kennedy campaign aide Fred Dutton returned to the Marott Hotel, he told Martin and Greenfield what Kennedy had said to the crowd. Martin and Greenfield threw the statements they had so carefully composed into the wastebasket. "What he had said was so much better than anything we had written," Martin remembered.[14]

The news of King's violent death at the hands of a white gunman, James Earl Ray, sparked outrage and violence across the country. Black activist Stokely Carmichael told a crowd in New York: "Go home and get a gun! When the white man comes he is coming to kill you. I don't want any black blood in the street. Go home and get you a gun and then come back because I got me a gun."[15] Riots broke out in a number of cities, including the nation's capital, Washington, D.C. Regular army troops were called into action by President Johnson to bring the situation under control. But in Indianapolis the crowd at Seventeenth and Broadway had taken Kennedy's words to heart: they quietly left the rally and returned home. "We walked away in pain but not with a sense of revenge," said Crawford.[16] There were no riots in the Circle City.

Kennedy's remarkable speech marked the beginning of a whirlwind time in Indiana. "It was perhaps the most exciting month of politics ever in this city and state," noted Keating, who later became a columnist for the *Star*.[17] For most of April and early May, the eyes of the nation turned to the Hoosier State. Reporters and television correspondents from around the country flocked to Indiana to report on what Kennedy and his staff hoped would be the first in a series of primary victories in the senator's effort to capture the 1,312 delegates needed to win the Democratic presidential nomination. Kennedy hoped that Indiana would provide the same validation for his presidential ambitions that West Virginia had for his brother when it accorded him the primary victory over Hubert Humphrey in 1960, undermining the assumption that no Roman Catholic could attract the support of Protestant voters. "Indiana is the ball-game," Kennedy told Martin. "This is my West Virginia." In his campaign literature and at rallies before Hoosier voters, Kennedy emphasized that Indiana had the opportunity to once again play a vital role in the country's presidential contest. "Indiana can help choose a president," Kennedy repeated again and again in his speeches.[18]

Kennedy wanted to gain enough of a mandate in Indiana to knock McCarthy out of the race for good. Because he could not pick up enough delegates from primary states to win the nomination, Kennedy also needed to have enough strong showings to impress the heads of city and state Democratic organizations, such as Chicago mayor Richard Daley, who controlled the majority of delegates at the convention through caucuses and state conventions. Kennedy sought to prove to these party stalwarts that he could attract the support not just of African Americans and college students, but of working-class white voters who were worried about violence in their communities and fearful of the gains made by African Americans in civil rights. This was the "white backlash" vote George Wallace, the segregationist governor of Alabama, had depended on when he captured approximately 30 percent of the Democratic vote in the 1964 Indiana presidential primary. (Indiana governor Matthew E. Welsh, running as a stand-in for Johnson, won the primary with 376,023 votes to Wallace's 172,646.) Wallace had run particularly well in the northwest section of the state, in the steel towns of Hammond and Gary, and garnered a majority of the vote in both Lake and Porter counties.[19]

A number of Kennedy's advisers cautioned him against entering the Indiana primary. They saw the state as too conservative, and pointed to the strength of the Ku Klux Klan in the state during the 1920s, the fact that in 1960 John Kennedy had lost Indiana to Republican Richard Nixon by more than two hundred thousand votes, and Wallace's strong showing in parts of Indiana in the 1964 primary. His staff also worried that Kennedy's antiwar beliefs would clash with Hoosiers' political views, as they noted that Indianapolis was home to the national headquarters of the American Legion and the place where Robert Welch Jr. had founded the ultra-conservative John Birch Society on December 9, 1958, to fight Communist infiltration of the American government. Venturing into such foreign territory seemed to be a daunting task for both Kennedy's mainly East Coast staff and the media that reported on the campaign. Jules Witcover, who had covered the presidential campaigns in 1960 and 1964, recalled being put off because Indianapolis was home to two huge war memorials, the Indiana War Memorial and the Soldiers and Sailors Monument. He articulated the feelings of many national media figures about Indiana in 1968 when he commented: "Were a Martian to land his flying saucer in Monument Circle, he might well take one look, climb back in and beat a fast retreat."[20]

Pondering all the obstacles facing the Kennedy campaign in Indiana, John Bartlow Martin, the author of a well-regarded history of the state, believed Branigin might well win the primary, with Kennedy's best chance to come in second, ahead of McCarthy. The rest of the senator's campaign staff was also pessimistic about their candidate's chances. Echoing Martin's prediction, they attempted to lower expectations by telling anyone who would listen that they did not expect to win, but just hoped to run even with the governor. Kennedy's late start and the chaotic nature of the campaign might have prompted the staff's doubts. "The 'smooth-running, well oiled Kennedy machine' got to be an office joke very quickly," said Frank Mankiewicz, Kennedy's press assistant.[21] Kennedy himself had no illusions about what faced him in Indiana, and in other primaries to come in states such as Nebraska, Oregon, California, South Dakota, and New York. Warned by his advisers that entering the Indiana primary would be a gamble, he replied, "The whole campaign is a gamble."[22]

In addition to showcasing such national political figures as Kennedy and McCarthy, the Indiana presidential primary shone a spotlight on some fascinating Hoosier politicians, especially Governor Branigin, a Harvard-educated lawyer from Franklin, Indiana. An engaging, witty speaker with an encyclopedic knowledge of the state's history, Branigin had initially agreed to run as a stand-in for President Johnson in the primary. With Johnson's announcement that he would not seek or accept his party's nomination for president, a stunned Branigin nevertheless decided to remain in the race as a favorite-son candidate. He hoped to win some influence for Indiana's sixty-three delegates at the Democratic convention in Chicago, to be held in August 1968. Time and time again during the campaign he repeated that national issues were not at stake in Indiana. "What is at stake here," he told his supporters, "is who is going to represent the state of Indiana in Chicago."[23]

Branigin enjoyed several advantages over his opponents in the primary. With his tight control over patronage in the state, the governor could count on the expertise of Democratic Party regulars in each of Indiana's ninety-two counties. To fund his campaign, Branigin could draw upon the funds raised by several thousand patronage employees "voluntarily" kicking back to the party 2 percent of their salaries. Democratic officials throughout the state also feared that if Kennedy was nominated for president, his candidacy would hurt local candidates in the November election. With these factors in mind, Democratic Party chairmen in all but one of Indiana's counties threw their support to the governor.

In addition to the support of elected officials, Branigin enjoyed the unwavering editorial assistance of Eugene C. Pulliam, the powerful owner and publisher of the state's leading newspapers, the *Indianapolis Star* and the *Indianapolis News*, as well as newspapers in Muncie and Vincennes. Pulliam did all he could in his newspaper to aid Branigin and defeat Kennedy, whom the newspaper labeled a carpetbagger ready to buy the election with unlimited cash. The newspaper gave the governor's effort page-one coverage and even peddled him as a possible candidate for vice president. Referring to his time delivering copies of the *Star* as a young man, Branigin joked: "I used to carry Pulliam, and he has been carrying me ever since."[24] Negative coverage in the Indianapolis newspapers caused Kennedy to declare them "the worst newspapers in the country."[25]

The combination of an unwillingness to challenge an incumbent president and, later, Branigin's ability to wield patronage power, including the staffing of license branches throughout the state, was strong enough to keep even liberal officeholders such as Indiana's two U.S. senators, Vance Hartke (an early critic of the war in Vietnam) and Birch Bayh, from openly supporting Kennedy's efforts in the state. With the Indiana governor's stranglehold on the normal method of staffing a campaign, through party regulars (the backbone of any run for office), the Kennedy staff had to turn to a loose assemblage of young liberal Democrats who chafed at the conservatism of their elders Branigin and Gordon St. Angelo, the party's longtime state chairman. These low-level officeholders played a key role in finding the necessary signatures to secure a spot on Indiana's primary ballot for Kennedy, and later provided contacts for other like-minded individuals who also helped on the petition drive and then went on to volunteer their time to help him win the primary.

Of course, these political neophytes were not called upon to lead the charge in Indiana. For that, Kennedy early on called upon a person wise in the ways of the cutthroat world of Massachusetts politics, and a person who had skillfully aided his brother Ted's campaign for the Democratic nomination for the U.S. Senate in 1962—Gerard Doherty. A former member of the Massachusetts legislature and chairman of the state's Democratic Party, Doherty initially came to Indiana to gauge the likelihood of gaining enough signatures to place Kennedy's name on the primary ballot. "If RFK gets on the ballot," Doherty confidently stated in one memorandum, "we can beat Branigin."[26] Doherty then set about building a Kennedy organization in the state, bringing with him a host of seasoned political veterans from Massachusetts to head the Kennedy organization in each of Indiana's eleven congressional districts. The Kennedy campaign could also rely on the expertise of those who had worked in John Kennedy's 1960 presidential campaign—such famous figures as Pierre Salinger, Arthur Schlesinger, Theodore Sorenson, and Lawrence O'Brien—as well as staff from Kennedy's U.S. Senate office.

Both Kennedy and McCarthy turned to Hoosier literary figures for advice in the primary campaign. The two men, John Bartlow Martin, for the Kennedy camp, and Jeremy Larner, on McCarthy's staff, were both natives of Indianapolis. Martin, who had come of age during the Great Depression and had engaged in a love–hate relationship with his home state, made his living as a freelance writer for national magazines and had earned a reputation as one of the country's best true-crime reporters. He had been involved in every Democratic presidential campaign since 1952, serving as a speechwriter and editorial advance man, who informed candidates about the history and culture of the places they visited. Martin came to consider Kennedy's effort in Indiana "the climatic event" of his own life, and he played a vital role in advising Kennedy on the best way to reach Hoosier voters. Kennedy listened closely to Martin's advice, particularly when it came to emphasizing his experience in enforcing law and order as U.S. attorney general in his brother's administration.[27]

Before joining McCarthy's staff as a speechwriter, Larner had written short stories and achieved some acclaim for his 1962 novel *Drive, He Said*, which examined the relationship of college roommates, one a basketball star and the other a revolutionary. Although he spent most of his formative years in Indianapolis, where he won the city's high school tennis championship in 1954, Larner, like Martin, never seemed comfortable with his Indianapolis upbringing. The wariness may have dated from his first day in the city when an official from the American Legion made him stop playing on its grassy mall.[28] Larner, who joined the McCarthy campaign during the Wisconsin primary, had become disenchanted with his candidate by the time they reached Indiana. In *Nobody Knows*, the book he wrote on the McCarthy campaign, Larner noted McCarthy's "hidden iceberg qualities" and in one telling anecdote tells of a young campaign aide who, although approached by the Kennedy staff and asked to switch sides, stuck with the Minnesota senator. "I thought McCarthy had a secret," Larner quotes the aide as saying. "I thought one day the secret would explain it all."[29]

McCarthy and his campaign never seemed to hit their stride in Indiana. One key McCarthy staff member called his time in the state a "frustrating, painful experience, lacking the spontaneity of New Hampshire and the organization and enthusiasm of Wisconsin." Workers had to endure poor press coverage, ineffective cooperation with local supporters, and a pending strike by telephone installers that hampered the campaign's communication efforts. Those who canvassed the state seeking votes on McCarthy's behalf were usually met with blank stares and the question "McCarthy who?" The senator wasted much of his time attempting to draw crowds in smaller rural communities and hampered his own efforts by making last-minute decisions to alter or cancel his planned schedule.[30]

Focusing on appearances in small communities, McCarthy encountered small crowds and appeared uncomfortable connecting with Hoosiers. He seemed put off by what he called "a rather general defensiveness in Indiana against outsiders. In northern Indiana . . . people seemed worried about the prospect of being taken over by Chicago. In the south, they were threatened by Kentucky, in the west, by Illinois, in the east, by Ohio. It was as though in Indiana they have to think Indiana for fear that if they do not it will be absorbed by the outside world."[31] Erratic scheduling that made him late for some appearances and entirely miss the large crowds waiting for him in others did not help matters. Later, McCarthy summed up his unease while campaigning by noting that he kept hearing from people about a poet, and asked if they were referring to William Shakespeare or perhaps his friend Robert Lowell. "But it was James Whitcomb Riley," he said. "You could hardly expect to win under those circumstances."[32]

During the early days of his campaign Kennedy, too, had a difficult time getting his message through to Indiana voters. Martin had warned him that Hoosiers were "phlegmatic, skeptical, hard to move, with a 'show me' attitude."[33] Kennedy decided to break through voters' defensiveness by throwing himself into the campaign, barnstorming around the state in motorcades, making quiet stops at sites important to Indiana history in the southern portion of the state, and even resurrecting railroad whistle-stop campaigning on the Wabash Cannonball. "He always does better in person," campaign aide Fred Dutton said of the candidate. "Because Bob is so misunderstood, he has to show himself."[34] Kennedy did his best in hostile situations where he faced tough crowds skeptical about his policies, such as a famous confrontation with medical students at the Indiana University Medical Center. "He went yammering around Indiana about the poor whites of Appalachia and the starving Indians who committed suicide on the reservations and the jobless Negroes in the distant great cities," Martin remembered, "and half the Hoosiers didn't have any idea what he was talking about; but he plodded ahead stubbornly, making them listen, maybe even making some of them care, by the sheer power of his own caring. Indiana people are not generous nor sympathetic; they are hardhearted, not warm and generous; but he must have touched something in them, pushed a button somewhere. He alone did it." The candidate was also affected by his experiences with Hoosiers. John Douglas, the son of Paul Douglas, U.S. senator from Illinois, and a key Kennedy aide during the Indiana primary, marveled at Kennedy's ability to overcome numerous obstacles—hostile press coverage from Indianapolis newspapers, little support from local party leaders, and resentment from college students opposed to the Vietnam War about his late entry into the race—through the force of his own character. "By the end of that Indiana campaign he was an attractive, effective, articulate candidate, entirely capable of presidential leadership," said Douglas.[35]

The night before Indiana voters went to the polls, Kennedy, exhausted from a full day of campaigning that started in Evansville and ended with a nine-hour motorcade through a series of communities in northwest Indiana, stopped for an early-morning dinner at an Indianapolis restaurant with campaign aides and members of the media. Kennedy, his hands red and swollen after shaking thousands of hands, ruminated on his experiences and the next day's election, which might end his fledgling effort at the White House once and for all. In a mellow mood, according to *Village Voice* reporter Jack Newfield, the candidate expressed a fondness for the state and its people. "I like Indiana. The people here were fair to me," Kennedy said. "I gave it everything I had here, and if I lose, then, well, I'm just out of tune with the rest of the country."[36]

1 **2** 3 4 5 6 7

The Decision

Very early in the morning on Friday, March 22, 1968, Gerard Doherty, a Boston attorney, stepped off a plane that had just landed at Indianapolis's Weir Cook Municipal Airport. At the behest of Ted Kennedy, U.S. senator from Massachusetts, he had left Washington in a snowstorm to come to Indiana to investigate whether there might be enough support for Robert Kennedy to run in the state's May 7 Democratic primary. Five days earlier, Robert Kennedy had announced his intention to seek the Democratic presidential nomination. Doherty, the former chairman of the Massachusetts Democratic Party, was up against a tight deadline: just one week later all candidates for the Hoosier State primary had to submit to the secretary of state's office the signatures of 5,500 registered voters—500 signatures from each of Indiana's eleven congressional districts.

Before flying to Indianapolis, Doherty had stopped at the new Kennedy for President campaign headquarters in Washington, D.C., to be briefed on his assignment. Days earlier, after hearing that Robert Kennedy had decided to run for president, he had called Ted Kennedy's office to volunteer his services. "I had just returned to the law business and I was chasing after ambulances," Doherty recalled. "But, I said, I'm not going to . . . take apart paper clips and put them back together. Whatever you want me to do, I'll do, but it has to be meaningful." Doherty got his wish. He flew on to Indianapolis expecting to be "greeted by thousands of cheering people"—the multitudes needed to run a successful political campaign. When he arrived, however, he soon discovered he could initially only count on the assistance of three young Hoosier Democrats: Michael Riley, Louie Mahern, and William Schreiber.[1]

The paucity of help for Doherty early on in Indiana reflected the chaotic nature of Robert Kennedy's campaign. Time was short; Kennedy's staff had to prepare for six primaries in just three months. Kennedy had vacillated about taking on incumbent president Lyndon Johnson. "It's all so complicated," Kennedy lamented to Jack Newfield, a reporter for the *Village Voice*. "I don't know what to do." History was against the success of such an attempt. The last time a challenger had unseated a sitting president for his party's nomination had been in 1884, when James G. Blaine won the Republican nomination over President Chester A. Arthur.[2] As Kennedy wavered, two student activists, Allard Lowenstein and Curtis Gans, were desperately trying to find someone to take up the banner of their "Dump Johnson" movement and face off against the president. The prime candidate for their organization, the Conference of Concerned Democrats, was Kennedy, who had been an articulate critic of America's growing involvement in Vietnam. Urged on by some members of his Senate staff, Kennedy had been flirting with the possibility of opposing the president. "How can we possibly survive five more years of Lyndon Johnson?" Kennedy asked his adviser, the historian Arthur M. Schlesinger Jr. "Five more years of a crazy man?" Other advisers, however, warned him that if he ran for the presidency in 1968 he would be committing "political suicide." Even Kennedy's family was divided: his wife and his sisters urged him to tackle Johnson, but his brother Ted was opposed. A family friend asked Ted Kennedy during a dinner what John Kennedy might have done in the same situation. "He would have advised against it," Ted Kennedy responded. "But he would have done it himself."[3]

In September 1967 Lowenstein met with Robert Kennedy at Hickory Hill, his home in Virginia, to ask him to consider opposing Johnson. Kennedy listened sympathetically but turned down the offer. Although he called the president "a coward" and believed Johnson might quit if challenged by a fellow Democrat before the convention, Kennedy said he could not be the first to take him on. If he did, he said, everyone would believe he had split the party not out of concern for the numerous problems facing the country, but only because of his ambition for high office and his personal dislike for Johnson. The

two men had a long history of conflict; each despised the other. "You understand, of course," Lowenstein told Kennedy, "that there are those of us who
think the honor and direction of this country is at stake. We're going to do it
without you, and that's too bad, because you could have become president of
the United States." Lowenstein remembered storming from the room, but being caught and turned around by Kennedy. He said the senator told him:
"Well, I hope you understand I want to do it, and that I know what you're doing *should* be done; but I just can't do it."[4]

Rebuffed by Kennedy, Lowenstein unsuccessfully broached the idea to civil
rights leader Martin Luther King Jr. before turning to such liberal Democratic
senators and critics of the war in Vietnam as Vance Hartke of Indiana, Frank
Church of Idaho, and George McGovern of South Dakota. McGovern believed
he had no chance of winning the nomination, but considered the effort worth-
while. "So I suggested they pick a Senator who was not up for election," McGovern recalled. "Just off the top of my head I said, 'How about [Lee] Metcalf [of
Montana], or Gene McCarthy.'"[5] Eugene McCarthy, the poetry-writing fifty-
one-year-old U.S. senator from Minnesota, was at first reluctant to take on Johnson, believing Kennedy might do best against the president. McCarthy suggested
that perhaps other senators who opposed the war could run against Johnson as
favorite sons in their home states. Most of them, however, faced tough reelection
campaigns and declined. Facing pressure from his family members, particularly
his daughter, Mary, McCarthy accepted the daunting task of running against an
incumbent president of his own party. "There comes a time when an honorable
man must raise the flag," McCarthy later said of his decision to run. "There
comes a point when you can't let people be denied a voice in a democracy. If you
do, you can be pushed into complete ineffectiveness or utter submission."[6]

Born in the rural central Minnesota community of Watkins, McCarthy
had been an excellent student and a skilled baseball player. "We worried a
great deal about baseball," he recalled of his hometown. "You started worrying
about whether you'd make the team when you were about 11, and stayed on
through it." A devout Roman Catholic, McCarthy spent nine months studying
to become a Benedictine monk but eventually left the monastery. He studied
English at Saint John's University in Collegeville, Minnesota, and earned a
master's degree in sociology from the University of Minnesota. A professor of
economics for a time at Saint John's, McCarthy served in military intelligence
for the War Department during World War II and, in 1948, successfully ran
for Congress on the Minnesota Democratic-Farmer-Labor Party ticket, representing the Fourth Congressional District. He won election to the U.S. Senate
in 1959. Five years later at the Democratic convention, Johnson considered
McCarthy as a possible running mate in the campaign against Republican

challenger Barry Goldwater. The nod went instead to the other U.S. senator from Minnesota, Hubert Humphrey—a decision that caused a furious McCarthy to vow that he would "get that son of a bitch"—meaning Johnson.[7]

McCarthy had also been growing more and more skeptical about the country's role in Vietnam. "I had had some doubts about the accuracy of the Administration's reports about conditions in Vietnam almost from the beginning of our involvement in that country," he noted in his memoir about the 1968 campaign. All of the government's calculations and statistics about the war could not "measure the power and the strength and the willingness to die in a cause."[8] As early as January 1967, McCarthy, joined by fourteen other Democratic senators, had signed a public letter urging the president to continue a bombing halt begun over the Christmas holiday. "I felt that the debate over our involvement in Vietnam, occasioned by the prospect of renewed bombing of the North, was a proper point for the beginning of a much deeper and much more extensive discussion not only on Vietnam but also of the whole role of America in this second half of the twentieth century," McCarthy said later. He was outraged when Nicholas Katzenbach, a State Department official, testified before the Senate Foreign Relations Committee in August 1968 that the Johnson administration could take any course of action it deemed fit in Vietnam without congressional approval because of the Gulf of Tonkin Resolution. After the hearing, McCarthy told a reporter that Katzenbach's remarks were the "wildest testimony I have ever heard. There is no limit to what he says the President could do. There is only one thing to do—take it to the country."[9]

Before committing himself to such a vast undertaking, McCarthy had attempted to ascertain Kennedy's plans for the upcoming election. In a private, seven-minute meeting in the Senate cloakroom in October, McCarthy, after seeking the opinions of some of his fellow senators, told Kennedy he planned on running in some of the upcoming primaries. "I didn't ask him what he was going to do," McCarthy recalled. "I just said, 'I'm not worried as to whether I'm a stalking horse for you,' meaning if Bobby were to enter later on I would not say I'd been tricked. I left it open to him." Kennedy offered neither encouragement nor obstacles. "He just accepted what I'd said," McCarthy noted. For his part, Kennedy, who had run his brother's campaign for the White House in 1960, appeared perplexed that McCarthy had failed to seek his advice on the upcoming campaign. "He's a very strange fellow. After all, I don't want to blow my own trumpet, but I have had a little experience running primaries," Kennedy said later.[10]

Kennedy believed that McCarthy might do very well in New Hampshire, that voters there would respond favorably to the Minnesota senator's calm and reasoned manner. "All he has to do is drive around those little towns, alone, talking to people about Vietnam," said Kennedy. McCarthy's campaign needed only one piece of literature to distribute to voters in New Hampshire, according to Kennedy: a single sheet with a photograph of John Kennedy and the words "This is the state that launched John Kennedy's movement toward the presidency. This is what we hoped for—and this is what we got."[11]

Most political prognosticators laughed at McCarthy's audacity when, on November 30, 1967, he made his formal campaign announcement in the Caucus Room of the Old Senate Office Building in Washington, D.C. "I am hopeful," said McCarthy, who had grown tired of life in the Senate, "that a challenge may alleviate the sense of political hopelessness and restore to many people belief in the processes of American politics and American government." The president's policies regarding Vietnam, including his failure to negotiate a settlement with North Vietnam to end the fighting, had helped prompt McCarthy's decision to run. "I am concerned that the administration seems to have set no limits on the price that it is willing to pay for military victory," McCarthy said. He told reporters he did not view his underdog campaign as "any great threat to the unity and the strength of the Democratic party." McCarthy originally planned to run in four primaries—Wisconsin, Oregon, California, and Nebraska. Asked by a reporter if he believed he had a chance to win, McCarthy blithely responded: "I think the President is the leading candidate for the Democratic nomination right now." When another reporter wondered if the senator might be committing political suicide with his quixotic quest to unseat Johnson, McCarthy demurred, noting he did not believe it would be suicide, but perhaps it "might be an execution."[12]

Now that there was a candidate willing to challenge Johnson, Allard Lowenstein barnstormed across the country to gather support for McCarthy. In late December 1967 Louie Mahern, a former marine who for a long time had been involved in Indiana Democratic politics, received a phone call from Jim Beatty, the Marion County Democratic chairman. Beatty told Mahern that there was to be a meeting in the basement of the Merchants Bank branch on Thirty-eighth Street in Indianapolis to hear someone talk about a possible insurgency against Johnson for the presidential nomination in 1968. Eight or ten Hoosier Democrats were at the meeting to hear from the mystery man—Lowenstein—who arrived thirty minutes late "wearing a suit that looked like he had slept in [it] and very much in need of a shave," Mahern recalled. Although Lowenstein's appearance "did not inspire a great deal of confidence," Mahern was intrigued by the activist's argument that Johnson had to be removed if the Democrats wanted to hold on to the White House and put an end to the war. "I decided to be for Senator McCarthy," said Mahern.[13]

As word spread about the effort to provide an alternative choice for Democrats, McCarthy reevaluated his campaign strategy. He had avoided making any commitments to enter the New Hampshire primary, as the state seemed supportive of the war in Vietnam and its only statewide newspaper was the fiercely conservative *Manchester Union Leader*. Some voters in the state even confused McCarthy with the late Joseph McCarthy, the U.S. senator from Wisconsin famous for his witch hunts of Communists in the federal government during the 1950s. On January 3, 1968, however, McCarthy decided to enter the New Hampshire race. "Those of us who wanted him to enter did so on the belief that he would make a respectable enough showing to better win subsequent primaries," noted Curtis Gans, who became McCarthy's campaign director in the state.[14] In New Hampshire McCarthy would indirectly battle Johnson, who did not appear on the ballot by name, but instead ran a write-in campaign overseen by the state's top Democratic leaders, including Governor John W. King and Senator Thomas McIntyre. King declared that the president would "murder" McCarthy in the coming primary. McIntyre predicted McCarthy would receive less than 10 percent of the state's Democratic vote.[15]

Other Democrats did not regard the senator as a serious threat to Johnson's renomination. After all, when asked, approximately 60 percent of the American public had never heard of the senator from Minnesota. In a poll taken of Democratic voters in New Hampshire, only 17 percent supported McCarthy, against a formidable 63 percent for the president. The opposition candidate did not seem to take seriously the immense task before him. A Kennedy aide used to the hustle and bustle of a political campaign was stunned one December morning to see McCarthy eating breakfast alone at a New York hotel. McCarthy's own supporters complained that their candidate's campaign had so far been a disaster. A reporter who covered Congress said McCarthy seemed to believe he could campaign "by just traveling around all alone like some medieval minstrel singing his songs." A *New York Times* reporter covering McCarthy could not get his articles published because his editors back in Manhattan did not consider McCarthy a credible candidate. A delighted White House aide told Johnson that he was "tempted to float a rumor that he [McCarthy] is actually working for you to dispirit the 'peace movement.'" The president's strength seemed so durable that Kennedy told reporters he "would not oppose Lyndon Johnson under any foreseeable circumstances."[16] There seemed little doubt that Johnson would again be the Democratic Party's candidate for president. In just a few short days all of these political considerations would be shattered by events in an Asian country thousands of miles away.

On the evening of January 31, the pop of fireworks could be heard throughout Saigon, the capital of South Vietnam. The fireworks celebrated Tet, the lunar new year. Shortly before three o'clock in the morning, two vehicles, a Peugeot truck and a taxicab, rolled up to the gates of the four-acre U.S. Embassy compound. In the vehicles were approximately nineteen Vietcong fighters who leaped out and began firing automatic weapons at the military policemen guarding the entrance. The MPs—Specialist Fourth Class Charles L. Daniel and Private First Class William E. Sebast—fired back at the attackers and radioed for assistance. Daniel shouted: "They're coming in! They're coming in! Help me! Help me!" Despite the fierce opposition from the American MPs, Vietcong sappers were able to blow a hole in the wall that surrounded the compound and the fighters stormed in to attack the embassy with rockets and grenades. Both Daniel and Sebast were killed. The Tet Offensive had begun.[17]

Over the next few days, approximately seventy thousand North Vietnamese soldiers and their Vietcong allies struck not only the American embassy, but also the South Vietnamese presidential palace and army headquarters. Enemy soldiers also attacked a majority of the provincial capitals and five of South Vietnam's six largest cities, holding Hue, the old imperial city, for twenty-five days. U.S. Marines retook Hue, but most of the city lay in ruins and thousands of civilians either lay dead or had become refugees. The offensive proved to be a crushing military defeat for the North Vietnamese, who lost approximately forty thousand men and failed to achieve the uprising they had hoped for against the ruling South Vietnamese regime. The breadth and ferocity of the assault, however, stunned the American public. Many Americans were perplexed by an army major's reasoning that U.S. forces had to use their massive firepower to destroy Ben Tre, a village in the Mekong Delta, "in order to save it." The Johnson administration had led the public to believe that there was "light at the end of the tunnel"—that the half a million American forces and their South Vietnamese allies were winning the battle against their Communist foes. Reading the reports of the desperate fighting as they came in over the teletype in the newsroom of the *CBS Evening News* in New York, Walter Cronkite, the esteemed anchorman, asked: "What the hell is going on? I thought we were winning the war!"[18]

The image that burned itself most indelibly into the American mind was captured by an NBC television camera crew and Associated Press photographer Eddie Adams in Saigon. On February 1, General Nguyen Ngoc Loan, chief of South Vietnam's national police, walked along a Saigon street. Communist forces had recently killed several of his men, including his best friend, a major who was gunned down along with his wife and children. South Vietnamese troops had captured a suspected Vietcong guerrilla and had tied his hands behind his back before taking him to Loan. In a shocking sequence, Loan walked up to the suspected guerrilla, drew his revolver, pressed it against the man's head, and fired. Loan turned to those who had witnessed the execution and said: "Many Americans have been killed these last few days, and many of my best Vietnamese friends. Now do you understand? Buddha will understand." An estimated twenty million people saw the brutal shooting on NBC's *Huntley-Brinkley Report*. Adams's picture of the incident ended up on the front page of newspapers around the world and won the photographer a host of awards, including the Pulitzer Prize.[19]

Obviously the Johnson administration had not been forthright with the public about the progress it had claimed to be making in winning the war. How could the United States be winning if American generals were requesting the deployment of an additional two hundred thousand more troops in Vietnam? Critics of the war pointed to Johnson's declaration four years earlier, in a speech at the University of Akron, that his administration was "not about to send American boys nine or ten thousand miles to do what Asian boys ought to be doing for themselves." A "credibility gap" was growing between reality on the ground in Vietnam and the administration's carefully groomed, optimistic pronouncements about the war's progress. That gap worsened, noted Joseph A. Califano Jr., a Johnson speechwriter, because the president himself became "the most gullible victim of his own revisionist claims. He would quickly come to believe what he was saying even if it was clearly not true."[20]

The devastating images from Vietnam further damaged Johnson's approval rating with the American public, which had already fallen in the wake of the riots that swept a number of major cities—Newark, Detroit, Boston, Cincinnati, Milwaukee, and Tampa—during the summer of 1967. To investigate the causes of the riots, Johnson had appointed a special commission headed by Mayor John Lindsay of New York and Governor Otto Kerner of Illinois. The Kerner Commission, as it came to be known, issued its report on February 29 and pointedly reported that America was rapidly developing into "two societies, one black, one white—separate and unequal." The commission called for increased taxes to help create two million new jobs over the next three years and the addition of more African Americans to police forces throughout the country. Some white Americans were outraged that the report failed to condemn black radicals who had threatened to use violence against police aggression and racism. Johnson had tried to remain noncommittal on the commission's findings. Kennedy was outraged. The president, Kennedy told his friends, had failed to find a solution for the war in Vietnam and "he's not going to do anything about the cities either."[21]

Before the Tet Offensive, a Gallup poll noted that Americans agreed with the way Johnson handled his duties as president by 48 percent to 39 percent. In early February 1968, 41 percent approved of Johnson's performance and 41 percent disapproved.[22] The shocking news from Vietnam also took its toll on

Johnson. Califano talked of a "sense of siege" developing in the White House. "The nights are very long," Johnson lamented before a crowd at the annual presidential prayer breakfast in Washington, D.C. "The winds are very chill. Our spirits grow weary and restive as the springtime of man seems farther and farther away."[23]

Worries about the situation in Vietnam brought new life to the McCarthy presidential campaign. A growing number of college students protesting American involvement in Vietnam flocked to the senator in New Hampshire. McCarthy's early attempts at persuading students to join his cause had been uninspiring. At a national meeting of the Conference of Concerned Democrats in Chicago in December 1967, Lowenstein had delivered an impassioned blast against President Johnson before more than two thousand attendees crammed into the ballroom at the Conrad Hilton Hotel. "When a President is both wrong and unpopular, to refuse to oppose him is both a moral abdication and a political stupidity," said Lowenstein. He added that if a "man cheats you once, shame on him. But if he cheats you twice, shame on you!" When McCarthy arrived to give his speech, he listened to some of Lowenstein's fevered words and appeared upset at what he heard. Students saw him angrily kicking a Dixie cup backstage while listening to Lowenstein. Jeremy Larner, later a speechwriter for the senator's presidential campaign, said McCarthy possessed "deep misgivings about a group of young rebels using him as a battering-ram against his party." For his own part, McCarthy said Lowenstein's speech was an "overstatement of the case against Johnson and was not in the spirit of the campaign which I intended to wage." McCarthy laid out the basis for his campaign in a calm, measured approach that failed to stir many in the audience. But, as McCarthy said, "it was not a time for storming the walls, but for beginning a long march."[24]

McCarthy's "long march" toward the nomination began with some early triumphs. In March his supporters won the party caucuses in three of the five Minnesota congressional districts. On March 5 Johnson decided not to place his name on the ballot for the April 30 Massachusetts primary. When Massachusetts Democrats could find no takers to run as a stand-in for Johnson, McCarthy was left as the only viable candidate; he was thus assured of control of the state's seventy-two delegates for the first ballot at the national convention. In California, McCarthy supporters organized an impressive effort to gather signatures to place the senator's name on the state's primary ballot; thirty thousand signatures were collected in just nine hours.[25] Meanwhile, student volunteers from across the country were leaving their campuses and traveling to New Hampshire to work for McCarthy's campaign. "I detected early that my campaign was giving a sense of purpose to young people," said McCarthy. "The students came into New Hampshire like early spring."[26]

Stirred by the campaign's slogan of "New Hampshire Can Help Bring the Nation Back to Its Senses," the students, mostly unpaid volunteers who made sure to shave off beards and mustaches, cut their long hair, and wear conservative clothing (no miniskirts) so they could be "Clean for Gene," canvassed many of the state's ninety thousand registered Democrats and its hundred thousand independent voters. "I was thinking of turning in my draft card, but then the campaign began," said Dan Dodd, a twenty-three-year-old who dropped out of a seminary school to campaign for McCarthy. "We're not going to build grass-roots politics in time to end the war by November, but if we can end the present President's career, maybe we can do it by then."[27] Dodging angry dogs and slippery, snow-covered streets and sidewalks, the students went door to door talking with people about McCarthy or distributing campaign literature if no one was home. "Not only were there many canvassers; they were unbelievably enthusiastic," said Ben Stavis, a Columbia University graduate student who helped organize the students. "They would stay up all night preparing maps and then canvass the next day. Not even sub-zero temperature or snow storms could keep them from voters' doors."[28]

By early March the McCarthy campaign could count on the assistance of two thousand students on a full-time basis, plus another five thousand working on weekends. "My campaign may not be organized at the top," McCarthy said, "but it is certainly tightly organized at the bottom."[29] In addition to canvassing, students worked on a variety of specialized tasks, including translating McCarthy literature into French for New Hampshire's large French-Canadian population. Those assigned to lead the student volunteers quickly learned that this was a new way to campaign. As campaign director, Gans had avoided engaging in any common tasks such as addressing envelopes. After staying up till midnight addressing invitations for a reception, Stavis, a Chinese history scholar, went to Gans and asked him if he had ever heard how the emperor used to open the agricultural season in China. He noted the emperor had a special silver shovel that he used to go out and turn one shovelful of soil to symbolically participate in the work. Gans got the message and helped with the mailing until the staff ran out of stamps. "That night united the staff and defined how we would work," said Stavis. "We would work until the work was done; we would do whatever work there was."[30]

Political veterans who had worked in other campaigns were impressed by what they saw. After Robert Kennedy decided to stay out of the race, Richard Goodwin, who had been part of both the Kennedy and Johnson administrations, traveled to New Hampshire in late February to work for McCarthy, offering the campaign advice on press relations and advertising. "I wanted to go down fighting," Goodwin noted in his memoir. "And New Hampshire was the only battlefield left." Meeting Seymour Hersh, McCarthy's press secretary, upon his arrival in the state, a confident Goodwin took him outside to his car, opened his trunk, pointed to his Smith-Corona portable typewriter, and stated: "You, me, and this typewriter, Sy; together we're going to overthrow the president of the United States." Although some of the young people working for McCarthy worried that he might be a spy for Kennedy, Goodwin had nothing but praise for the students' dedication to their cause. "It was the biggest and best field organization ever assembled for a political campaign, before or since," he said.[31]

In addition to the student volunteers and his paid staff, McCarthy also had the assistance of celebrities such as Paul Newman, Myrna Loy, Tony Randall, and Rod Serling, who traveled throughout the state to promote his cause. Newman proved to be a particularly effective campaigner, telling voters, "I didn't come here to help Gene McCarthy. I need McCarthy's help. The country needs it." The candidate, however, proved to be his most effective advocate. He charmed New Hampshire residents by playing hockey with a local semi-pro team and publicized the event by distributing free windshield ice scrapers emblazoned with a picture of McCarthy on skates with the slogan "McCarthy Cuts the Ice." The candidate rarely made personal attacks on Johnson. Instead, he pointed out the high cost in money and lives of what seemed to be a never-ending conflict and asked voters to judge for themselves if the war was worth fighting. "What you want to do," Gans said of McCarthy's strategy, "is pit the image of an honest man against the image of a dishonest man." McCarthy began to think he had a chance to achieve success in New Hampshire when he realized that a person could walk into any bar in the country and "insult Lyndon Johnson and nobody would punch you in the nose."[32]

Johnson's supporters in New Hampshire aided the opposition far more than they did their own candidate. One of the Johnson for President organization's first errors in judgment was deciding, with the approval of Johnson's aides, to distribute numbered pledge cards for registered Democrats to sign indicating they intended to cast their vote for the president. The cards had three parts, one to be kept by the voter and the other two to be sent back to the state Democratic committee. The campaign committee would keep one portion of the pledge card for itself and send the other one on to the White House. Voters who signed the card received a note of thanks from Governor King and Senator McIntyre and an autographed photo of the president and first lady. Although benign in intent, the pledge cards were immediately attacked by McCarthy as a violation of a voter's right to a secret ballot. "It's not at all inconsistent with administration policy to kind of put a brand on people," said McCarthy. The senator's staff countered the pledge cards with a poster that read "You Don't Have to Sign Anything to Vote for Gene McCarthy."[33]

The negative publicity engendered by the pledge cards led to further errors by the Johnson camp. They panicked as they learned through their private polling of voters in the state that McCarthy's popularity had grown. Hoping to stem the tide, Johnson supporters attempted to smear McCarthy with charges that a vote for him, as King asserted, "would be greeted with great cheers in Hanoi." The governor went on to call McCarthy "a champion of appeasement and surrender" and radio advertisements cautioned voters not to cast their ballots for "fuzzy thinking and surrender." A newspaper advertisement warned that the Communists in Vietnam were watching the New Hampshire primary to see "if we at home have the same determination as our soldiers in Vietnam. To vote for weakness and indecision would not be in the best interests of our nation." These tactics, reminiscent as they were of 1950s McCarthyism, boomeranged, as New Hampshire residents sympathized with McCarthy and considered the attacks against him to be unfair; a Portsmouth newspaper called the comments "disgraceful political tactics." Goodwin said that the McCarthy campaign did not have to answer the "slanders," as the candidate himself "was the answer." Voters contrasted the bombastic statements of the Johnson backers with a heartfelt McCarthy radio advertisement during the final days of the campaign: "Think how it would feel to wake up Wednesday morning to find out that Gene McCarthy had won the New Hampshire primary—to find out that New Hampshire had changed the course of American politics."[34]

On March 12, defying a snowstorm, New Hampshire voters cast a record number of ballots in the state's Democratic primary and delivered a result that shocked the country. McCarthy could feel that the tide had turned in his direction. When an aide told him that officials had discovered the names of three dead men voting in one city, McCarthy said not to release the information to the press. "It was the resurrection," he said. "They came back to vote for us." Even the town that traditionally cast its votes first in the state, Waterville, went for McCarthy, giving him nine votes and none for Johnson (Kennedy received two write-ins). A Johnson campaign official had prophesied before the voting that the McCarthy effort would be a failure if it captured less than 40 percent of the vote. McCarthy won 42.2 percent of the vote to Johnson's 49.4 percent. Adding the 5,511 Republicans who wrote in his name, McCarthy finished only 230 votes behind Johnson, 28,791 to 29,021. (On the Republican side, Richard Nixon, the former vice president, easily won the GOP primary with 84,005 votes to 11,691 for Nelson Rockefeller, the governor of New York.) Another tactical error by Johnson supporters—allowing forty-five candidates to run as pro-Johnson candidates for the twenty-four positions as delegates to the national convention—made it possible for the McCarthy team, which fielded exactly twenty-four candidates, to capture twenty of New Hampshire's twenty-four delegates. "People have remarked that this campaign has brought young people back into the system," McCarthy told a crowd of three hundred cheering supporters in the ballroom of the Sheraton-Wayfarer Inn in Manchester. "But it's the other way around: The young people have brought the country back into the system." He promised that if they "went to Chicago [the site of the upcoming Democratic convention] in this strength, there will be no violence and no demonstrations, but a great victory celebration." McCarthy praised his young volunteers for their efforts on his behalf and noted that if he had failed in New Hampshire, it would have been a personal failure on his part because he possessed "the most intelligent campaign staff in the history of American politics, in the history of the world!"[35]

President Johnson attempted to downplay the New Hampshire results. He noted that the state seemed to be the only place where "candidates can claim 20 percent as a landslide, 40 percent as a mandate, and 60 percent as unanimous."[36] The president, however, had missed the true significance of McCarthy's success. Although he had not technically won the primary, McCarthy and his dedicated mass of student volunteers had been able, as Goodwin noted, to expose "the subterranean discontent" with Johnson and his policies. The results also revealed a widespread desire among the voting public for change in the nation's capital. Even those who supported the war cast their ballots for McCarthy as a way to protest the president's handling of the conflict. "I was now certain," Goodwin said, "that whatever McCarthy's personal destiny, Lyndon Johnson would not be the next president of the United States."[37]

McCarthy's strong showing in New Hampshire boosted his confidence for the effort ahead. "I think I can get the nomination," an ecstatic McCarthy told reporters as he prepared to move his campaign to Wisconsin for that state's April 2 primary. "I'm ahead now. There's no point in being anything but optimistic."[38] Unfortunately, the senator had little time to bask in the glow of his achievement. When McCarthy arrived at National Airport in Washington, D.C., the day after the New Hampshire vote, his administrative assistant, Jerome Eller, handed him a copy of a statement from Robert Kennedy: because of recent events Kennedy had decided to reassess the possibility of running against Johnson. "The [New Hampshire] primary demonstrated that there is a deep division within the party," Kennedy said. "It clearly indicates that a sizable group of Democrats are concerned about the direction in which the country is going both in the fields of foreign and domestic policy." Kennedy added that he would make a final decision before March 22, the final day he could remove his name from consideration for the Oregon primary. (Under Oregon law in 1968, the state's secretary of state had the authority to place on the primary ballot the name of any presidential candidate "generally advocated or recognized in the national news media."

Those who wished to remove their names from the Oregon ballot had to file affidavits to do so by 5 PM, March 22.) Reporters at National Airport clamored for McCarthy's reaction to Kennedy's startling remarks. Asked if he welcomed Kennedy's entry into the campaign, McCarthy said, "Well, I don't know. It's a little crowded now." He later pointed out, with some feeling, that Kennedy, with the timing of his announcement, had not allowed him to have even one day to celebrate his New Hampshire triumph.[39]

But the news did not come as a total surprise to the Minnesota senator. Almost a week before New Hampshire voters went to the polls, Kennedy had called Richard Goodwin to let him know he had not totally abandoned the idea of joining the presidential race and asked him to relay the information to McCarthy. An uncomfortable Goodwin later told McCarthy of the conversation, and McCarthy responded, "Why don't you tell him that I only want one term anyway. Let him support me now, and after that he can have it." When a surprised Goodwin expressed disbelief about the offer, McCarthy reaffirmed that he was serious; he believed the presidency should be a one-term office. "Then the power would be in the institution," he said. "It wouldn't be so dependent on the person."[40]

The morning after the New Hampshire primary, Kennedy called McCarthy's Senate office to arrange a meeting. The two senators decided to meet late that afternoon in Ted Kennedy's office on the fourth floor of the Old Senate Office Building. To avoid the crush of reporters waiting for him, McCarthy ducked into the Senate gymnasium—off-limits to the media—and left by another door before proceeding to Ted Kennedy's office. The two men talked for approximately fifteen minutes. McCarthy reiterated the statement he had made to Goodwin that he intended to serve only one term in office if elected, and perhaps Kennedy should wait and try his luck in the 1972 presidential contest. McCarthy noted that Kennedy did not specifically indicate he would join the race for the White House, but McCarthy had "the definite impression" Kennedy had made up his mind to seek the nomination. "Now, at least three people in Washington are reconsidering their candidacy," McCarthy joked after the meeting. The next day, anticipating Kennedy might soon formally announce his entry into the campaign, McCarthy confirmed his desire to remain as a candidate by indicating he planned to add the Indiana and South Dakota primaries to his schedule. "He would not give Kennedy any presents, or, above all, show fear of any kind; he would make Kennedy fight for everything," noted Arthur Herzog, a journalist and McCarthy volunteer. McCarthy left Washington to campaign in Wisconsin, where he faced off once again with Johnson.[41]

According to Kennedy's recollection of the meeting, which he related to *Village Voice* reporter Jack Newfield, there had not been much communication between the two men. He did say he told McCarthy he "was probably going to run, and that I hoped we might work together in some coordinated way." Kennedy added that he offered his support for McCarthy's effort against Johnson in Wisconsin, but McCarthy failed to respond except to indicate Kennedy could do what he wanted to do, as he planned on continuing in the race come what may. "I would say he was cold to us," Kennedy said of McCarthy.[42]

Kennedy held off on making a formal announcement of his entry into the race to pursue another avenue to alter the Johnson administration's policies in Vietnam. Theodore Sorenson, a valued speechwriter for President John Kennedy and a close adviser to Robert Kennedy who opposed his running for the presidency in 1968, devised a plan to appoint a presidential commission to study and provide recommendations on the war. The panel would include members that might be acceptable to both Johnson and Kennedy—such influential figures in politics and the military as Senator Mike Mansfield of Montana and General Matthew Ridgeway. Richard Daley, the powerful Democratic mayor of Chicago, had proposed a similar idea to Kennedy in February. Although Kennedy thought the commission plan would ultimately fail, he said he "had to go the last mile, to prove I was not running out of ambition, or some petty feelings about Johnson." Johnson and his new secretary of defense, Clark Clifford, considered the idea, but Johnson eventually rejected it, believing that it would be considered as nothing but a "political deal" by the American public and that it would usurp the president's authority. "The President of the United States can't select a group of citizens hand-picked by somebody else, and apparently agree in advance that these men could come in, study a problem, make a recommendation which would in turn be the president's decision," Clifford said. "You wouldn't need a President of the United States if that's the way our government worked." Clifford called Kennedy and informed him of Johnson's decision.[43]

The failure of the commission proposal made Kennedy realize that as long as Johnson remained president, the administration's Vietnam policy "would consist of only more war, more troops, more killing, and more senseless destruction of the country we are supposedly there to save."[44] Before making a public announcement of his entrance into the campaign, Kennedy attempted to work out an arrangement with McCarthy to divide the upcoming primary states between the now two antiwar candidates. The two men would then face off against each other in the crucial California primary on June 4. Ted Kennedy traveled to Wisconsin to meet secretly with McCarthy and tell him his brother had decided to run and to seek an agreement on a joint anti-Johnson effort. Joining Kennedy on the flight were members of the McCarthy campaign staff, including Richard Goodwin, Curtis Gans, and Blair Clark, the national campaign manager. The commercial flight from Washington, D.C., to Chicago arrived late, so the men missed their connecting flight. Clark used a personal credit card to charter a Learjet for the late-night flight to Green Bay, Wisconsin, where McCarthy was staying at the Northland Hotel.

The meeting between the two camps turned into a comic opera. David Schoumacher, a correspondent for CBS News, had learned of the meeting and attempted to obtain a scoop on the proceedings. McCarthy had gone to bed leaving orders that he didn't want to be disturbed, but he finally agreed to get up and meet with Kennedy. "It was like a family gathering for a matchmaking," McCarthy observed, "some of them hoping an engagement would take place, others not." Kennedy had a draft of a reconciliation statement in his briefcase perched on his knees, but McCarthy never let him take it out and refused any sort of compromise arrangement between the two campaigns. McCarthy's wife, Abigail, compared Ted Kennedy to an insurance salesman or lawyer anxious to pass on important documents to his client. She added that later the briefcase held by Kennedy became a catchphrase in the campaign: staff members could always get a laugh by asking, "What was in that briefcase?" Gans remembered McCarthy telling Kennedy that he had to "go along the way I've been going." Kennedy left the meeting to fly back and report to his brother. Left alone in the room with his wife and daughter, McCarthy turned to his wife and said, "That's the way they [the Kennedys] are. When it comes down to it, they never offer anything real."[45]

On Saturday morning, March 16, from the Senate Caucus Room, where his brother had begun his candidacy for the presidency eight years before, Robert Kennedy, with his wife, Ethel, and nine of his ten children by his side, declared: "I am announcing today my candidacy for the presidency of the United States." His announcement outlined Kennedy's goals for the coming campaign, including an end to the bloodshed in Vietnam and an enhanced focus on closing the wide gaps that existed "between blacks and whites, between rich and poor, between young and old in this country and in the rest of the world." His decision to challenge Johnson reflected "no personal animosity" toward the president, Kennedy insisted to a crowd of skeptical reporters, but he did point out their "profound differences over where we are heading and what we want to accomplish." Kennedy also stressed that his campaign would not be run in opposition to, but in harmony with, McCarthy's effort, and stressed the importance of the Minnesota senator's achieving large majorities in the Wisconsin and Pennsylvania primaries. Kennedy had no illusions about the difficulties facing him as he sought to wrest the nomination from Johnson. "But these are not ordinary times," Kennedy said, "and this is not an ordinary election."[46]

Kennedy's decision to wait until after McCarthy's dramatic showing in the New Hampshire primary reinforced in many people's minds old charges of Kennedy's ruthlessness in pursuing his ambitions. His critics were reminded of his days as an assistant to Senator Joseph McCarthy in his reckless hunt for Communists in government and of Kennedy's relentless pursuit of Teamsters union boss Jimmy Hoffa. It also made for sharp questions from the assembled media. Mary McGrory, a columnist for the *Washington Evening Star* and one of the first reporters to write about the "children's crusade" supporting McCarthy, asked Kennedy if he would be willing to stay out of the Wisconsin primary if Gene McCarthy asked him to do so. After the senator replied that he would be willing, McGrory was heard to say: "So he could have the victory for himself." Another columnist, Murray Kempton, blasted Kennedy for his action and compared him to a coward coming down from the hills "to shoot the wounded."[47]

On the campaign trail McCarthy pointed out to newsmen that any "Irishman who announces the day before St. Patrick's Day that he's going to run against another Irishman shouldn't say it's going to be a peaceful relationship." He pointed out that at a time when other politicians were afraid to take on Johnson, he had been the one to take the bold step of direct opposition. "They were willing to stay up on the mountains and light signal fires and bonfires and dance in the light of the moon, but none of them came down," said McCarthy, who indicated he was the best potential president in the field. "They weren't even coming in from outside, just throwing a message over the fence." The students who had campaigned with such enthusiasm for McCarthy greeted Kennedy's announcement with scorn. They had once looked upon Kennedy as the rightful heir to his brother's legacy, but now treated him as a usurper who might even be conspiring with Johnson to end McCarthy's campaign. One student volunteer spoke for many when she said: "We woke up after the New Hampshire primary like it was Christmas Day. And when we went down to the tree, we found Bobby Kennedy had stolen our presents." The students remained loyal to their new leader. "We'll fight him [Kennedy] the same way we fought Johnson," vowed Joel Feigenbaum, a twenty-five-year-old Cornell University physicist.[48]

Johnson tried to greet Kennedy's opposition to his renomination with humor. At a businessmen's conference in Washington, D.C., the president commented that there were days when a person had to take chances. "Some speculate in gold—a primary metal—and others just speculate in primaries." The antiwar candidacies of his two Democratic opponents hardened Johnson's feelings about completing the task in Vietnam. In a March 17 speech before the National Farmers Union in Minneapolis, the president called upon his audience and the nation to join his administration "in a total national effort to win the war, to win the peace, and to complete the job that must be done here at home. Make no mistake about it . . . we are going to win." Just a few days later, he reiterated his belief in the cause at a conference at the State Department. "Today we are the Number One Nation," Johnson said. "And we are going to stay the Number One Nation."[49]

Behind the scenes, however, the pressures of the war and the campaign were weighing heavily upon the president. Johnson later revealed to Doris Kearns, a White House fellow who assisted the president with his memoirs, that he had felt he was being chased by a "giant stampede coming at me from all directions." On one side stood the American public clamoring for him to do something about the war in Vietnam, while inflation grew out of control and there were danger signs that there would be more riots in the inner cities during the coming summer. "I was being forced over the edge by rioting blacks, demonstrating students, marching welfare mothers, squawking professors, and hysterical reporters," Johnson said. The final straw was when the one thing Johnson had feared from the first days of his presidency came true: Robert Kennedy announced his candidacy. "And the American people," said Johnson, "swayed by the magic of the name, were dancing in the streets. The whole situation was unbearable for me."[50]

In spite of his secret fears, Johnson seemed determined to seek another four years in office. Although his campaign in Wisconsin seemed fated to fall to McCarthy and his youthful volunteers, Johnson did not really need to win any of the remaining primaries. There were enough uncommitted delegates controlled by party bosses allied with the president to ensure his renomination. Administration officials were also confident Johnson could defeat Nixon in the general election, especially since George Wallace, the avowedly segregationist former governor of Alabama, seemed determined to seek the presidency as a third-party candidate with his new American Independent Party. (Wallace, who eventually earned a place on the general election ballot in all fifty states, hoped his candidacy might receive enough electoral votes to deadlock the election and throw it to the House of Representatives.) But for now, to help stem the surging wave ridden by McCarthy and Kennedy, the president and his team of advisers turned for help to a popular governor from a conservative midwestern state: Roger D. Branigin of Indiana.

1 2 **3** 4 5 6 7

The Governor

Politics has always played an important role in Indiana. For a century the state furnished candidates for national office for an assortment of American political parties. From 1840, when the Whig William Henry Harrison captured the White House with his "Tippecanoe and Tyler Too" campaign, to 1940, when Wendell Willkie won the Republican presidential nomination and challenged incumbent President Franklin D. Roosevelt in his try for a third term in office, Hoosiers were on some party's national ticket in approximately 60 percent of the elections. By the 1880s Indiana had become such a pivotal state in securing political success for presidential candidates that the Democratic and Republican parties did everything they could, including buying votes, to win the state's allegiance for their candidates. Loyal party workers in the nineteenth state were proud to say they had risked going to jail in pursuit of their cause. Politics became so ingrained in the state's character that the noted humorist and journalist George Ade once joked—playing off General William Tecumseh

Sherman's famous quote—that the first words of every Hoosier child upon birth were "If nominated I will run, if elected I will serve."[1]

When county chairmen and other faithful members of the Indiana Democratic Party gathered for a leadership meeting at the French Lick Springs Hotel on March 16, 1968, however, they faced an uncertain future. Party loyalty no longer seemed to matter: Eugene McCarthy and his legion of young supporters had nearly defeated President Lyndon Johnson in the New Hampshire primary and seemed poised to deal another blow to Johnson's flagging popularity with voters in the upcoming Wisconsin primary. News had also filtered into the meeting that another antiwar candidate, Robert Kennedy, had declared his intention to join the race to deny Johnson renomination. McCarthy had already decided to enter Indiana's May 7 primary, and there were rumblings that Kennedy might select Indiana as the first test for his young campaign. No Hoosier politician seemed willing to represent the state Democratic Party's interest by volunteering to serve as a stand-in for President Johnson.

The Democrats gathered in southern Indiana without their leader, Governor Roger Branigin, who was on his way to Fort Lauderdale, Florida, for a short vacation. But the meeting's main speaker, Vice President Hubert Humphrey, had a surprise in store for his nervous audience, which numbered approximately five hundred. After months of back-and-forth negotiations, Branigin had, in a last-minute telephone conversation with Humphrey and state party chairman Gordon St. Angelo, agreed to run as a stand-in for Johnson. "I'm happy to tell you, Governor Roger Branigin stands with the President—and he's a winner," Humphrey said. The vice president confidently declared that with the support of Branigin and St. Angelo, the state could "demonstrate that when we have a president who shoulders responsibility . . . who knows what he's doing, that Indiana will back him." According to Paul M. Doherty, a reporter from the *Indianapolis Star* who covered the meeting, Humphrey's announcement of Branigin's decision had "brought the crowd of organization Democrats to a state of stomping, cheering excitement." St. Angelo had never seen anything like it in the many years he had been involved in Indiana politics. "They were literally standing on the tables and chairs," said St. Angelo, who had managed Branigin's gubernatorial campaign four years earlier. He compared the tumult to a crowd at the final game of the Indiana high school basketball tournament.[2]

In Branigin, a World War II veteran and a Harvard-educated attorney, Johnson had a partner with a proven track record for attracting the attention of Hoosier voters. Before he turned to politics, Branigin had been well-known as one of the state's premier public speakers at events ranging from political conventions to church conferences and 4-H club meetings. "When you get a reputation and don't charge anything, you get deluged," he explained when asked about his oratorical success. St. Angelo noted that Branigin possessed the "greatest sense of humor" of anyone he had ever met—a talent he sometimes used without considering the possible harmful consequences to his political life. St. Angelo remembered one occasion during Branigin's run for governor when a woman kept accosting the candidate about women's rights. Tired of the interruptions, Branigin turned to the agitator and said, "I'm not interested in a woman's rights, I'm interested in a woman's wrongs." Luckily for the candidate, the press covering his campaign did not make an issue of his ill-timed quip. Branigin, however, managed to avoid any major gaffes, and in the 1964 gubernatorial election he had defeated his Republican opponent, former lieutenant governor Richard Ristine, by more than 260,000 votes—at that time the largest plurality in the state's history. The Democrat had also received a front-page endorsement from the normally Republican *Indianapolis Star*, whose publisher, Eugene C. Pulliam, had been a friend of Branigin's since his days as editor and publisher of the *Franklin Evening Star*. All of these factors pointed to Branigin doing well in the Indiana Democratic presidential primary.[3]

Branigin appeared to be the quintessential Hoosier. Born in Franklin, Indiana, on July 26, 1902, he was the third of four sons raised by Elba and Zula Branigin. All four boys followed in their father's footsteps by becoming lawyers, earning the elder Branigin the moniker "the Barrister of Branigins." A former schoolteacher, Franklin College graduate, and amateur historian, Elba Branigin maintained an extensive library, which all of his sons used. Later in life Roger Branigin also amassed an impressive book collection, including many volumes on Indiana history that he later gave to the Franklin College library. Branigin attended the Franklin public schools and during his senior year in high school was a cheerleader for the school's basketball team, the "Wonder Five," when it won the first of its three straight state championships. As a young man Branigin earned money delivering the *Indianapolis Star*. After graduating from high school in 1919, Branigin attended Franklin College, where he majored in French, Spanish, and history, and also pursued an interest in dramatics. Although an excellent student, Branigin did sometimes clash with school authorities: he refused to attend the school's compulsory chapel and was placed on probation after being caught smoking.

Upon his graduation from Franklin, Branigin attended Harvard Law School, receiving his law degree in 1926. For the next three years, he worked in the prosecutor's office in Franklin. On November 2, 1929, Branigin married Josephine Mardis of Shelbyville; the marriage would produce two sons, Roger Jr. and Robert. The next year, Branigin began work as an attorney with the Federal Land Bank and Farm Credit Administration's Louisville office, which served a five-state area. Branigin traveled extensively in his work, giving speeches throughout Indiana and other states. "By the time I was 36," he later said, "I knew everybody in Indiana."[4] In 1938 he left the land bank and joined a law firm in Lafayette. Volunteering for service in World War II, Branigin worked in the contract division of the Judge Advocate General's Office in Washington, D.C. He subsequently became chief of the legal division for the army's transportation corps. In 1946 he became a partner in the firm Stuart, Branigin, Ricks, and Shilling.

A longtime Democrat and an admirer of former Indiana governor Paul McNutt, Branigin honed his political skills in a variety of non-elective positions. He served as permanent chairman of the Democratic State Convention in 1948, was appointed by Governor Henry Schricker as chairman of the state conservation commission, and was president of the Indiana Bar Association. He also served on the board of trustees for both Franklin College and Purdue University. In 1956 Branigin attempted to win the Democratic nomination for governor, but was defeated by Ralph Tucker. Branigin had better luck in June 1964, when he captured the nomination on the first ballot at the state Democratic convention, which was held at the Fairgrounds Coliseum. The 1964 gubernatorial campaign pitted Branigin against another Hoosier political veteran, Richard Ristine. As lieutenant governor under the Democratic governor Matthew Welsh, Ristine had cast the tie-breaking vote in favor of the establishment of a sales tax in Indiana. This unpopular decision, coupled with the strong showing of incumbent president Johnson over GOP opponent Barry Goldwater, helped Branigin defeat Ristine in the general election.

During his four-year administration, Branigin, who had declared upon his election he would not seek any other political post, shunned the usual trappings of the governor's office. He turned down offers of complimentary tickets to athletic events and the free use of corporate aircraft, and also kept a sharp eye on such state expenditures as out-of-state travel by members of his administration. At his inauguration as governor, he noted: "It should never be necessary for anyone to make gifts in order to do business with the state of Indiana. Conflict of interest should be forbidden and absolute civic morality must be the order of the day."[5] Criticized for spending too much time on such trivial matters, Branigin responded: "Perhaps we are saving peanuts, but we may save enough to open a peanut-vending business."[6] The governor's common touch extended to often handwriting, addressing, and posting his correspondence, dialing his own telephone calls, and preferring train travel to flying. When one day the heating system failed in his office, he remained as repairs were made, doing his work dressed in his hat and coat. "I am a Democrat, Irish and a lawyer," said Branigin. "You can't get more common than that."[7]

Branigin's popularity, and his continued support for the war in Vietnam, made him the perfect stand-in for Johnson in the 1968 Indiana primary. Four years earlier Johnson and his campaign team had arranged a similar role for Branigin's predecessor, Matthew Welsh, who had then stood successfully against the insurgent campaign of Alabama governor George Wallace. Johnson had met with Branigin several times in Washington, D.C., from the late fall of 1967 to the early spring of 1968, trying to get Branigin to commit his services for the primary. But Branigin had never warmed up to the president; he observed that Johnson was "always and forever being distant. When he asked you down there it was not to ask you your advice, it was to tell you what he had concluded. Hell, he never asked any questions."[8] The governor later confided to an interviewer that he could never be close to Johnson because he considered the president "a selfish, opinionated man of considerable mediocrity. As a matter of fact, he's rather a triumph of mediocrity."[9]

Other political leaders in the Hoosier State also urged Branigin to assist the president's reelection efforts. Birch Bayh, one of Indiana's two Democratic U.S. senators—Vance Hartke was the other—made a personal trip to meet with the governor in his State House office to "suggest that he was the only one that could really give us a chance to protect the president's flank." Bayh preferred not to serve as Johnson's stand-in because he and his staff were preoccupied with his own reelection effort. "I would have if it had been necessary," said the senator, "but the Governor was the head of the party and he was the one to whom the party machinery owed its primary allegiance."[10]

Johnson's desire to have Branigin as his stand-in gave the governor an opportunity to obtain concessions from the Johnson administration on Indiana's behalf. "I didn't need to make any deals involving me," he recalled, "but I did want some things done for Indiana and I listed them." Branigin's want list included more than twenty items. Among them: financial aid to help fund Branigin's efforts in the Indiana primary; a prominent ambassadorship for Frank McKinney Sr., the former national chairman of the Democratic Party; finally paying $25 million of the federal government's share for work on the Burns Harbor port on Lake Michigan; federal highway funds for several projects in the state, including road improvements in Gary and Vincennes and a new highway from South Bend to Indianapolis; funding for a new federal park at the Falls of the Ohio River at Jeffersonville; and reconsideration of an administration decision to award Illinois a nuclear research center.[11]

In mid-March, having obtained no firm commitment from the Johnson administration to meet his conditions, Branigin left Indianapolis for a brief trip to Florida. Before he left the state by train, however, a telegram arrived at his office from Robert Kennedy. The message indicated Kennedy would be seeking the Democratic presidential nomination. The governor was shocked. "This is a change in policy—and position," he wrote in his daily journal. "Like a carrion crow he descends to eat the wounded bird." The governor predicted that Kennedy would "lose the friendship of many of his ancient allies in Indiana. He should have waited—until 1972. But a Kennedy has never lost a primary or an election!"[12]

In preparing for his vacation Branigin had signed a "consent to run" form and secured the number of signatures required by law to place him on the ballot. He cleared his decision with his advisers and with Eugene C. Pulliam. "But I had not agreed to *go*—because I still did not have any assurances on the many promises the Johnson coterie had made," he recalled. Eager to secure Branigin's cooperation, Vice President Humphrey traveled to Indiana to appear at the gathering of Hoosier Democrats at the French Lick Sheraton Hotel on March 16. All that day administration officials had been attempting to contact Branigin via telephone to finally secure his agreement to run. According to St. Angelo, the Johnson administration had dispatched Secret Service agents to stop the train carrying Branigin somewhere in Alabama. It is unclear, however, whether the agents were successful, as some reports have Branigin calling from his hotel room in Fort Lauderdale. Dinner had been served when Humphrey and St. Angelo, sitting at the speaker's table, learned from John Nolan, manager of the hotel, that the governor had finally been reached. Humphrey, St. Angelo, a Secret Service agent, and a Humphrey aide retired to an area that had once been used as a locker room for golfers to hear the governor's decision. "All was tenseness and excitement," Branigin said. "After assurances—I agreed to go." Branigin later received a personal letter from Humphrey thanking him for standing in for the president and assuring him that all of the conditions the governor outlined for his agreement to run would be met.[13]

With Branigin's agreement secured, Humphrey delivered a stirring defense of the Johnson administration's social and international policies that drew frequent applause from the Hoosier Democrats. Although he did not mention McCarthy or Kennedy by name, the vice president compared the political situation in 1968 with the Progressive Party and Dixiecrat challenge faced by President Harry Truman in 1948. "Everybody was against us except the people on election day," said Humphrey. "I stand by my President, and we shall fight and we shall win." He also criticized Republican presidential candidate Richard Nixon, who claimed to have a solution for the problems in Vietnam. "If any man can produce the enemy at the conference table," Humphrey said, "let him step forth."[14]

Branigin was a formidable foe for anyone foolish enough to challenge him in his home state. As governor, he had enormous power over the distribution of the approximately seven thousand patronage jobs in state government. Patronage employees were required to "voluntarily" kick back 2 percent of their salaries to the coffers of the party in control—a system established under the administration of Democratic governor Paul V. McNutt in the 1930s. Until the practice ended in 1986, the governor also wielded power over the awarding of the operation of approximately 180 license branches in Indiana's ninety-two counties to county chairmen, who could use part of the profits from these operations to help finance their local organizations; branches in large urban areas could net profits of $20,000 or more. No county chairman wanted to incur the governor's wrath and risk losing such an essential moneymaking machine.[15]

When deciding whether or not to enter the Indiana primary, the Kennedy campaign took the Branigin threat seriously. On March 19 Kennedy adviser Ted Sorenson discussed the situation with three key Indiana Democratic congressmen, John Brademas, Lee Hamilton, and Andy Jacobs. All three agreed that Branigin would be able to easily defeat McCarthy, and could well do the same to Kennedy. They did hold out some hope that delegates committed to Branigin on the first ballot at the convention might later switch to Kennedy. The following day Ted Kennedy and David Hackett, a friend of Robert Kennedy's, met with Jim Beatty, chairman of the Marion County Democratic Party. Beatty shared a poll taken of people who had previously voted in primaries that showed Kennedy winning 28 percent, Branigin 24 percent, and McCarthy 5 percent.[16]

There were some Hoosier Democrats, however, who stood ready to work against Branigin in the primary. These Democrats were younger and more liberal than conservative party elders such as Branigin and St. Angelo and had been inspired by the energy of John F. Kennedy's New Frontier. When Robert Kennedy announced his candidacy for the presidency in March 1968, this younger generation rallied to his cause. One of this new breed was Michael Riley, a native of the coal country around Linton, Indiana. Riley's father, a dragline operator for a coal company, worshipped United Mine Workers boss John L. Lewis and fiercely supported the Democratic Party. After completing his freshman year at Indiana State University, Riley had gone home and told his father he had decided to support the Republican Party. His father sat his son down on the screened porch of the family home and talked with him for three hours about the history of the Democratic Party and why his son should support its work. At the end of the talk, Riley turned to his father and said, "Dad, I'll always be a Democrat."[17]

After earning his law degree, Riley found work in a variety of state government patronage jobs, including positions in the Department of Revenue and the secretary of state's office. He also found time to work as a precinct committeeman. In 1965 Riley moved up the ranks a bit in the party when he was elected president of the Marion County Young Democrats. Two years later, he became president of the state Young Democrats organization, defeating a candidate favored by St. Angelo. While in Gary, Indiana, attending a fund-raiser for the Young Democrats, Riley heard the news about Kennedy's announcement on television. When he returned home to Indianapolis, he called Jim Beatty and told him that if Kennedy came to Indiana, Riley wanted to be involved in the campaign. (Beatty often battled over political matters with both Branigin and St. Angelo.)

On the morning of March 21, shortly after his conversation with Beatty, Riley was sitting in his Indianapolis law office on the second floor of the Circle Tower building when he heard a phone ring. His secretary answered it and informed him that a gentleman identifying himself as Ted Kennedy wanted to speak with him. Riley picked up the phone and heard a man with a Boston accent on the other end telling him that Robert Kennedy planned to run in the Indiana primary and asking if the thirty-year-old Riley would take the job as chairman of the Indiana Committee to Elect Robert Kennedy. Riley suspected that one of his friends was playing a practical joke on him: he was "just waiting for someone to laugh," Riley recalled. After about two or three minutes Ted Kennedy realized that Riley questioned whether he really was the senator from Massachusetts. Kennedy laughed and said he would have Frank Mankiewicz, Robert Kennedy's press secretary, call and tell him more about what was expected of him. Mankiewicz called Riley and asked him to schedule a press conference to announce that Senator Kennedy had expressed an interest in exploring the possibility of running in the Indiana primary; Riley, said Mankiewicz, would be helping Kennedy make a decision. On Friday, March 22, the *Indianapolis Star* included an article noting that the first steps were being taken toward launching a statewide petition drive to place Kennedy on the primary ballot. Riley was quoted as saying that "more than 75 percent" of the activists involved in the Young Democrats organization were ready to throw their support behind Kennedy.[18]

One of the activists Riley intended to involve in the campaign was Louie Mahern, a former U.S. marine whose family had long been involved in Indianapolis politics. Mahern's maternal grandmother had worked as a Democratic precinct committeeman in Beech Grove in the 1930s. While he was growing up, Mahern also heard stories about political battles from his uncle Paul Cantwell, who served as a Marion County commissioner and as a representative in the state legislature. "He brought some pretty interesting people around the house," Mahern remembered. "I told my mother when I was eleven that I wanted to be a politician." Mahern received his first experience in politics after World War II, when he assisted another uncle in the Democratic primary for a seat in the state legislature. He placed cards on the windshields of those attending mass at Saint Catherine Catholic Church, urging people to vote for his uncle.[19]

In 1968 Mahern worked as the Democratic chief deputy at the Marion County Board of Voter Registration, a job usually filled by county chairman Beatty as a way to groom promising politicians. A veteran who opposed the war in Vietnam, Mahern found himself supporting the presidential candidacy of Eugene McCarthy, but like many Democrats he harbored the "secret hope that Bobby Kennedy would run." At that time approximately thirty Marion County Democrats would gather for lunch every Thursday in the basement of the Indiana State Teachers Association building. "There was usually a speaker," Mahern said, who also served as chairman of the Young Democrats for the Eleventh Congressional District, "but the principal feature of the lunch was getting together with other Democrats and trading information and rumors." At about eleven o'clock in the morning on March 21, Mahern was sitting in his office at the City-County Building. Michael Riley phoned to ask if Mahern would be attending the regular Thursday luncheon. When Mahern said he planned to be there, Riley suggested that they meet on the Circle downtown and walk over together. On the way, Riley told Mahern about his conversation with Ted Kennedy. He wanted Mahern to get and have copies made of the petition forms needed to place Robert Kennedy's name on the Indiana ballot. The Young Democrats had only a week to obtain certified signatures of five hundred registered voters in each of Indiana's eleven congressional districts— this new, tougher requirement had been enacted by the Indiana General Assembly to make it harder for non-serious candidates to place their names on the ballot. The certified signatures had to be in the Indiana secretary of state's office before midnight on March 28.

After lunch, Mahern returned to the Board of Voter Registration, picked up a blank Branigin for President petition, and walked over to Commercial Printing, on East Ohio Street just west of Alabama Street. Behind the counter that day was the owner's son, Tom Ash, who was just a few years older than Mahern. "I went in there and I saw him and said, 'Tom, I need one of these things, but at the top here instead of where it says Roger Branigin, West Lafayette, Indiana, I want you to put Robert Kennedy of New York, New York.' He looked at me and said, 'No kidding?'" Mahern replied that his request was not a joke, that it should be kept secret, and that he needed approximately eight thousand petitions by the next morning. Ash promised the order would be ready on time.[20]

The Young Democrats were joined in their efforts by a representative from the Kennedy campaign, Gerard Doherty of Boston. Doherty had earned the Kennedys' trust during Ted Kennedy's first run for the U.S. Senate in 1962, to fill John F. Kennedy's unexpired term. During that race for the Democratic nomination against Edward J. McCormack Jr., Doherty prepared a detailed report on each of the state's congressional districts. Ted Kennedy shared the report with his brother President John Kennedy, who said, "You know, whoever wrote this knew what he was talking about." Subsequently Robert Kennedy put Doherty in charge of brother Ted's primary campaign; he gave Doherty his home and office number and told him to call if he had any problems. Doherty used this information as leverage during the campaign, warning recalcitrant campaign workers that he would notify Robert Kennedy directly if they failed to follow Doherty's instructions. After Ted Kennedy won the nomination, Robert Kennedy told Doherty: "You know I asked you to do something; you did it, you did very well. Our family will be forever grateful to you."[21]

Doherty was practicing law in Boston in 1968 when he received another assignment from the Kennedys: to head to Indiana and see if there might be any chance for Robert Kennedy to enter the May 7 primary there. Doherty flew into Indianapolis and met with Riley, Mahern, and another Indiana Young Democrat, William Schreiber. These three men became the core group Doherty worked with on the petition drive. In Massachusetts Doherty could always find some politicians to help out during a campaign, but in Indiana "they just pulled the shades down." Mahern pointed out that senior members of the Democratic Party who would have normally supported Kennedy were stymied by Branigin's decision to serve as a stand-in for Johnson and by the need to protect, at all costs, Congressman Andrew Jacobs Jr., "the most important progressive officeholder in Marion County," said Mahern. Jacobs faced a potentially tough opponent in the primary, a young attorney named Dave Foley, who received some support from the Branigin administration. "That's why it fell to the Young Democrats to essentially run the Kennedy campaign in Indiana," Mahern explained. Doherty also reported to Ted Kennedy that a February 14, 1968, redistricting by a panel of three judges (which Democrats dubbed the St. Valentine's Day Massacre) had badly hurt such Democratic congressmen as Jacobs, John Brademas, and J. Edward Roush. "And for this reason," Doherty said, "many of their friends, although sympathetic [to Robert Kennedy], do not want anybody in making waves. It seems everybody is with us on a voice vote but no one wants us on a stand up vote."[22]

Riley recalled Doherty as "just a great guy, funny, but all business. [He] knew how to run a campaign, [he] knew the ins and outs. We set up shop in my law office." Riley used his Indiana contacts to find volunteers to circulate petitions. Doherty also received under-the-table assistance from Senator Vance Hartke's office, which provided names of Hoosiers who might be willing to support Kennedy. In order to make the most effective use of their limited resources, Doherty and his advisers decided to solicit signatures in the most populous county in each congressional district. William Schreiber was assigned to the Third Congressional District in northern Indiana; he set out for South Bend in a heavy snowstorm, carrying the names of two University of Notre Dame undergraduates, Chuck Naus and Michael Kendall.[23]

A sophomore at the University of Notre Dame when Kennedy entered the presidential contest, Kendall had already formed a Notre Dame Students for Kennedy organization. He received the necessary petitions from Schreiber on a Friday and with other students went out over the weekend to collect signatures. Kendall, who went on to serve in the Indiana State Senate, and another student were set upon and punched in downtown South Bend by local Democrats backing Governor Branigin. "So we got beat up in the United States of America trying to get petitions signed," Kendall said. Undeterred by the physical assault, Kendall and other members of the student group were able to obtain more than a thousand signatures for Kennedy's nomination papers; many of them were gathered at area Catholic churches. Looking back on the experience, Kendall still finds it hard to believe that the Kennedy campaign allowed him to play such a vital role in its Indiana primary effort. "Can you imagine a person running for president today doing that?" he asked.[24]

The First Congressional District, most of which centered on Lake County in northwest Indiana, also proved difficult. According to Mahern, the Democrats in Lake County "lived and died on patronage" and no politician wanted to risk angering Branigin. In addition, many Lake County Democrats harbored resentment toward Kennedy for an investigation undertaken by the Justice Department while he was attorney general: as a result, George Chacharis, the popular longtime mayor of Gary, had been indicted and sent to prison for tax evasion. Democrats in the region felt betrayed because Chacharis had aided John F. Kennedy in his quest for the presidency and helped deliver a sixty-thousand-vote plurality in the region for Kennedy in the 1960 general election. In addition, white members of the county Democratic machine opposed to Mayor Richard Hatcher, Gary's first African American mayor, remembered that Kennedy had sent his political aide, Dick Tuck, to assist Hatcher during his campaign for the mayor's office. To circulate petitions, the Kennedy campaign had to rely upon volunteers from Chicago, a group organized by Richard Wade, a professor of history at the University of Chicago, who headed the Kennedy office there. Getting the petitions to the district was the first challenge. At about ten o'clock Friday morning, Mahern had gone to the Greyhound bus station in Indianapolis to express-ship blank Kennedy petitions to Chicago. Later that afternoon, Mahern and Riley received word that the shipment had not arrived, so Mahern returned to Greyhound with a duplicate shipment—which also failed to reach its destination. (Riley later learned that there was a work stoppage at the Chicago depot and baggage handlers weren't sorting packages.) In order to get the petitions to the Chicago volunteers, Mahern borrowed Riley's car—he feared his own would not survive the trip—and left Indianapolis at about two o'clock in the morning for the northwest part of the state. He arrived at a Hammond, Indiana, service station four hours later and handed off the petitions to the Chicago volunteers through the car window. "We didn't even get out of the car," said Mahern, who then turned around and drove back to Indianapolis.[25]

Kennedy's entrance into the presidential contest had prompted a number of people to call Wade's Chicago office to volunteer their services. "When they would call up the Chicago office," said Wade, "they would say, 'What can I do for Kennedy?' I'd said, 'Forget Illinois. Can you get down? Do you have a car? Can you get down to Gary? Can you get to Whiting?'" The volunteers were especially important because any signatures submitted by those loyal to Mayor Hatcher were sure to be scrutinized with a fine-tooth comb by Lake County officials opposed to the mayor, Wade pointed out. In addition, the Branigin and McCarthy campaigns had already been working for several weeks to obtain signatures from registered Democratic voters.[26]

After talking with Doherty, Wade went to Whiting, Indiana, a majority-white area, and went door-to-door with a non-official Kennedy for President petition to gauge public opinion. "You could see it was do-able," Wade said. "The people responded very fast to it." Once the official petitions were ready, Wade's volunteers returned to the homes of people who had signed previously and had them sign again. "To get those petitions signed we put four busloads down there in two straight days," Wade recalled. "That's probably four hundred people."[27]

Doherty himself had spent most of Friday calling seminaries and Catholic high schools in the state asking for help and sending out petitions to those who volunteered. "It was just people working—all sorts of people," said Doherty. "I had eighteen, twenty seminarians out in the northeast getting signatures in the snow. It was one of those things you see movies about." In Indianapolis, the Kennedy forces had the able assistance of an African American self-styled minister named Joe Turner, a nattily dressed man never seen without a clerical collar. Turner took petitions to Kokomo and gathered the needed signatures for the Fifth Congressional District. That done, he performed the same stellar job in Terre Haute for the Seventh Congressional District. "Reverend Turner may have been the con man he was reputed to be," said Mahern, "but he sure as hell knew how to get petitions signed." In case Kennedy could not make it to the state in time to file his candidacy, the campaign gave power of attorney to Turner, Riley, and Schreiber to file on his behalf.[28]

In reports to the Kennedy campaign from his room at the Marott Hotel, Doherty outlined the political picture in the state and noted that the Kennedy campaign could expect "a hell of a battle." He did express confidence that if Kennedy could garner enough signatures to be put on the ballot, he could defeat Branigin. "NEED BODIES. NEED MONEY," he wrote. Doherty did worry that problems might arise with the petition drive, because "in all probability the county clerks will make it difficult to certify names." (Kennedy supporters did have to go to court to obtain a writ of mandamus to force Lake County clerk John G. Krupa to certify the approximately twenty-five hundred signatures gathered in Lake County.) By late Sunday evening Doherty had determined that the volunteers had accumulated almost ten thousand signatures—more than enough to place Kennedy's name on the ballot. As the signature drive continued, Doherty received a call from the Kennedy campaign to return to Washington, D.C., for a meeting on whether or not to enter the Indiana primary. The meeting involved most of Kennedy's Senate staff and a number of old friends of President Kennedy.[29]

Most of those present, including Ted Sorenson and Ted Kennedy, opposed making Indiana the first test for Robert Kennedy's presidential campaign. They were put off by the state's conservative reputation and the lack of assistance from the state Democratic Party. The campaign might survive a defeat in Indiana by Branigin, they thought, but if McCarthy ran ahead of Kennedy his race for the nomination would be finished before it could begin. Doherty was the lone voice arguing in favor of going into Indiana. A veteran of ward politics in Boston, Doherty faced opposition from fellow party members in his campaign for the legislature. He had to go door-to-door to win support. By working so hard, Doherty said he began to develop what he called "a sense of the people who live on the second floor." He had developed such a feeling in Indiana. "You just can't get that many signatures, people working for you, if you're a dud," Doherty said.[30]

In his meeting with Kennedy's advisers, Doherty argued that with just the initial help of three people, and with the entire state apparatus arrayed against them, he could guarantee that they would have enough certified signatures before the March 28 filing deadline. As the argument continued, Robert Kennedy entered the room. He asked a tired Doherty, who had gone without sleep for several days, "Gerry, what do you say?" Doherty responded: "I say we go in and I think we can win." Kennedy turned to the others in the room and said that as a candidate for president, he needed to know if he had any support. "The best thing to do," Doherty recalled Kennedy saying, "is to run, so I'm going to run in Indiana."[31]

On Thursday, March 28, Kennedy, wearing a gray glen plaid suit and fresh from campaign stops in Denver, Colorado, and Lincoln, Nebraska, stepped off an airplane at Indianapolis's Weir Cook Airport to officially file to enter the Indiana primary. It was 8:25 PM; he was little more than a half an hour behind schedule. There to greet the candidate was a crowd of about four thousand, many with homemade signs bearing slogans such as "Anybody over Johnson," "All the Way with RFK," and "Sock It to Them Bobby." Earl Conn, an assistant professor of journalism at Ball State University, had brought his family with him to witness the senator's arrival. "We could see him about 100 feet away speaking into a microphone but we couldn't hear him," Conn said. The crush of the crowd grew so great as Kennedy prepared to leave that some children were at risk of being trampled. "People were simply swept along; you could not stop moving if you wanted to," remembered Conn.

From the airport, Kennedy traveled by motorcade to the Indiana Statehouse, where another large crowd, this one numbering more than five thousand, was on hand to cheer the candidate at the south entrance to the building. James Tolan, an advance man for the Kennedy campaign, noted that the press of people made it almost impossible for the Kennedy entourage to enter the Statehouse. "Indiana is a terribly important state," Kennedy told the cheering crowd. "If we can win in Indiana, we can win in every other state, and win when we go to the convention in August." He asked for Hoosiers to help "start a new course, start a new path to peace in Vietnam."[32]

The overflow crowd also made it difficult for Kennedy and his party to leave the Statehouse after filing in Secretary of State Edgar Whitcomb's office on the second floor. Kennedy couldn't make it to his waiting car; he had to return to the Statehouse and leave by another exit. In the confusion, the candidate became separated from his wife, Ethel, who had to take a separate car for the short trip to the Marott Hotel on Meridian Street. At a press conference at the hotel, Kennedy gave a brief statement to members of the press. "I am not running against Governor Branigin. I consider him an outstanding governor, and a close personal friend." The issues in the campaign did not include the governor's stewardship of the state, he continued; they "are the divisions among us, between races, between age groups, and most of all over Vietnam."[33]

That evening, Riley, Mahern, and Schreiber met with the candidate in his room at the Lincoln Hotel on East Washington Street. "I immediately noticed how swollen his hands were and the scratch marks that ran up his arms and disappeared under his sleeves, souvenirs from adoring airport crowds that clutched at him," said Mahern. Although Ethel Kennedy expressed concern about her husband losing his voice and suggested that he write down his answers to the Hoosiers' questions, Kennedy waved away her concerns; he said he would speak with them. He asked them a number of questions about the petition drive and the political situation in the state. When Kennedy asked why so many people were so anxious to sign the petitions, Mahern said, "I don't think the people in Washington have any idea how detested Lyndon Johnson is and how upset people are with this war." Mahern added that a number of the signatures came from Lawrence Township, a normally Republican area. "They were falling all over themselves trying to sign these petitions," Mahern recalled, attributing this enthusiasm to uneasiness with what was happening in Vietnam. Looking back on his encounter with Kennedy, Mahern said the most remarkable aspect "was the piercing nature" of the candidate's eyes. "When I spoke to him he looked at me as though there was no one else in the world," said Mahern. "I felt as though he could see the inside of the back of my skull." Kennedy left Indianapolis the next day for campaign appearances in New Mexico.[34]

Branigin's entrance into the Indiana primary proved to be a low-key affair compared to the hubbub surrounding Kennedy's appearance. The governor's sons—Roger D. Branigin Jr. and Robert M. Branigin—filed the necessary paperwork (more than twenty thousand signatures) for their father, joined by Thomas DeMoss of Franklin, a close friend of Branigin's. In a statement issued by Branigin, the governor said he agreed to enter the race because he believed "it to be the duty of every patriotic American to support his President and this country in time of crisis as well as calm." Dr. James A. Bogle, a professor of political science at the University of Notre Dame and chairman of Hoosiers for a Democratic Alternative, filed on behalf of the McCarthy campaign. Bogle called Kennedy's entrance into the campaign "cutthroat competition," and predicted that Branigin would fail to receive the majority of votes in the primary. Bogle added that McCarthy could have won the Indiana contest if pitted against either Branigin or Kennedy, but a three-person race would make it an "uphill fight."[35]

Once Kennedy had secured a spot on Indiana's ballot, Doherty turned his attention to organizing for the primary campaign. One of his initial challenges involved obtaining lists of Democratic voters—an essential tool for recruiting potential volunteers. Acquiring such lists had been an easy task in Doherty's home state of Massachusetts, but in Indiana they were not public records. The Kennedy campaign finally got its hands on the lists thanks to the assistance of Indiana Democrats opposed to Branigin's leadership. Because Branigin had tried to cut off any aid from the regular state Democratic Party organization, Doherty brought in political professionals from Massachusetts—people with strong ties to Ted Kennedy—to serve as heads of the Kennedy campaign in each of the state's eleven congressional districts. "I picked all the guys, they all responded to me," Doherty remembered, "they all knew that their reward was going to come from me, and that nobody was trying to take my job so you didn't have that rivalry where guys hide papers on one another. Everybody was clear as to what they were to do. So we were a very mobile kind of thing. That made it a lot easier." These outside professionals could seek help from those who had worked on the petition drive, and also from other contacts provided by Riley. The lack of cooperation from local Democratic officials proved to be a blessing in disguise: Doherty noted that he did not have to bother with clearing matters with them before getting things done or talking to people who might be of assistance to the campaign.[36]

As the Kennedy campaign progressed, however, rifts developed among Doherty's Massachusetts professionals, those who had been involved in John F. Kennedy's 1960 campaign and presidential administration, and Robert Kennedy's Senate staff. In addition, the candidate himself sometimes seemed unsure about Doherty. "You know, he'd say, 'Teddy, does Gerry know what he's doing?'" Doherty recalled. Ted Kennedy would reassure his brother and then call Doherty in Indiana to say, "Hey, Gerry, I hope you know what you're doing." Doherty noted that the source of the unease was that he "was not his [Robert Kennedy's] guy; I was his brother's guy." The candidate, however, soon developed faith in Doherty and the Indiana organization he created. "The greatest strength the Kennedys have is if they have confidence in you and you know what you're doing," said Doherty, "you can tell them to walk down the street in the altogether and they'll do it."[37]

At approximately nine o'clock in the evening on Sunday, March 31—just three days after Branigin, McCarthy, and Kennedy filed to run in the Indiana primary—President Johnson went on national television to deliver a major statement on the war. Early drafts of the speech had been hawkish, defending the administration's handling of the conflict and calling for more bombing raids and more troops. Tet, however, had changed the minds of many in the

administration, including Defense Secretary Clark Clifford, about further es-
calation. "After Tet," said Clifford, "there was no suggestion that we could see
any light at the end of the tunnel." On March 26 various respected political
and military figures who had advised the president on the war in the past—
among them former secretary of state Dean Acheson; Douglas Dillon, diplo-
mat, philanthropist, and former treasury secretary; General Omar Bradley;
and politician-diplomat Henry Cabot Lodge, who had served both JFK and
LBJ as ambassador to South Vietnam—met with Johnson and expressed the
opinion that the time had come to disengage from a war that had begun to
weaken America at home and abroad. Johnson was shocked. "I had always re-
garded the majority of them as very steady and balanced," he said. "If they had
been so deeply influenced by the reports of the Tet offensive, what must the
average citizen in the country be thinking?" Frustrated, he angrily asked Clifford, "Who poisoned the well with these guys?"[38]

The lack of progress in the war, the insurgent candidacies of McCarthy
and Kennedy, and his always fragile health all weighed heavily on his mind as
Johnson prepared to address the nation. The president also faced the distinct
possibility of a devastating loss to McCarthy in the Wisconsin primary. On a
trip to Wisconsin to assess the situation, Postmaster General Lawrence O'Brien
had driven by a dark and empty Johnson headquarters. A few blocks away he
saw about a hundred young volunteers hard at work for McCarthy. "It was not
a good sign," said O'Brien, telling the president he faced losing the state primary by a two-to-one margin. Johnson was coming to believe he could not survive another four years "of the long hours and unremitting tensions" he had
endured as president. Whenever he walked through the Red Room at the
White House and saw the portrait of Woodrow Wilson hanging there, his
mind turned to a scene with Wilson stretched out in bed "powerless to move,
with the machinery of the American government in disarray around him." At
the beginning of 1968 Johnson had considered including in his annual State
of the Union message to Congress a statement that he was withdrawing from
the presidential race. When he journeyed to the Capitol to give his remarks he
thought he had the statement with him, but when he reached into his pocket
at the end of his speech the statement was not there. Joseph A. Califano Jr., a
Johnson speechwriter, theorized that his boss had decided to refrain from
making the announcement because he did not want to harm his legislative
program before Congress by becoming a lame duck.[39]

There also existed another challenge to Johnson's presidency. On February 8 George C. Wallace, the former segregationist governor of Alabama, had
announced that he would run for president as the candidate of the American
Independent Party; there existed, he said, "not a dime's worth of difference"

between the Democrats and Republicans. Wallace had been a thorn in Johnson's side during the 1964 election, when he surprised political pundits by running well in Democratic primaries in Wisconsin, Indiana, and Maryland. He railed against the federal government's intrusion into state affairs, particularly with respect to civil rights legislation, and against the breakdown in law and order. "People always say that George Wallace just appeals to the crackers, the peckerwoods and the rednecks," Wallace said in stumping for votes. "George Wallace says there's an awful lot of us rednecks in this country—and they're not all in the South!" In 1968 Wallace hoped to do well enough in southern and border states to deny either the Republican or the Democratic presidential candidate the required 270 electoral votes, thereby throwing the election to the U.S. House of Representatives. "If it is thrown into the House," said Wallace, "we have all to gain and nothing to lose." Wallace's campaign appeared to be well funded, with contributions flowing into his Montgomery, Alabama, headquarters from individual donors, and larger contributions from such national figures as Colonel Harland Sanders of Kentucky Fried Chicken fame and actor John Wayne.[40]

As the pressures continued to mount, Johnson began to seek opinions from his aides on whether or not he should run. Califano and Harry McPherson, White House counsel, urged the president in a meeting to seek another term in order to avoid gridlock with Congress. Johnson demurred, comparing his relationship with the legislative branch to that of an old married couple who have "lived together so long and we've been rubbing against each other night after night so often and we've asked so much of each other over the years we're tired of each other." Later, Johnson asked Califano who he thought would be the likely winner of the Democratic nomination if he decided to step aside. When Califano expressed the opinion that Kennedy would ultimately triumph, the president pointed out that at least the senator would keep fighting for his Great Society programs and once he "sat in this chair he might have a different view on the war."[41]

As the time approached for Johnson's March 31 speech, Clark Clifford attempted to convince the president that the time had come to soften his stance on the war and turn toward peace by announcing that bombing would be restricted to north of the demilitarized zone. Such a move by the United States, Clifford believed, might finally persuade the North Vietnamese government to sit down at the negotiating table. Clifford and McPherson prepared a conciliatory draft from which Johnson could work. The president, however, had a surprise in store for his aides. Discussing the speech with McPherson and Clifford, Johnson asked why the speech had no ending. When McPherson explained that the original ending proved to be too long and no longer fit the address's theme, the president told McPherson to write a new ending but not worry about its length. "I may have a little ending of my own," he said. An astonished McPherson turned to Clifford and asked, "Jesus, is he going to say sayonara?" McPherson remembered Clifford looking at him "with pity, as if I were too tired to be rational."[42]

Johnson had indeed decided to withdraw from the presidential race. If he pulled out of the fight for the nomination, the president believed he might be able to rise above politics, gaining leverage with both Congress and North Vietnam, and also start to "heal some of the wounds and restore unity to the nation." During his speech, Johnson announced his administration's decision to de-escalate the conflict in the hope that this would lead to talks with North Vietnamese leaders. As a nationwide audience watched at home, Johnson ended his address with his belief that he should not devote any time as president to partisan political matters. "With American sons in the fields far away, with America's future under challenge right here at home, with our hopes and the world's hopes for peace in the balance every day," said Johnson, "I do not believe I should devote an hour or a day of my time to any personal partisan causes or to any duties other than the awesome duties of this office—the Presidency of your country. Accordingly, I shall not seek, and I will not accept, the nomination of my party for another term as your President." After completing his fifty-five-minute speech, Johnson felt that a large weight had been lifted from his shoulders. "I had done what I knew ought to be done," he said. "Now it was history and I could do no more."[43]

Although some of his staff, including Vice President Hubert Humphrey, knew that Johnson had decided to withdraw from political life, the president's statement caught most of his staff and the cabinet by surprise. There was a politician in Indiana, however, who had been forewarned of Johnson's surprise announcement: Governor Branigin. For most of March 31 Branigin felt uncharacteristically out of sorts and lethargic. About eight o'clock in the evening, while home at the governor's mansion in Indianapolis, he received an urgent message from a Johnson aide, calling from the White House; he refused to accept it because he had become "a little tired of urgent messages" from the Johnson administration. "Well—they called back soon and announced LBJ would not run for the Presidency—the bombshell of the century," said Branigin in his journal. "We listened to his television address . . . and we enjoyed it more because we were of the very few—perhaps 50 in America who knew what he would add to his script at the end." Johnson's seemingly sudden decision to end his campaign left the governor in the lurch. "The roof had fallen in—and there I lay in the debris!" Branigin wrote in his diary. "The phone rang off the wall." The next day the governor received a call from Humphrey, who asked how the governor was doing. "How the hell do you think I am?" Branigin responded, according to his son, Robert. "I have a noose around my throat—I've just fallen from the attic—and my feet are three feet from the basement floor—and I feel the rope tightening around my neck."[44]

The candidate who had almost bested Johnson in New Hampshire, Eugene McCarthy, had spent most of March 31 making speeches in Wisconsin for that state's April 2 primary, where sixty delegates were at stake. The McCarthy effort in Wisconsin had been going well—more than eighteen thousand people (five thousand more than capacity) jammed together for a rally on March 25 at the Dane County Memorial Coliseum in Madison. Approximately thirteen thousand canvassers had gone to more than a million homes in the state on McCarthy's behalf. Volunteers reported that some towns in rural areas were totally devoid of Johnson supporters. "We were headed for a landslide," said Richard Goodwin, who remained on McCarthy's staff even after Kennedy entered the race. Polls indicated that the Minnesota senator should capture 63 percent of the vote. McCarthy supporters could also count on support from some Republicans, who could legally cross over and cast ballots in the Democratic primary. Such glad tidings boosted the candidate's belief in his cause to such an extent that after a speech at Whitewater State University, he said that the contest for the presidency was now between him and Republican Richard Nixon. When a student asked about Kennedy, McCarthy smiled and said that the New York senator might be "a problem along the way." He added that a win in Wisconsin would make "most all of the intermediate problems . . . disappear."[45]

As Johnson spoke to the nation, McCarthy prepared to address students at Carroll College in Waukesha. Shortly after he began, McCarthy heard a commotion from the back of the auditorium. Over the ruckus came the news that Johnson had abandoned his attempt for another four-year term. McCarthy seemed nonplussed. "Things have gotten rather complicated," he said. Later, at his hotel in Milwaukee, McCarthy tried to ignore the television newsmen clamoring for him to comment. It was, he said, "a night for reading poetry—maybe a little Yeats." The students who had worked so hard for McCarthy, however, reacted with unalloyed joy at their triumph. Ben Stavis, who had come to Wisconsin to work the same magic he had wielded in New Hampshire with the student canvassers, remembered that while he watched Johnson's speech at McCarthy headquarters in Milwaukee, he was desperately trying to stay awake after many long evenings on the campaign trail. When the president announced his withdrawal from the race, the crowd at the headquarters erupted with joy. "We jumped, shrieked, kissed, laughed, and cried," said Stavis. "We could not believe that we, a group of young, inexperienced students, had helped engineer the downfall of the world's most powerful politician."[46]

Jeremy Larner, a native Hoosier who had joined the McCarthy campaign in Wisconsin as a speechwriter, lay on the floor of his hotel room nearly asleep only to be snapped awake by journalist Theodore White, who was pointing to the television screen and declaring that Johnson's nerve had snapped. An exultant Richard Goodwin could not believe the news; he had believed the president "wouldn't fold for two months more." Sympathy for Johnson's action did cause McCarthy's expected percentage of the vote to dip slightly from what had been predicted by his campaign's earlier polls, but McCarthy went on to win a decisive victory in Wisconsin, polling 412,160 votes (56.2 percent) to 252,696 for Johnson (34.6 percent).

The day after his victory, McCarthy met with Larner and Jonathan Schell, another young speechwriter. "It's narrowed down to Bobby and me," McCarthy confided. "So far he's run with the ghost of his brother. Now we're going to make him run against it. It's purely Greek; he either has to kill him or be killed by him. We'll make him run against Jack. . . . And I'm Jack." Both Larner and Schell were perplexed by McCarthy's comments, and Schell, unsure of the campaign's direction, decided to leave the campaign and return to his studies at Harvard. Larner said he understood only half of what McCarthy had been talking about, and went to think more about what he had said. "I still got only half," he said, "and there wasn't any more, then or later."[47]

In a conversation with Shana Alexander from *Life* magazine, McCarthy elaborated on his view of Kennedy by quoting from a poem he had written in 1967 called "Lament of an Aging Politician," particularly a section stating: "I have left Act I for involution / and Act II. There mired in complexity / I cannot write Act III." According to the rules of classical Greek drama, McCarthy said, problems were presented in Act I, complications in Act II, and a solution in Act III. "I'm an Act II man," he told Alexander. "That's where I live—involution and complexity. In politics, I think you must stay in Act II. . . . When you get into Act III you have to write a tragedy."

Robert Kennedy, however, could be categorized as stuck in Act I, presenting problem after problem. "He never really deals with Act II," McCarthy said of his opponent, "but I think maybe Bobby's beginning to write Act III now. Bobby's tragedy is that to beat me, he's going to have to destroy his brother. Today I occupy most of Jack's positions on the board. That's kind of Greek, isn't it?"[48]

As Johnson was making his nationally televised remarks on the war, Kennedy, the other declared Democrat in the race, was flying toward New York's John F. Kennedy International Airport on an American Airlines flight from

Phoenix, Arizona. Kennedy had been in Arizona campaigning and holding hearings for a U.S. Senate subcommittee on Native American education. Kennedy knew nothing about Johnson's decision until John Burns, New York State Democratic Party chairman, rushed onboard and cried, "Johnson isn't running." As newsmen on the plane waited to hear his reaction, Kennedy remained in his seat. "I don't know quite what to say," he said. Instead, he decided to withhold comments on the situation until a hastily arranged press conference at ten o'clock the next morning. On the drive to Kennedy's apartment on United Nations Plaza in Manhattan, Dick Dougherty, a reporter for the *Los Angeles Times*, heard Kennedy mutter, "I wonder if he'd have done this if I hadn't come in."

That night in the Kennedy apartment, Burt Drucker, a campaign worker, went into the kitchen with Ethel Kennedy, who wanted to open a bottle of champagne to celebrate. Another aide, Fred Dutton, came into the room and said that the senator did not believe it was a night for celebrating with champagne. "She turned around and looked at me and looked at him, and with a twinkle she said, 'Scotch?'" Drucker recalled. Anticipating the entrance of Vice President Humphrey into the presidential contest, Robert Kennedy telephoned a number of Democratic Party leaders who were expected to play important roles at the August convention, but failed to receive any pledges of support. Kennedy also called Lawrence O'Brien, who had been part of John Kennedy's administration, to ask for his help. "Here we go again, Larry," O'Brien remembered Kennedy saying. "It's going to be like the old days. You'd better get a good night's sleep tonight because I'm not going to let you sleep from now on. It's a new ball game now."[49]

The news of Johnson's withdrawal also caused a flurry of telephone calls by Kennedy supporters in Indianapolis. Louie Mahern and Jim Beatty watched Johnson's address from the anteroom of Ted Kennedy's suite in the Marott Hotel. In the suite were Michael Riley and Earl Graves, a Special Forces veteran of Vietnam. When the president announced he would not accept his party's nomination for the presidency, "a whoop went up in both rooms simultaneously." According to Mahern, Kennedy, still clutching a Heineken beer and a ham sandwich, ran from the other room and immediately went to the telephone to try to call his brother. When he discovered that all of the phone lines were jammed, Kennedy and the rest of the group decided to go to Riley's law office, where more lines might be available.

Once they got there, the Kennedy supporters also persuaded the attorneys in the office across the hall to let them use their telephones. After finally getting through to his brother and talking to him for about twenty minutes, Ted Kennedy had a list of twenty-five to thirty people he wanted to try to reach.

"We divided the names, went to various offices and started calling the Democratic governors, senators, and state chairmen on the list," Mahern recalled. "Once we got the person on the phone, we asked them if they would hold for Senator Kennedy. A few of them asked, 'Which one?' We would then yell down the hall, 'Senator, I have Governor So and So on the line.'" Mahern remembered placing several calls, and noted that Riley had the honor of calling Mayor Richard Daley in Chicago and Gordon St. Angelo in Indianapolis. Riley remembered that the total long-distance bill for the night came to $4,000.[50]

Once the telephone calls were completed at about eleven o'clock that evening, Beatty drove Kennedy and Mahern back to the hotel. The trio walked from Riley's offices east on Market Street toward the Union Federal parking garage. As they walked, Mahern could hear Kennedy repeating the phrase "What startling developments." As they passed a Dunkin' Donuts shop at the southwest corner of Pennsylvania and Market streets, Kennedy said, "This has been an amazing year. What more could possibly happen?"[51] Kennedy would have his answer in just a few days.

1 2 3 **4** 5 6 7

The Speech

Robert Kennedy's quest for the presidency in 1968 began in utter chaos. His campaign had started more than a year behind the normal schedule for such an effort, and Kennedy lacked a national organization and the backing of any key Democratic Party officials. "I have to win through the people," he explained to a reporter from the *New York Post*. "Otherwise I'm not going to win." Kennedy also faced the difficult task of balancing the talents and egos of those who had been on his Senate staff since his election in 1964 (talented speechwriters Adam Walinsky and Jeff Greenfield and press secretary Frank Mankiewicz, for example), with former officials from President John F. Kennedy's administration (who included such notable figures as Ted Sorenson and Pierre Salinger). Joseph Kraft, a national newspaper columnist, noted that Kennedy's campaign had too many celebrities. "There were more chiefs than Indians," Kraft said. "It was very hard to fit all these people together." The frantic and disconnected nature of those early days of Kennedy's campaign was perhaps best summed up by a question posed by Arthur Schlesinger Jr. in a memo: "IS ANYONE IN CHARGE OF ANYTHING, ANYWHERE?"[1]

With Lyndon Johnson's decision not to seek reelection, the Kennedy campaign hoped that the way might now be clear for important Democratic leaders to switch their support from the president to the New York senator. Now that Johnson was out of contention, perhaps Governor Roger Branigin could be persuaded to stand aside and allow Kennedy to meet Eugene McCarthy one-on-one in the May 7 Indiana primary. "The smartest thing he can do now is not campaign," Michael Riley, chairman of the Indiana Committee to Elect Robert Kennedy, told a reporter for the *Chicago Daily News*. "Branigin should just say, 'Look, fellows, I don't want the presidency but I'm stuck on the ballot.' He should tell the voters to forget him and choose between Kennedy and Mc-Carthy." If the governor sat on the sidelines, Kennedy might then be able to garner enough of a majority in the Hoosier primary to deal a deathblow to the McCarthy campaign.[2]

Branigin, however, with no legal way to remove his name from the ballot—the deadline for doing so had passed—decided to remain in the race as a favorite-son candidate. Although most political observers saw Branigin's move as serving the needs of Vice President Hubert Humphrey, who was seriously considering entering the nomination fight—he finally announced his candidacy on April 27—the governor claimed otherwise. "I'm running and I'm running to win," Branigin told reporters. Even without the Johnson administration's support, Branigin and his advisers believed he could win the primary over Kennedy and McCarthy. With a victory, Branigin could control the Indiana delegation and bargain from a position of strength at what was likely to be a wide-open Democratic convention in Chicago. The Hoosier delegation might even have enough leverage to play a vital role in the selection of the vice presidential nominee. Speaking to a Chamber of Commerce dinner in Fowler, Indiana, Branigin made a point that he continued to stress for the rest of the campaign: "I feel the governor is the best person to represent Indiana's position at a national political convention—not some outsider." He planned on presenting his favorite-son candidacy to Hoosiers "as much as prudence and good judgment dictate. The polls show I'm not doing very well. But I never cared for polls. When they say I'm ahead I don't believe 'em. When they say I'm behind, I don't like 'em." Asked if he planned on importing any political figures or movie stars to aid in his effort (a dig at the Kennedy and McCarthy campaigns), Branigin said, "No movie stars and no animal acts." At a news conference, Gordon St. Angelo, Indiana Democratic Party chairman, predicted that other states might follow the same path and run their own favorite-son candidates in their primaries, in order to wield more influence at the national convention. "He is absolutely uncommitted," St. Angelo said of Branigin. "I'm sure there will be no commitment to anyone before the convention. Even then he would consult with the delegation before acting."[3]

In spite of the new political landscape, Branigin continued to receive solid support from Hoosier Democrats. Telegrams poured into the governor's office in Indianapolis from county chairmen offering assistance in the campaign. "We in Delaware County will give complete organization support to your favorite son candidacy," promised a telegram from Robert W. Stewart, Delaware County Democratic Committee chairman. "The comments I hear from the man on the street seem to be definitely anti-Kennedy. So I feel confident of your success in the coming primary." Robert Mahowald, a state senator from South Bend, also told the governor he could count on his help. "I just heard McCarthy. I don't want to see or hear Kennedy," Mahowald said. "I urge you to campaign actively as an alternate candidate."[4]

Branigin could also rely on the backing of the state's two largest newspapers, the *Indianapolis Star* and the *Indianapolis News*, for much of the coming primary campaign. The publisher of the two newspapers, Eugene C. Pulliam, offered the governor behind-the-scenes advice and actively promoted Branigin in his editorial pages and news columns. The governor noted in his daily journal that Pulliam agreed with his position to "hold the line for the Indiana delegation so as to be more effective in Chicago—and press my candidacy as far as prudence and good judgment permits." The Democratic governor was amazed that Pulliam, a strong supporter of Republican causes, was promoting his candidacy day after day in his newspaper, "sometimes when there was no news—or reason. You can't purchase such support." Although he did not know what the long-term effect might be for the primary contest, Branigin noted in his diary that Democrats should remember that "Republicans can elect you!" He also was surprised, and delighted, to receive a donation for his campaign from conservative Indiana businessman Eli Lilly. "I knew that he approved of much that I have tried to do—but a gift of $1,000—overwhelms me," Branigin wrote in his daily journal. In a conversation with St. Angelo, the governor also expressed the opinion that "it is a coalition of your enemies who hate the common foe more than they hate you—and *not* an association of your friends and idolaters which gets you elected."[5]

Born in Ulysses, Kansas, Pulliam had attended DePauw University in Greencastle, Indiana, before leaving after his junior year to work in newspapers. He quickly rose in the industry, working for the *Kansas City Star* and serving as editor of the *Atchison Champion* before buying a number of newspapers in Indiana, including the *Lebanon Reporter*, the *Franklin Evening*

Star, and the *Indianapolis Star.* According to his grandson, Pulliam was at heart "an old fashioned editor who went into political battles with both fists swinging." During the 1968 Indiana primary, Pulliam used his power as publisher to bolster Branigin's efforts in Indiana, and to hamper the Kennedy campaign at all costs. During John Kennedy's administration, Pulliam, who also owned newspapers in Phoenix, Arizona, had developed a liking for the president's wit, but he never developed any such warm feelings for Robert Kennedy. In Pulliam's mind, the younger Kennedy possessed an unattractive personality that sorted people into two distinct categories: those who were with him, and those who were against him. "You could never relax and just be with him, like you could with Jack," Pulliam said. Although warned by both his assistant publisher—his son, Gene—and the *Star's* managing editor, William Dyer, that his efforts against Kennedy might harm the newspaper's reputation, the publisher refused to pull any punches. Longtime *Star* city editor Lawrence "Bo" Connor remembered receiving a memo from Pulliam that read: "I think whenever Senator [Eugene] McCarthy comes to Indiana that we should give him as full coverage as possible—but this does not apply to a man named Kennedy."[6]

McCarthy, the challenger whose success in wooing Democratic voters had helped to force Johnson from the contest, had attempted to minimize the effect Kennedy's entry might have on the race for the nomination. The Minnesota senator had compared Kennedy's campaign to a quick-burning grass fire. "Mine is like a fire in a peat bog," noted McCarthy. "It will hold on for six months." McCarthy also dismissed the possibility of Humphrey joining the contest, terming it as "irrelevant" and not making "much difference one way or the other." Despite his bravado, McCarthy realized the importance of the Indiana primary to his campaign's future. After Johnson's withdrawal, McCarthy had taken Richard Goodwin's advice and telephoned some Democratic Party leaders asking for support. Goodwin did not expect leading establishment Democrats such as Mayor Richard Daley of Chicago to back McCarthy, but believed the attempt might "dissipate . . . the hostility that McCarthy's candidacy had aroused among party leaders." Once he returned from placing his calls, McCarthy opined to Goodwin that the Indiana primary would be "decisive." Goodwin agreed, pointing out that the state represented a "crucial confrontation between the pretenders."[7]

Before Kennedy entered the race, McCarthy had planned only three days of campaigning in the Hoosier State. Now he drastically revised his schedule. Those working with the state's Citizens for McCarthy group were "encouraged to expect" the senator to double and perhaps triple his effort in Indiana, noted Robert Toal, a member of the group's steering committee.

These last-minute changes meant that McCarthy volunteers in South Bend only had a day's notice that the candidate would be visiting the city on April 3.[8]

Faced with an antagonistic local press and two tough opponents, Robert Kennedy began his Indiana primary campaign with a busy day of appearances beginning at noon on Thursday, April 4. His schedule called for speeches at the University of Notre Dame in South Bend and Ball State University in Muncie, followed by the formal opening of the Indiana Kennedy for President headquarters at 36 East Washington Street in Indianapolis and ending with a rally at the Broadway Christian Center at Seventeenth and Broadway streets. After Indiana, the Kennedy campaign would move on to six other states, including Ohio, Louisiana, Michigan, and Oregon. John Bartlow Martin, the native Hoosier and veteran of many previous Democratic presidential efforts who had joined the Kennedy entourage for the trip to Indiana, remembered Kennedy coming up the aisle of the aircraft on the flight to South Bend and sitting beside him to ask, "Do you think it can be done?" Martin said that victory could be achieved and the two men discussed the coming effort. Kennedy told Martin that the speeches he produced could not be the same as the ones he had written when he worked on Adlai Stevenson's presidential campaigns in 1952 and 1956. Kennedy suggested that Martin travel with him for the next several days "to get the rhythm." Martin shared a draft of an earlier speech he had sent Kennedy with a statement saying the question before the country was whether there would be one nation or two or none. "He especially liked three or four sentences in it, one quoting Adlai Stevenson as saying that self-criticism is the secret weapon of democracy," Martin wrote later. Kennedy liked the line so much he told Martin to give it to speechwriter Jeff Greenfield to include in his talk before Notre Dame's students. Unfamiliar as yet with the campaign staff, Martin gave the quote by mistake to another speechwriter, Adam Walinsky, who could not believe Kennedy—never a big fan of the former Illinois governor—wanted to use a Stevenson quote in his speech and so left it out. Martin later noted that after the speech Kennedy grew angry with Walinsky and Greenfield for cutting part of his speech without first informing him. "This campaign promised to be like others I'd been through," Martin wrote.[9]

Upon his arrival at the South Bend Airport on board a chartered Electra aircraft, Kennedy drew a crowd of a thousand people, double the number that had gathered the day before for an appearance by McCarthy. "If I can win here in Indiana," Kennedy said, "I could go on to win the Democratic presidential nomination and turn this country around with your help." From the airport, Kennedy drove in an open convertible to the Stepan Center for a speech sponsored by the Notre Dame Academic Commission, an arm of the university's student government that handled campus lectures.[10]

Along the ride to the Notre Dame campus, Kennedy's motorcade received an enthusiastic greeting from students at Central High School. According to *South Bend Tribune* political reporter Jack Colwell, Kennedy's aides had to keep him from toppling out of the car as he tried to reach the outstretched hands of the students—many of whom, unfortunately for Kennedy, had not reached voting age. Kennedy received a subdued greeting, however, from local Democratic officials, who remained solidly allied with Governor Branigin. "I was honest with him," said Ideal Baldoni, Saint Joseph County Democratic chairman and secretary of the Democratic State Central Committee. "I pointed out he came in the picture late. We were committed to work for Branigin. And we keep our commitments." If Kennedy went on to win the nomination in Chicago, Baldoni said Saint Joseph County Democrats would "back him 100 percent."[11]

Approximately five thousand people crowded into the geodesic-domed Stepan Center, which had been prepared for an audience of thirty-eight hundred. Another thousand gathered outside, some climbing onto the center's entrance to catch a glimpse of the candidate. Kennedy's speech touched only lightly on the war in Vietnam, focusing instead on the plight of the impoverished in America. As students held signs reading "Up Tight with Kennedy" and "Rate in '68 with RFK," Kennedy pointed out that in one of the most affluent nations in the world, one with an unrivaled capacity to produce food, there were still American children so hungry that their minds and bodies had been damaged almost beyond repair. "If we cannot feed the children of our nation," he said, "there is very little we will be able to succeed in doing to live up to the principles which our founders set out nearly two hundred years ago." To help feed the hungry, Kennedy called for the creation of more meaningful jobs so fathers could "support their families with dignity and pride and buy the food that children need." Asked what he thought of the draft laws, Kennedy called them "unjust and inequitable" and, despite boos from the gathered students, argued the case for ending college deferments because they discriminated against those who could not afford a college education. As Martin noted, "He was nearly always at his best when trying to convince people who disagreed with him."[12]

Before leaving South Bend, Kennedy unsuccessfully attempted to elude the press horde following him long enough to pay a forty-five-minute visit to the Saint Joseph County Home for the Aged. The scene at the home was a far cry from the frantic nature of his appearances earlier that day. As a camera crew hired by the Kennedy campaign filmed the scene, about a hundred of the

home's residents gathered in the dining room to ask questions about such issues as Social Security, medical care, and the war. "If this country amounts to
anything now," Kennedy said, "it's because of what you've done." He called for
funding Social Security from general government revenues instead of from
payroll taxes, saying it would be the "fairest way" to fund the program. To a
question about the war from a resident who had sons who had fought in both
World War II and Vietnam, Kennedy expressed the hope that peace could be
attained and called for negotiations to start soon "so that no more American
boys are sent there."[13]

Meticulous planning stood behind each stop by Kennedy, and it was no
different for the senator's visit to Ball State University. Earl Conn, an assistant
professor in Ball State's journalism department, had helped establish a Students for Kennedy organization at the university. Through his connections
with Marshall Hanley, a local attorney and Tenth Congressional District coordinator for John Kennedy's presidential campaign in 1960, Conn became involved in making local arrangements for Robert Kennedy's Muncie campaign
stop. He found himself working closely with Bill Foley, a Kennedy advance
man. "The Kennedy advance people were unlike anything I had ever seen in
politics," said Conn, "really good." Foley made sure that every detail was covered; he even took a tape measure to find out if the airstrip at the local airport
was long enough to handle Kennedy's plane. (It wasn't; Kennedy had to trans-
fer to a smaller aircraft in order to safely land at Delaware County Airport–
Johnson Field.) "In confirming every detail, more than 200 telephone calls went
out of his room at the Ball State Student Center," Conn said.[14]

In investigating possible locations for Kennedy's speech at Ball State,
Foley considered both Emens Auditorium and the Men's Gym. Foley expressed concerns about being able to fill the vast Men's Gym. "Only when he
was assured that empty seats on the second floor could be curtained off so the
gym would appear full did he agree to its use," said Conn. Foley need not
have worried; a crowd estimated at twelve thousand packed the gym's bleach-
ers, balconies, lobbies, and the entire basketball floor for Kennedy's speech.
"It was beyond anybody's expectations," Conn said. Students began filling the
gymnasium in anticipation of Kennedy's arrival late Thursday morning and by
5 PM the building was full. To the strains of "Born Free" and "Downtown,"
played by the Scecina High School marching band from Indianapolis, Kennedy stepped off his chartered Convair 550 aircraft at 5:40 PM, about a half
hour behind schedule. Kennedy gave no speech to the seven hundred people
at the airport, moving briskly instead to a waiting red convertible that trans-
ported him and his wife the two miles to the Men's Gym. En route, Kennedy
had Muncie police chief James Carey stop the car so he and his wife could

greet the students who had begun to pour out of their residence halls when they spied the candidate driving by.[15]

After Hanley introduced him to the crowd at the gym, Kennedy gave an approximately half-hour talk. He prefaced his remarks by joking that he had given his brother Ted the assignment of having campaign buttons made so he could distribute them on his visit to Ball State. Unfortunately, after Johnson's withdrawal, Ted Kennedy had decided to put his own picture on the buttons. As the crowd laughed and applauded, Robert Kennedy said he told his brother it "was too late for him to get in this campaign. He gave me his slogan, which he put on a paper: 'The candidate's ready; it's not Bobby but Teddy.'" Turning to more serious matters, he reiterated some of the same main themes he had discussed earlier in South Bend. He asked his audience to look upon the disadvantaged not as statistics, but as individuals. "Men and women and children, condemned to suffer by our inaction," Kennedy said, "leading lives of deprivation as we live in relative comfort." If America could spend millions of dollars on the development of a supersonic jet, he added, it "can afford to feed the hungry children of the state of Mississippi."[16]

In a question-and-answer session after his prepared remarks, Kennedy deftly handled pointed statements from one student who called the senator's remarks "opinions and double-talk" and asked if he had any solutions for the problems he outlined. As the crowd booed the questioner, Kennedy noted that the student was "perfectly entitled to express his view, and he's perfectly entitled to disagree with me." Then he launched into a discussion of a program to offer tax credits to the private sector to encourage building factories and housing in areas, both rural and urban, that were suffering from massive unemployment. While agreeing with most of Kennedy's ideas, an African American student pointed out that the senator seemed to be placing a great deal of faith in white America, and wanted to know if such faith was justified. Kennedy responded: "I think that there are extremists on both sides. . . . I think that there are black people and there are black extremists who do not like white people. And I think they are teaching violence and lawlessness and disorder and say that there's no future under our government or under our society. I think that they are to be condemned, and I think they're performing a disservice for their own people. I think that there are white people who say they are concerned about black people and that the black people are inferior and therefore they don't want to treat them as equally. I think that is a small minority of the white people, and I think the vast majority of American people want to do the decent and the right thing here within our country."[17]

Students swarmed close to the stage at the conclusion of Kennedy's talk, making it difficult for the senator and his wife to leave. Conn, who was responsible for helping to escort Ethel Kennedy, noted that William Barry, Robert Kennedy's personal security officer, tried to lower himself off the raised platform to clear a space. "In doing so," said Conn, "he swung around and his forearm struck Ethel Kennedy full across the face. She staggered backward." Barry realized what he had done and apologized before finally making it to the floor and clearing a little room. Robert Kennedy jumped down successfully, but the swell of the crowd made it impossible for his wife to follow. "It seemed that thousands of persons were attempting to reach, to touch Kennedy and his wife," said Conn. Instead of fighting through the crowd, Conn led Ethel Kennedy to the back of the platform and out of the gymnasium through another door.[18]

As Kennedy was preparing to speak at Ball State, a white assassin shot Dr. Martin Luther King Jr. as he stood on the balcony outside his room, number 306, on the second floor of the black-owned Lorraine Motel at 420 South Main Street in Memphis, Tennessee. King had come to Memphis the week before in support of thirteen hundred striking African American sanitation workers. On the evening of April 3 King had delivered an emotional sermon before two thousand cheering supporters at the Mason Temple. As a thunderstorm raged outside, the civil rights leader spoke of the threats made against his life. He noted that on the flight to Memphis from Atlanta that day the pilot had announced over the public address system that because King was on the plane, the flight had to be delayed in order to make a security check. "Well, I don't know what will happen now. We've got some difficult days ahead," King warned. "But it really doesn't matter with me now. Because I've been to the mountain top. . . . I just want to do God's will. And he's allowed me to go up to the mountain. And I looked over and I've seen the Promised Land. I may not get there with you. But I want you to know tonight that we as a people will get to the promised land."[19]

On the afternoon of April 4 King worked on plans for a march in support of the striking sanitation workers. A similar march a week earlier had ended in violence, and local authorities had gone to federal court to stop King's plan for another protest. "We stand on the First Amendment," King told reporters. "In the past, on the basis of conscience, we have had to break injunctions, and if necessary we may do it. We'll cross that bridge when we come to it." Early in the evening, the thirty-nine-year-old King and others in his party prepared to go out to dinner at the home of a local minister, Samuel Kyles. King stepped out on the balcony and spotted Ben Branch, a local musician, standing in the parking lot with Jesse Jackson, Andrew Young, Hosea Williams, and other Southern Christian Leadership Conference aides. After dinner the men planned to attend a rally to support the strikers. As King leaned over the railing, Jackson called up and asked if he remembered Branch. "He'd heard us play 'Precious Lord' up in Chicago," Branch said. "So he told me, 'Man, tonight . . . I want you to play that 'Precious Lord' like you never played it before.' And I said, 'Dr. King, you know I do that all the time.' He said, 'But tonight especially for me. I want you to play it real pretty.'" King's local driver advised him to wear a jacket in the cool evening and King had turned to return to his room when, shortly after 6 PM, a shot rang out from a nearby rooming house. James Earl Ray's bullet had hit and mortally wounded King in the neck. Ralph Abernathy rushed to King's side and saw his friend try to say something, but all he could do was look at him. "It was like he was talking through his eyes—and what they were saying was, 'It has come. It has happened,'" Abernathy said. Although aides rushed King to Saint Joseph's Hospital, doctors could not save his life, and he died shortly after 7 PM.[20]

After his Ball State speech, Kennedy made his way back to the Delaware County Airport for a flight to his next stop on the campaign trail—the opening of his headquarters in Indianapolis. When they arrived at the airport, Kennedy and his wife climbed out of their car and went over to a nearby fence to shake hands with people gathered to catch a glimpse of the candidate. Hanley, who had ridden with the Kennedys to the airport, heard a news flash over the car's radio that King had been shot; he informed the senator as he prepared to board his waiting airplane. "He seemed stunned and dropped his head," Hanley recalled. "'Is he dead?' he asked. I said I didn't know and then he went up the ramp to the plane."

Kennedy may already have heard the news. According to the *Muncie Star*, while Kennedy shook hands with well-wishers at the airport, someone in the crowd asked if he had heard about King. "Was he shot?" the newspaper reported Kennedy as asking. The spectator answered that the Nobel Peace Prize winner had been wounded and appeared to be in critical condition. "The senator shook his head and walked on," the *Star* noted.[21]

Kennedy volunteers in Indianapolis were eagerly awaiting his arrival in the capital city. James Tolan, an advance man for the campaign, had been in the state since April 1 making arrangements for the senator's visit. He had hunkered down in his room at the Marott Hotel for a day, equipped with a map and a "breakdown of the figures on the various universities, trying to set up a schedule for him for April the fourth." Tolan met with other Kennedy staff members and decided to finish the day with two events in Indianapolis: the opening of the new headquarters and a rally at the Broadway Christian Center in the heart of the Indianapolis ghetto, which would tie into a voter registration effort led by Walter Sheridan and John Lewis, former chairman of the Student Nonviolent Coordinating Committee. "The kickoff rally here was held in the Negro neighborhood because it is an area of weak registration," said Pierre Salinger, who aided the Kennedy campaign in press relations in the state. Despite the inner-city location for the rally, Sheridan had "no real fears that there was going to be any problem." Tolan also arranged for a meeting between Kennedy and local African American leaders, to take place at the Marott after his speech. "Some of them were real militants and others were not," recalled Tolan.[22]

Kennedy appeared to have solid support among even the most radical elements of Indianapolis's African American community. Charles "Snooky" Hendricks, president of the Radical Action Program, believed that Branigin had ruined his chances of attracting black voters when he placed the Indiana National Guard on standby because of rumors of potential violence during the Gary mayoral election the previous November; on that day voters chose Richard Hatcher to become the city's first African American mayor. Hendricks also charged that the governor had shown no interest in helping with such problems as housing, jobs, and education. "The mere fact that Kennedy will come into the heart of the ghetto will pull the whole black vote," said Hendricks, whose organization assisted the Kennedy campaign with planning the rally at Seventeenth and Broadway streets. Benjamin Bell, treasurer for the Radical Action Program, said the group would not "blindly follow" the Democratic Party. Still, he added, "We dig Kennedy. His brother's image still lingers with us."[23]

Tolan had gone to Indianapolis's Weir Cook Airport to wait for Kennedy's arrival. Before Kennedy's plane landed, Tolan received word from Salinger that King had died. The news threw the campaign's carefully planned schedule into total disarray. Should Kennedy cancel both of his planned appearances in Indianapolis, go directly to the Marott Hotel, and issue a statement on the tragedy? Should he proceed to the rally at Seventeenth and Broadway? Or should he do nothing? Tolan managed to contact Sheridan at the rally site; Sheridan reported that the crowd seemed quiet and a number of them seemed to be unaware of the King shooting. Upon his arrival at the Indianapolis airport, Kennedy finally learned that King had died. "Oh God," a reporter heard Kennedy say. "When is this violence going to stop?" David Murray, a newsman seated across from Kennedy, saw him break down when he heard the news. "It was unbearable to watch him," said Murray, "to know that he was thinking about his brother getting it the same way. I don't want to go through that again." Speaking to reporters at the airport, Kennedy read the following statement: "Dr. King dedicated himself to justice and love between his fellow human beings. He gave his life for that principle, and it's up to those of us who are here—his fellow citizens and public officials, those of us in government—to carry out that dream, to try and end the divisions that exist so deeply within our country and to remove the stain of bloodshed from our land."[24]

As Kennedy dealt with reporters at the Indianapolis airport and tried to decide what to do next, frantic calls were being dispatched between city officials and representatives of the Kennedy campaign. Mayor Richard Lugar had called Gerard Doherty asking that the speech at Seventeenth and Broadway be canceled because he was concerned for the candidate's safety and feared a riot might break out. Michael Riley, who was not used to such high-level negotiations, heard the mayor say that if Kennedy did choose to speak, he would do so entirely at his own risk. "You're not going to get him to do anything he doesn't want to do," Riley remembered telling the mayor.[25]

At the Marott Hotel—dubbed the "Marat de Sade because the phones never worked," according to one Kennedy staff member—speechwriter Jeff Greenfield listened as Adam Walinsky and John Bartlow Martin argued about a foreign policy speech being written for Kennedy. They were still arguing when they learned of King's assassination. "I jotted down a few notes because I figured he [Kennedy] might want to have some," said Walinsky. "I jotted down a few notes and some words. God knows what they were." Walinsky hopped into a car to drive to the rally site to meet Kennedy and make sure he knew King had died so he could try to calm what might become a restless crowd. "We were all convinced that there were going to be riots," Walinsky said. Martin and Greenfield stayed behind at the hotel to work on a prepared statement for the candidate to deliver later to the press about the tragedy.[26]

At the airport, Kennedy had decided to cancel his stop at his campaign headquarters and instead head directly to Seventeenth and Broadway for the rally. Ethel Kennedy wanted to accompany her husband, but he sent his pregnant wife on to the Marott. Kennedy told Tolan he did not want any police going with him. A motorcycle escort did accompany the Kennedy motorcade, but peeled off as the car approached the rally site. "He had no prepared speech," said Fred Dutton, Kennedy's right-hand man for much of the campaign. "He had planned a fairly standard stump talk." On the approximately twenty-five-minute drive from the airport, Kennedy sat alone in the backseat staring out of the window at the dark city and attempting to find the right words for the occasion. "What should I say?" he asked. "I made a couple of inadequate responses," Dutton remembered responding. Kennedy managed to scribble out a few ideas for his talk on the back of an envelope.

The rally site, according to Adam Walinsky, who had pulled up just a few minutes before Kennedy's arrival, was a "phantasmagoric scene." There was almost no artificial lighting, "just a couple of floodlights on the platform," noted Walinsky, who could not remember if there were one thousand, three thousand, five thousand, or ten thousand people waiting to hear from the candidate. "I just don't know to this day," Walinsky said.[27]

The predominantly African American crowd at the Broadway Christian Center had been waiting nearly an hour and a half for Kennedy when he finally began his remarks shortly after nine o'clock in the evening. John Lewis noted that early on the throng appeared "upbeat, eager and excited to see the man who might well be the next president of the United States." About an hour before Kennedy's scheduled arrival, Lewis learned from Walter Sheridan that King had been shot. Those with the Kennedy campaign huddled together to discuss the situation; they debated whether or not to cancel the event and send the crowd home. "Somebody has to speak to these people," Lewis argued. "You can't have a crowd like this come, and something like this happen, and send them home without anything at all. Kennedy has to speak, for his own sake and for the sake of these people." It was agreed that the rally would go on, and that Kennedy himself would inform the crowd of King's death.[28]

Those packed near the flatbed truck that served as a makeshift stage had not heard the news from Memphis. Those on the periphery of the crowd, however, were listening to the latest bulletins about the shooting on transistor radios pressed to their ears. "People were jamming in groups of six or seven listening to developments," noted Reverend Lewis Deer, the white pastor of the Christian Brotherhood Center. An African American woman grabbed Deer's arm and said, "Dr. King is dead and a White man did it, why does he [Kennedy] have to come here!" Some who attended the rally later reported hearing threats being made by blacks to whites on the crowd's outskirts, including such statements as "What are you doing here, whitey?" and "Get out of here, you white son-of-a-bitch."[29]

Mary Evans, a white North Central High School student, had come to the rally with fellow North Central student Altha Cravey. The friends shared an abiding interest in politics and distaste for the war in Vietnam. Both had decided to volunteer their time and talent on behalf of McCarthy for the Indiana primary, but were curious to hear what Kennedy had to say. "I was keenly interested in national politics," said Cravey, "and he was a key figure in the debates about what the nation would do next and how it could be accomplished." Cravey's father, Gerald, a mechanical engineer who worked for Reilly Tar and

Chemical Company, had attempted to persuade his daughter not to attend the event because he feared for her safety. "When he saw that he could not deter us," Altha Cravey said, he decided to go with them. According to Evans, the trio "stuck out like sore thumbs" because they were among the few white people in the throng.[30]

Upon Kennedy's arrival, Walinsky went up to the senator, who was huddled under a dark overcoat, to tell him about King's death, but learned he already knew. Walinsky thrust the notes he had made to Kennedy, who took the paper and shoved it into his pocket before walking up onto the platform. Once at the microphone, Kennedy first told the crowd that he would only be talking for a few minutes because he had some sad news to impart, and asked those waving signs to lower them. He then said: "I have bad news for you, for all of our fellow citizens and people who love peace all over the world, and that is that Martin Luther King was shot and killed tonight."

Kennedy's shocking news resulted in great cries of astonishment and gasps from those in attendance, with many crying "No! No!" The noise reached such a level that a woman driving her car two blocks away, who had not heard about King's death, wondered what Kennedy had said to elicit such a response. "I could hear the oooo," said the woman, "it just filled the air." Mary Evans remembered thinking, "Oh my God, I'm going to be killed," as a wave of hostility and anger began to flow through the audience in its overwhelming grief. "It was such an eerie scene with the lights and the wailing in the background," Walinsky said. As the noise gradually died down, Kennedy continued with his remarks. "The quiet was partly due to the fact that everyone strained to hear Kennedy's words," said Altha Cravey, "and that people were absorbing the terrible facts of his message."[31] Kennedy glanced only briefly at the envelope he clutched in his hands throughout his extemporaneous talk, which lasted about six minutes. He continued:

"Martin Luther King dedicated his life to love and to justice for his fellow human beings, and he died because of that effort.

"In this difficult day, in this difficult time for the United States, it is perhaps well to ask what kind of a nation we are and what direction we want to move in. For those of you who are black—considering the evidence there evidently is that there were white people who were responsible—you can be filled with bitterness, with hatred, and a desire for revenge. We can move in that direction as a country, in great polarization—black people amongst black, white people amongst white, filled with hatred toward one another.

"Or we can make an effort, as Martin Luther King did, to understand and to comprehend, and to replace that violence, that stain of bloodshed that has spread across our land, with an effort to understand with compassion and love."

The next few sentences in Kennedy's talk marked a first for him. Since November 22, 1963, he had not spoken in public about the assassination of his brother, President John F. Kennedy. In the following years, Robert Kennedy had attempted to assuage his great grief by looking for meaning in the works of classical Greek dramatists and the writings of French novelist and essayist Albert Camus. "He knew the Greeks cold," Greenfield said of Kennedy. From time to time Kennedy would cite a quotation from a Greek play and ask his young staff members if they knew it. "We didn't at all. I think he got some delight out of that," Greenfield recalled. Now, in the heart of the Indianapolis ghetto, Kennedy drew upon what he had learned during the awful years following his brother's death and used that knowledge to console an audience of hurt and angry people—for the first time he shared his great sense of loss with a crowd of strangers. "That was something Bobby Kennedy never, ever did in public—he never talked about the murder of his brother," said Lewis. "To do it that night was an incredibly powerful and connective and emotionally honest gesture. He stripped himself down. He made it personal. He made it real."[32] Some in the crowd remembered seeing tears in his eyes as Kennedy continued:

"For those of you who are black and are tempted to be filled with hatred and distrust at the injustice of such an act, against all white people, I can only say that I feel in my own heart the same kind of feeling. I had a member of my family killed, but he was killed by a white man. But we have to make an effort in the United States, we have to make an effort to understand, to go beyond these rather difficult times.

"My favorite poet was Aeschylus. He wrote: 'In our sleep, pain which cannot forget falls drop by drop upon the heart until, in our own despair, against our will, comes wisdom through the awful grace of God.'

"What we need in the United States is not division; what we need in the United States is not hatred; what we need in the United States is not violence or lawlessness, but love and wisdom, and compassion toward one another, and a feeling of justice toward those who still suffer within our country, whether they be white or they be black.

"So I shall ask you tonight to return home, to say a prayer for the family of Martin Luther King, that's true, but more importantly to say a prayer for our own country, which all of us love—a prayer for understanding and that compassion of which I spoke.

"We can do well in this country. We will have difficult times; we've had difficult times in the past; we will have difficult times in the future. It is not the end of violence; it is not the end of lawlessness; it is not the end of disorder.

"But the vast majority of white people and the vast majority of black people in this country want to live together, want to improve the quality of our life, and want justice for all human beings who abide in our land.

"Let us dedicate ourselves to what the Greeks wrote so many years ago: to tame the savageness of man and make gentle the life of this world.

"Let us dedicate ourselves to that, and say a prayer for our country and for our people."[33]

As Kennedy climbed off the flatbed truck on which he had been speaking, people close to him stretched out their arms to try and touch him. "And you could see the awful magnetic power that he had—the charismatic quality that he had," Tolan said. There existed within the crowd a belief that Kennedy represented the "last hope" for the poor and dispossessed. Kennedy was the only white politician at that time who enjoyed a degree of trust from the African American community, said Michael Riley, chairman of Kennedy's Indiana campaign committee. "He had a definite total affection for African Americans and they for him," he added. "He was just a genuine caring person, and I think that came across." As Lewis left the rally site, he felt devastated by King's death, but consoled himself with the thought that "at least we still have Senator Kennedy."[34]

Across the nation, the report of King's death resulted in an outbreak of violence in more than a hundred American cities, including Boston, Chicago, New York, Baltimore, Pittsburgh, and Oakland. President Johnson had to use more than four thousand federal troops to quell the disturbance in the nation's capital. Nationwide, approximately seventy thousand army and National Guard troops attempted to restore some semblance of order; nevertheless, thousands of people were injured and the property damage soared into the millions of dollars. But in Indianapolis the streets were quiet. There had been some at the Indianapolis rally who were ready for violence. "Man there was going to be trouble," one militant recalled. "They kill Martin Luther and we was ready to move." Yet in just a matter of minutes, the multitude that had come so close to exploding in anger had quietly dispersed and returned peacefully to their homes. Both whites and blacks who witnessed the speech described what they experienced in religious terms. "They were in common grief together; they share[d] a common experience; he reminded them of that; he communicated," said Reverend Deer. One African American woman compared Kennedy to a figure out of the New Testament, saying her life would not have been complete without standing in the "presence of such a man." Another black woman who saw the speech on television said the feeling of the moment "comes right through the TV, when he speaks it's just like Mr. [Billy] Graham." Mary Evans said she has long held an "emotional memory" of Kennedy's remarks and remembered feeling as if the candidate had "laid his hands upon the audience" and healed them, deflating the powerful anger that surged through the packed audience. "It was worth the wait," Evans said.[35]

When he arrived at the Marott Hotel, Kennedy went to his room and placed a call to Coretta Scott King, the slain civil rights leader's widow, to offer his condolences and help. "What should I say to her?" John Bartlow Martin remembers Kennedy asking those assembled in his room. When nobody seemed to have an answer, Martin told Kennedy that whatever he said had to come from his heart. When Kennedy asked Mrs. King if there was anything he might do to assist her in her time of need, she asked if he could help in moving her husband's body from Memphis to their home in Atlanta. "Let me fly you there, I'll get a plane down there," Mrs. King remembered Kennedy saying. "I'll be glad to do that." After hanging up Kennedy had his staff take the necessary steps for chartering an aircraft and also had Burke Marshall, one of his former assistants in the Justice Department, fly down to accompany Mrs. King. Kennedy also arranged to have more telephone lines installed at the King residence to handle the crush of condolence calls. "They were political figures; but, aside from that, they were human beings first," Mrs. King noted of the Kennedy brothers, "and that humanness in them reached out to the needs of other people."[36]

As his staff discussed what to do with the rest of his campaign schedule, Kennedy put his oratorical skills to the test once again in a two-hour meeting with about fourteen local African American leaders. He faced a hostile audience; the more militant members, including Hendricks, thought the only solution to the issue of race might be to burn the whole country down. Others in the group were willing to listen to what Kennedy had to offer. Gerard Doherty remembered walking to the meeting with Kennedy and hearing the rumbling from those present, questioning why they should listen to what this white man had to say. A tired Kennedy noted that he had left his home in Virginia at five o'clock in the morning despite pleading from his children to stay. When he got on the plane, he read a newspaper article criticizing him for being too friendly with minority groups, and now he had come under fire from this same group for being like all the other white leaders. "I happen to believe that I have something to offer to you and your people," said Kennedy. "Yes, you lost a friend. I lost a brother. I know how you feel. . . . You talk about the establishment. I have to laugh. Big business is trying to defeat me because they think I am a friend of the Negro. You are down on me because you say I am part of the establishment." When Kennedy had finished talking, one of the people in the room said that by the next day, he would have boarded an airplane and flown off to another city, while they would remain behind to deal with the

community's problems. Kennedy pointed to Doherty and told those in attendance that if they had any concerns to seek him out, the political professional
from Massachusetts: talking to him would be the same as talking with Kennedy. As Doherty and the candidate made the long walk back to the senator's
room, Kennedy turned to him and observed, "Well, Gerry, I certainly assured
your stay in Indianapolis to be a very interesting one."[37]

The senator's blunt approach made an impression on those who attended
the meeting. Hendricks later told reporters that the time he spent with Kennedy the night of King's assassination had led him to believe that the senator
was "completely sympathetic and understanding" of the problems faced by the
African American community in Indianapolis. Ben Bell, another member of
the Radical Action Program, noted, "The cat was able to relax"—an ability not
shared by McCarthy in later meetings with local black leaders and clergymen
to discuss such issues as unemployment, housing, and education.[38]

To his staff, Kennedy seemed unaffected by his emotional speech earlier
in the evening. "I almost don't think he realized what a tremendous impact it
was going to have," said Greenfield. The day's events had dredged up once
again for Kennedy that horrible day in Dallas; "You know," he said, "the death
of Martin Luther King isn't the worst thing that ever happened in the world."
At first, Greenfield considered the remarks to be callous, but later realized
Kennedy's thoughts had been concentrated on the memory of his slain brother.
As Walinsky and Greenfield worked late into the night to draft a speech for
Kennedy to give the next day in Cleveland, this one on violence in America,
the candidate wandered into the room in which they were working, something
Kennedy normally never did. Kennedy remarked to his speechwriters, "You
know, that fellow Harvey Lee Oswald, whatever his name is, set something
loose in this country." Greenfield remembered that the first news reports about
John Kennedy's death had transposed Lee Harvey Oswald's name. "And that's
the way he remembered it, because obviously he never took another look at it
again," said Greenfield. "But, it was quite clear that the thing he was ruminat-
ing on, what led him in the first place to say the death of King wasn't the worst
thing in the world, was that this was part of a link." Exhausted, Greenfield
later collapsed onto his bed to sleep, only to be awakened by Kennedy tucking
him in. Greenfield said to the senator, "You aren't so ruthless after all." He
said, "Don't tell anybody."[39]

1 2 3 4 **5** 6 7

The Campaign

As a young boy growing up in Angola, Indiana, Bill Munn took an active role in his family's support of the Democratic Party. Wearing a tiny straw hat, Munn handed out pamphlets urging people to vote for Adlai Stevenson in his 1956 presidential run against incumbent Dwight D. Eisenhower. Four years later, Munn's father served as coordinator of John F. Kennedy's presidential campaign in Steuben County. When Lyndon Johnson battled Republican Barry Goldwater for the presidency in 1964, Munn went door-to-door handing out brochures extolling Johnson's candidacy in a county that was a hotbed of GOP activity on Goldwater's behalf. "By the time I went off to college," said Munn, "I already had a lot of political experience."

At Ball State University in Muncie, Indiana, Munn decided to major in political science and history. "When I got to Ball State, I'd go anyplace to a [political] meeting. I'd love to hear people talk about politics," he said. In the spring of 1968, as many of his friends became enthralled by Eugene McCarthy's stand against the war in Vietnam, Munn found himself attracted to Robert Kennedy's advocacy on behalf of African Americans and working people. "McCarthy had done a great service in tackling Johnson," Munn said, "but he was like a one-horse candidate, and I never did quite figure out if he was opposed to Johnson or opposed to the war." Munn volunteered to aid Kennedy's attempt to win Indiana's sixty-three delegates to the national Democratic convention by running in the state's May 7 primary.

For three to four weeks in April and May, Munn, after his classes were finished for the day, went door-to-door in Delaware County soliciting votes for Kennedy. Years later, Munn particularly remembered the contrast in reactions from the African American neighborhoods he visited and the poorer white neighborhoods other canvassers covered for Kennedy. The minute Munn told an African American homeowner that he worked for Robert Kennedy, he or she invited him in and often offered him coffee or a beer while telling him stories of the obstacles they faced and overcame as members of a minority group in America. Hanging on the walls in many of these homes were framed pictures of John F. Kennedy. In some of the county's poorer white neighborhoods, however, Kennedy canvassers were threatened with guns; Munn himself was menaced by one person who told him to get off his porch or he would turn his dogs loose on him.[1]

Delaware County epitomized in microcosm the challenge faced by the Kennedy campaign in Indiana. How could Kennedy retain his strong support among the state's African American community while persuading white voters who were threatened by advances made by blacks in civil rights and fearful of violence in the streets that he could work for their welfare as well? Kennedy told Richard Goodwin, who had left the McCarthy campaign to join his friend in the fight for the nomination, that he had to convince disadvantaged whites that African Americans were not their enemies. "They're being discriminated against too," said Kennedy. "Not because of race. But because the people at the top don't care about them. They need what the blacks need—a decent home, medical care. If they waste their energy fighting against blacks, they're only going to sink themselves. But it's not easy."[2] Fortunately for Kennedy, he could draw upon the services of John Bartlow Martin.

Though born in Ohio, Martin grew up in a house on Brookside Avenue, Indianapolis, "a mean street in a mean city," he noted in his memoirs. "Most people who write their memoirs seem to have had happy childhoods," he later said. "I hated mine." His two brothers died at a young age. Martin particularly recalled one occasion where he observed "a seemingly endless parade of robed and hooded Klansmen marching around Monument Circle in dead silence." Derisively dubbed "the bookworm" by his father, a general contractor, Martin knew from his days in grade school that he wanted to become a writer. He eagerly read the works of such authors as H. L. Mencken, Theodore Dreiser, Sherwood Anderson, John Dos Passos, Thomas Wolfe, and Ernest Hemingway, and honed his writing skills as a reporter with the *Indianapolis Times*. He left the world of newspapers for a successful career as a freelance writer, an occupation he described as "champagne today, crackers and milk tomorrow." During the 1940s and the 1950s, from his home in Highland Park, Illinois, Martin earned a reputation as one of America's ablest reporters, producing at his peak a million words a year. His detailed, well-researched articles frequently appeared in the "big slicks," mass-circulation magazines such as the *Saturday Evening Post, Life, Look, Collier's, Reader's Digest*, and *Harper's*.[3]

What set Martin apart from his contemporaries was a deep and abiding concern for the common man. "Most journalists make a living by interviewing the great," he said. "I made mine by interviewing the humble—what the Spaniards call *los de abajo*, those from below."[4] Through the years the Hoosier journalist took his readers into the worlds of such people as a coal miner's widow, a mother who wondered why her teenage son had killed a nurse for no apparent reason, and a convict talking about his life behind bars. Martin's work showed that he possessed what he claimed was the one characteristic a writer couldn't do without: an inquiring mind. The economist John Kenneth Galbraith said of Martin that no one could "make a point more succinctly, support it more sharply with evidence and then, of all things, stop."[5]

In 1944 Alfred A. Knopf published the first of Martin's sixteen books, a history of Michigan's Upper Peninsula. Three years later, Martin produced *Indiana: An Interpretation*, a history of his home state. Although he assumed he would hate Indiana because of his unhappy days there as a child, Martin was surprised to discover "a certain affection suffusing parts of the book; and when I quoted the old saw 'Many good men come from Indiana, and the better they are the quicker they come,' it was more in jest than bitterness." Although historian Arthur M. Schlesinger Jr. praised the book, calling it the finest ever written about the nineteenth state, Hoosier reviewers were less kind, finding Martin's unsentimental depictions of the state's past unpalatable. An anonymous reviewer for the *Indiana Magazine of History* noted that the book administered "a shock treatment or, like Jove, hurls a bolt of lightning at the people of Indiana."[6]

Martin's life changed in the early 1950s when a friend asked him to edit a book of speeches by Illinois governor Adlai Stevenson. When Stevenson became a serious candidate for the Democratic Party's presidential nomination in 1952, Martin, described by one reviewer as "a devoutly liberal Democrat, unabashed and unregenerate," accepted an invitation to work for the governor.

Martin became a member of a group of speechwriters dubbed the "Elks Club" (so named because the Stevenson campaign rented space for them in a local Elks Club building in Springfield, Illinois). In addition to Martin, other members who worked for Stevenson's 1952 effort included Galbraith; Schlesinger; David Bell, a former member of President Harry Truman's administration; W. Willard Wirtz, a member of Stevenson's gubernatorial staff; and Archibald MacLeish, a noted poet. In Stevenson's 1952 and 1956 presidential campaigns, and in John F. Kennedy's 1960 run for the White House, Martin discovered a niche for himself—that of an editorial advance man, a position he invented during Stevenson's campaign in the 1956 California primary. "I'd go to a state in advance of the candidate to interview people, trying to find out what the local issues were," he said. "I would talk to the local Democratic leaders, businessmen, newsmen, taxi drivers, waitresses, bartenders anybody I could find. It was just like reporting." Once he was through ferreting out information, Martin produced a detailed report and then rejoined the campaign party as it traveled through the state he had just visited. The candidate could refer to Martin's work, which included such useful information as allusions to local history and famous figures and recommendations on what issues to emphasize and what issues to avoid. Through his work with politicians, Martin learned something about his former profession. "No reporter can ever know what's really going on; he is on the outside looking in," observed Martin. "As JFK used to say, the only man who knows what it's really like is the man that fights the bull."[7]

A seven-part series he wrote for the *Saturday Evening Post* on the U.S. Senate Rackets Committee investigations of Jimmy Hoffa and the Teamsters union led to Martin's connection with the Kennedy family. While working on the series, Martin met Robert Kennedy, then chief counsel for the Rackets Committee. "I had no way of knowing it at the time, of course, but meeting Bobby Kennedy on this story changed my life," Martin recalled. After John Kennedy won the Democratic presidential nomination, Martin became an editorial advance man for his campaign. After Kennedy was elected president, Martin received an appointment as U.S. ambassador to the Dominican Republic, a post he held until after Kennedy's assassination. "Ours was a house in mourning for several years after 1963," noted Martin's son, John Frederick Martin.[8]

The gloom that had fallen over Martin lifted in the spring of 1968 when Robert Kennedy decided to enter the Democratic presidential race. Over the years Martin had developed a deep fondness and respect for Robert Kennedy. "I liked Bobby Kennedy from the start," Martin said of their first meeting. "Though born to wealth and power, he had about him not a trace of superiority or affectation." Later, he learned of Kennedy's compassion and deep concern for the poor and disadvantaged, his devotion to justice, his interest in the concerns of young people, and his "brooding, almost tragic sense of life." As early as the fall of 1967 Martin had suggested that Kennedy should consider challenging Lyndon Johnson for the 1968 Democratic nomination by starting to round up convention delegates.[9]

Knowing of Martin's ties to the Hoosier State, both Kennedy and his close adviser Ted Sorenson called him several times after the candidate decided to enter the Indiana primary. Kennedy wanted Martin to do the same kind of editorial advance work that he had done for John Kennedy in the 1960 campaign. "Indiana is not Kennedy country," said Martin. Kennedy knew the odds were against him, but he also realized the importance of his first primary test, likening it to his brother's 1960 run against opponent Hubert Humphrey in West Virginia, where he had to prove to skeptical political pundits that a Roman Catholic could win the trust and support of Protestant voters. "Indiana is the ballgame," said Robert Kennedy. "This is my West Virginia." He also wanted to remind Hoosiers that John Kennedy never forgot what West Virginia had done for him in the primary, and had rewarded the state when he became president. Although Kennedy wanted to use such statements in his Indiana speeches, Martin advised against it; he believed Kennedy's best chance would be to finish second to Governor Roger Branigin, and that he should concentrate instead on running ahead of McCarthy in the three-man race. Kennedy noted that the national press following him would emphasize the point about the state being his West Virginia anyway, even if he eliminated it from his prepared remarks. Sorenson suggested that the candidate should tell Hoosiers that they had the chance to pick a president. "I liked this—Indiana's presidential primary had never before been important," said Martin. "He began saying in almost every speech, 'Indiana can help choose a president.'"[10]

In a memo to Kennedy and Sorenson, Martin warned that Indiana was a state "suspicious of foreign entanglements, conservative in fiscal matters, and with a strong overlay of Southern segregationist sentiment. Hoosiers are phlegmatic, skeptical, hard to move, with a 'show me' attitude." The frantic nature of Kennedy's early days on the campaign trail should be avoided at all costs in Indiana, Martin counseled. He sensed that the ordinary Hoosier watching television at home each night was "tired of excitement and, after watching pictures of killing in Viet Nam and rioting in the cities, doesn't want to watch pictures of kids pulling your clothes off."[11]

Instead of competing with McCarthy for young college students who opposed the Vietnam War, Martin wanted Kennedy to appeal to a broader constituency, including blue-collar workers. "The people, I thought," said Martin, "did not want to be excited." He reasoned that the 1968 election resembled that of 1952, the year of Stevenson's first presidential campaign. Then, the electorate, weary after years of the New Deal and two wars, had sought calm and turned to Eisenhower. After eight years of what Martin called Eisenhower's "do-nothingism," the voters were ready to follow a fresh, exciting, young leader and had turned to John Kennedy. "Not in 1968—once more they [voters] wanted change," said Martin, "change from Vietnam and from riots, but change and calm, not a summons to great adventures."[12]

With the assassination of Martin Luther King Jr., both Kennedy and McCarthy took some time to regroup, suspending their campaigns to attend King's funeral. By this time, Kennedy's staff realized just how critical the Indiana primary was. "I remember when we moved out in Indiana the theory was, 'God, well, you know, if we lose Indiana we lose everything,'" noted Kennedy campaign aide William Haddad. "So we all just went out there."[13] Kennedy resumed his visits to the state on April 10, with stops in Fort Wayne, Columbus, and Terre Haute. During these events, Kennedy reiterated the importance of the Indiana primary for his presidential effort. "We can win it here in the state of Indiana," he told the crowd in Fort Wayne that mobbed his car. "If we can win it here, we can go on to win in Oregon, win in California and win at the convention because of your help." In Columbus Kennedy told an older audience that in a poll of his ten children he had received only four votes. "Two votes went to my brother Teddy. Two went to my sister Pat. The others were reassessing their position," said Kennedy, drawing laughter from the crowd. The candidate also used humor to defuse potentially embarrassing situations on the campaign trail. While speaking in Columbus, Kennedy had pronounced Indiana as "Indianer." On a subsequent campaign stop in Gary, Kennedy noted that he was delighted to be in "In-dee-an-uh." He noted: "There was some fellow from Massachusetts that was here the other day that called it 'Indian-er.' That was my younger brother Teddy. He looks like me. But I call it Indian-uh! And we're going to elect a President of the United States that knows how to pronounce the name of this state!"[14]

As Kennedy made quick stops charming Hoosiers and voters in other primary states, including Nebraska and Oregon, Martin returned to Indiana from his home in Princeton, New Jersey, where he had moved to work on a draft of a biography of Adlai Stevenson and teach a seminar at the Graduate Center of the City University of New York. He dodged carpenters nailing up partitions and found office space in Kennedy headquarters, a loft over the old Indiana Theater in downtown Indianapolis (during the primary campaign, the theater showed *Gone with the Wind*) that the Kennedy campaign was renting for $2,500 per month. Martin met with Joe Dolan, a Kennedy aide in charge of scheduling the candidate, and two young staff writers and researchers,

P. J. Mode and Milton Gwirtzman, to help map out strategy for the rest of the Indiana campaign. At night, Martin retired for rest to the home of his mother, Laura B. Martin, at 208 East Kessler Boulevard.[15]

To eliminate the frenzied pace that had marked Kennedy's campaign to that point, Martin urged the senator to change his style to appear "sober and responsible" to Hoosier voters. (Kennedy agreed with Martin's assessment, at one point telling his staff he did not want to appear like Frank Sinatra running for the White House.) "For the middle-aged voters, and to be contemplative, Bob should try to identify with Indiana's past greatness," Martin wrote Sorenson. This included lauding such heroes as Abraham Lincoln and James Whitcomb Riley. Martin wanted Kennedy, accompanied by some of his children, to visit the memorials in Vincennes for George Rogers Clark, a hero of the Revolutionary War, and former president William Henry Harrison, followed by a visit to the grave of Lincoln's mother, Nancy Hanks Lincoln, where he could "walk around and kick leaves and muse about saving the Union, the house divided, kids, etc." To avoid being identified too closely with the concerns of the state's African Americans, Martin also wanted Kennedy to schedule stops at industrial communities he called "redneck backlash factory cities," including Kokomo, Muncie, and Marion. To play to Hoosier nostalgia, the Kennedy staff came up with the idea for an old-fashioned railroad whistle-stop trip to several cities. Mode suggested they use the route of the Wabash Cannonball. "John was trying to take the candidate's approach, his personality and his views on issues and placing them in some kind of historical setting or geographical context that would be attractive to Indiana voters," noted John W. Douglas, a former Justice Department official and troubleshooter for the Kennedy campaign in the state. Martin spent most of his first week in Indiana seeking support for his ideas with Goodwin, Ted Kennedy, and Larry O'Brien, who had resigned his job as postmaster general in Johnson's administration to help run Kennedy's campaign, and working on scheduling with Dolan. "Most of the stuff in the briefing sheets came from interviewing I did from my book on Indiana, and from Indiana fact books and the world almanac," said Martin. Kennedy later praised the Hoosier journalist for the documents, claiming they were a lifesaver, that they gave him a sense of confidence anywhere he appeared in Indiana. "When he came to a strange town," Martin noted, "he knew what to expect—what kind of town it was, who was in his audience, what kind of people they were, what was on their minds, and so on."[16]

On Saturday, April 21, Martin and Dolan had finished the schedule and briefing sheets for the whistle-stop trip to Hoosier historic sites that would begin at the start of the week. On Sunday, Martin traveled to Washington, D.C., and then on to Kennedy's Hickory Hill home, where a number of Kennedy's key staff had gathered. That evening at dinner, Martin told Kennedy about the schedule for the coming week. The senator expressed little enthusiasm for visiting the historic sites and balked at taking any of his children along. With the help of Fred Dutton, Martin convinced the candidate to include his children on the grounds that "every Hoosier takes his wife and kids to visit the Lincoln sites." Kennedy also expressed his dislike for Tuesday's schedule, which included stops in factory towns in central Indiana. Martin explained that the white backlash vote in these communities differed in composition from the Poles and other ethnic groups that had settled around Gary. In cities like Kokomo the white backlash vote consisted of workers who had come to Indiana from Kentucky and Tennessee ("red-necks and Klansmen," Martin called them) during World War II to find jobs in the war industry. "Why am I going there then?" Kennedy asked. Martin replied: "Because there are a lot of Democratic votes there and you've got to convince them." Kennedy, after reviewing Martin's briefing sheets, agreed to the schedule, and even decided to take three of his children, David, Courtney, and Michael, and his pet dog, Freckles, to visit the Hoosier historic sites.[17]

To attract the support of Hoosier voters, Martin also argued that Kennedy had to alter his message, speaking out against rioting and violence and emphasizing his law enforcement experience as attorney general. At the same time, Martin and others on the staff stressed, Kennedy should not neglect to include statements that injustice could not be tolerated either. Gwirtzman suggested that instead of saying "attorney general"—a government position some people didn't understand very well—Kennedy should just say he was the former chief law enforcement officer of the United States. Kennedy liked the recommendations, nodding and saying: "I can go pretty far in that direction. That doesn't bother me." According to Gwirtzman, Kennedy "just wanted to point out the fact that he had faced these kinds of problems in 1962, in 1963, even in 1964, that he had had some experience with it and that it was perfectly possible to preserve civil liberties . . . while enforcing the law." Martin also urged Kennedy to talk more about government working with private enterprise; as senator he had worked with white business leaders to help restore New York City's largest ghetto, Bedford-Stuyvesant. On the issue of Vietnam, Martin wrote for Kennedy a line indicating that the senator wanted to end the fighting and stop spending money in Vietnam and use it instead for programs in the United States, including Indiana. "This played to Indiana's natural isolationism and chauvinism and penny-pinching," Martin said. "It always got applause."[18]

Kennedy's decision to emphasize a more conservative tone while stumping in Indiana caused some dissension among his staff, particularly with his Senate speechwriters, Adam Walinsky and Jeff Greenfield. One night Martin found the young men composing limericks about Kennedy coming to Indiana and becoming a member of the Ku Klux Klan. An article by *New York Times* reporter Warren Weaver Jr., titled "Kennedy: Meet the Conservative," observed that Martin and Goodwin (who was not involved) had seemingly turned the liberal Kennedy into a Democratic version of George Romney, the Republican governor of Michigan who had dropped out of the presidential race. Although some in the media and on Kennedy's own staff viewed these changes as a struggle for the candidate's soul, Martin "conceived of it as an effort to win the Indiana election." Kennedy could not hope to achieve a victory in the Indiana primary by making speeches pleasing to the ears of liberals on the East Coast, something Martin said Schlesinger understood. Kennedy had the moral authority to take a firm stand against violence and rioting before white backlash voters because he stood as one of the few white men in America trusted implicitly by African Americans, noted Martin. "They knew that in his heart he was for them," he added. Kennedy also always followed his statements about his intolerance for violence and rioting with pleas to end injustice. "This may be viewed as a cynical effort to have it both ways; it may also be viewed as an effort to heal the country's wounds, to bring us together again," said Martin. As Kennedy himself later told reporters covering his campaign, rural and working-class whites were uninterested in hearing him talk about the problems of African Americans, but expressed time and time again their concerns about violence. "You have to get them listening by talking about what they're interested in," Kennedy pointed out, "before you can start to persuade them about other matters."[19]

Martin made sure to gauge what effect the ideas he presented to Kennedy had on Hoosiers. During the candidate's stops at county courthouses around the state, Martin often wandered around the edge of the crowds. There always seemed to be a claque of young girls screaming in the front rows, but most of the townspeople hung back with their hands in their pockets, as though they were daring Kennedy to make them respond. Martin noted: "He emphasized that violence could not be tolerated; and got big applause; then when he went on and said injustice could not be tolerated either and everybody was entitled to jobs and schools, they didn't applaud but they didn't mind—they had heard what they wanted to hear, that he was against violence in the streets, and that was enough. It worked." Kennedy usually ended his speeches with a paraphrase of a quote from George Bernard Shaw's *Back to Methuselah*: "Some men see things as they are and say, 'Why?' I dream things that never were and say, 'Why not?'"[20]

The disagreements on the emphasis of Kennedy's message reflected the sometimes disordered nature of his campaign in Indiana. The mixture of old hands from JFK's 1960 campaign, Robert Kennedy's Senate staff, the advance men headed by Jerry Bruno, a media group recruited by Pierre Salinger, and the Massachusetts professionals reporting to Doherty led to confusion over who was in charge. "We had a mixed kind of leadership; I mean you didn't know where the real power source was," said Haddad. On one occasion while in Indiana, he wrote a memo addressed to whoever was the leader of the campaign and sent it to ten people "because there was no really clear decision making process." To help ease the confusion, Kennedy called upon Douglas, the son of U.S. Senator Paul Douglas of Illinois, to go to Indiana to try to pull everything together. Douglas agreed, but only if he could work with Doherty, not over him, as the Massachusetts politician had done "an outstanding job building the local organizations from the ground up," noted Douglas. (Doherty praised Douglas, calling him a "minister without portfolio" and appreciated Douglas's support of his organizing efforts in the state.) During his three and a half weeks in Indiana, Douglas attempted to get the various components of the campaign "to mesh more smoothly, and by the end of the campaign we'd made some progress."[21]

Encouraging reports were being turned in to Kennedy headquarters by the student canvassers sent out around the state, to neighborhoods in such urban areas as Indianapolis, Anderson, Muncie, Wabash, and Kokomo, to promote Kennedy's candidacy. Although Indiana college students willing to canvass for Kennedy were often hard to come by, due to the appeal of McCarthy and a general apathy since Johnson's withdrawal from the race, special efforts were being made by the Kennedy organization to recruit students from out of state. Students from universities in Michigan, Ohio, Illinois, and Kentucky were bused in to canvass each of Indiana's eleven congressional districts. In addition, high school students "in substantial numbers" were able to play key roles in distributing tabloids promoting Kennedy, manning offices, and even canvassing in some areas. Jim Flug, a legislative assistant for Ted Kennedy, spent a weekend in the state accompanying the canvassers and debriefing them on their discussions with voters. "With minor exceptions," Flug reported, "operations both at senior and junior levels seemed fairly well organized, spirited and imbued with a feeling of optimism."[22]

In talks with the canvassers Flug discovered results that he thought at first were "too good to be true." After conducting a number of interviews with the canvassers in several areas, however, he became convinced by the consistency of their reports and their ability to cite specific instances to back up their claims. "And the recurring reports of [George] Wallace supporters who were willing to back RFK were confirmed by an interview I conducted in Kokomo," said Klug, "where my arguments as to RFK's record of 'laying down the law' domestically as AG [attorney general], and internationally in the Cuban missile crisis in fact left the Wallace supporters saying, 'If I do vote, it'll be for Kennedy.'" Those who opposed Kennedy were motivated less by his stands on substantive issues than by what Flug called the "RFK myth issues"—his youth, his long hair (which Kennedy eventually cut for the Indiana primary), his money, his coming late to campaign, and his "trying to be all things to all people." Those voters who were still undecided were craving specifics from Kennedy, Flug reported, including his exact stand on issues. "They want to hear and read his statements and know how his stand differs from others," said Flug. "They do not want generalities. This is especially true on the campuses."[23]

In addition to offering some pay to canvassers for their work, the Kennedy campaign found space in the basement of its headquarters to lodge them overnight on weekends. "We bunked two hundred to three hundred kids there every Friday or Saturday night," recalled Doherty. On one weekend before the canvassers left to do their work, a motivational psychologist who had attached himself to the campaign talked to Doherty about going out with the students. Doherty agreed, but had little faith that this "ivory tower" academic could offer any real assistance. When the psychologist returned, he seemed very excited about his experience. The students, he told Doherty, had come up with a phrase that seemed to click with voters in Hammond—"Robert Kennedy wants to give people a hand up rather than a handout." This simple statement resonated with the various ethnic groups in northwestern Indiana—Hungarians and Poles, for example. "I think you're going to get them," Doherty remembered the psychologist saying to him. "I think you're going to do pretty well."[24]

As the Kennedy effort began to gather steam in Indiana, the McCarthy campaign was struggling. Coming off emotional, thrilling battles for delegates in New Hampshire and Wisconsin, McCarthy and his legion of volunteers staggered into Indiana exhausted and ill. Campaign staff established a headquarters in Indianapolis on two floors of the former Claypool Hotel (a fire had destroyed the building's upper six floors in July 1967). Volunteers soon dubbed the building "the Cesspool" and were forced to subsist on peanut butter and other sandwiches donated by local families. On one occasion when funds were lacking, a group of housewives in Madison, Wisconsin, shipped 250 pounds of food by station wagon to Indianapolis. Most of the McCarthy staff stayed at the inexpensive Antlers Hotel, which quickly received the sobriquet "Ant Hill." Indianapolis, noted Ben Stavis, who had been with the campaign since New

Hampshire, was "simply not a comfortable city in which to live and work." Staff complained about the lack of good inexpensive restaurants and even about the taste of the local drinking water. "Somehow we're not made to feel as welcome here as we were in Wisconsin," said a McCarthy volunteer in New Castle, Indiana. A strike by telephone installers forced the campaign to rent offices around the state and install telephones before staff had a clear picture of where they were needed. "So over seventy-five storefronts were established in one week," Stavis said, "far too many, as it turned out, for us to supervise, staff, and finance."[25]

As with the Kennedy campaign, frictions developed among McCarthy's supporters. The national staff, headed by Curtis Gans, jostled for control with the Hoosiers for a Democratic Alternative (HDA) group, which was directed by Jim Bogle. "At times we were ready to shoot ourselves," said one of McCarthy's Indiana leaders. The rivalry grew so heated that the national staff started calling Bogle "Jim Bungle." According to Stavis, the HDA failed to produce promised lists of members, contributions, or effective staff assistance. "Indeed, they seemed always on the defensive and were hesitant using out-of-state resources," said Stavis. The Hoosier organization feared the national McCarthy campaign staff wanted to take over from them—a fear that was well-founded, according to Stavis, who believed that the HDA wasn't capable of running a large statewide campaign. "Eventually," he said, "the national staff became dominant simply by the sheer weight of hundreds of workers who went out into the field and worked."[26]

The disorder in the McCarthy camp was exacerbated in Indiana by the campaign's financial mismanagement. Literature promoting McCarthy sat idle because there were no funds for mailings. Automobiles were rented to transport staff from town to town, but there was no money to buy gas. What McCarthy speechwriter Jeremy Larner called the "telephone disease" often reached epidemic proportions. McCarthy's Senate staff was blocking all access to the candidate; McCarthy himself was offering no indication of what direction he wanted the campaign to take in the state. What could the staff members do? Make phone calls. Doing so, said Larner, helped to confirm a staff member's sense of belonging to a national operation. "You not only can, you must find out what's happening in other parts of the country, who is saying what, doing what, scheming what," said Larner. The phone bill accounted for approximately $78,000 of the $800,000 estimated to have been spent by the McCarthy campaign in Indiana.[27]

The changed political landscape seemed to throw McCarthy off stride. McCarthy had lost two of his most important issues: Johnson and the war in Vietnam. Johnson had abandoned the race; with a bombing halt and the

Robert F. Kennedy stops to address a crowd at Twenty-first and
Harding streets in Indianapolis during the waning days of the Indiana
primary, May 4, 1968. *Indiana Historical Society, DC 019.*

Los Angeles Rams defensive lineman Roosevelt Grier helps steady Kennedy as he
reaches out to shake hands from residents of the neighborhood near Twenty-first and
Harding streets in Indianapolis, May 4, 1968. *Indiana Historical Society, DC 019.*

Kennedy uses a microphone to address a crowd gathered to hear him speak at Twenty-first and Harding streets in Indianapolis, May 4, 1968. *Indiana Historical Society, DC 019.*

Carlo Defelice (left) and Ronnie Stenberger of the Stritto Sign Company hang a banner for Indiana governor Roger D. Branigin's presidential campaign outside the Sheraton-Lincoln Hotel headquarters of the Democratic State Central Committee, April 12, 1968. *Indianapolis Star.*

Workers for Governor Branigin's presidential campaign prepare materials at Branigin headquarters in Indianapolis. *Indianapolis Star.*

Governor Branigin on the campaign trail the day before Indiana voters went to the polls in the state presidential primary, May 6, 1968. *Indianapolis Star.*

Branigin reaches out to shake the hands of Hoosier voters at a campaign stop in Delphi, Indiana, on April 22, 1968. *Indianapolis Star.*

Union leaders and local officials listen to a Branigin speech in Highland, Indiana, on April 27, 1968. *Indianapolis Star.*

Branigin makes a point with Michael Dora, a Central Catholic High School student, during a stop in Vincennes, Indiana, on April 30, 1968. *Indianapolis Star.*

(Left to right) Karen Rariden, Annie Moore, and Carolyn Himes prepare campaign signs and posters at Branigin campaign headquarters in Indianapolis. *Indianapolis Star.*

Photos taken during Robert Kennedy's speech at the University of Notre Dame's Stepan Center on April 4, 1968. *University of Notre Dame Archives.*

Robert Kennedy visits
Evansville, Indiana, in
1966 to speak on behalf
of local congressman
Winfield Denton. *Indiana
Historical Society,* M 0681.

Senator Eugene McCarthy of Minnesota addresses a crowd of supporters at University Park in Indianapolis on March 18, 1968. *Indianapolis Star.*

Senator McCarthy talks to newsmen at Indianapolis's Weir Cook Airport during a campaign visit for the Indiana primary on April 25, 1968. *Indianapolis Star.*

McCarthy laughs as he prepares to answer a question from a reporter at a press conference at the Marott Hotel in Indianapolis on April 22, 1968. *Indianapolis Star.*

McCarthy supporters at a rally for the candidate in Indianapolis's University Park on March 18, 1968. *Indianapolis Star.*

McCarthy addresses his campaign staff and volunteers at his headquarters at the Claypool Hotel in Indianapolis on the night of the Indiana primary, May 7, 1968. *Indianapolis Star*.

A view of McCarthy campaign headquarters in the James Whitcomb Riley Room at the Claypool Hotel in Indianapolis, April 16, 1968. *Indianapolis Star*.

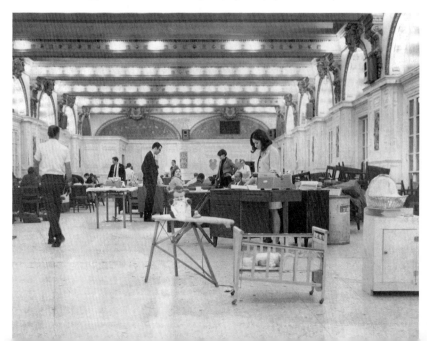

Views of the memorial *A Landmark for Peace* honoring Robert Kennedy and Martin Luther King in the Dr. Martin Luther King Jr. park on Indianapolis's north side. *David Turk.*

Robert Kennedy leaves after giving a speech to Indianapolis Democrats during the Indiana primary. Behind Kennedy is his aide, Fred Dutton. *Bass Photo Company Collection, Indiana Historical Society.*

Kennedy addresses Marion County Democrats in Indianapolis on crime and violence in America, May 1968. *Bass Photo Company Collection, Indiana Historical Society.*

Kennedy informs a crowd gathered for a political rally at Seventeenth and Broadway streets in Indianapolis that civil rights leader Martin Luther King Jr. has been shot and killed in Memphis, Tennessee, April 4, 1968. *Indianapolis Recorder Collection, Indiana Historical Society.*

Kennedy's speech at Ball State University's Men's Gym on April 4, 1968. *Archives and Special Collections Research Center, Bracken Library, Ball State University.*

Kennedy's car is mobbed by spectators as he campaigns on Indianapolis's Monument Circle on May 1, 1968. *Indianapolis Star.*

Kennedy is flanked by his wife, Ethel, and Indiana campaign coordinator Gerard Doherty, during a victory celebration with his volunteers at the Sheraton-Lincoln Hotel in Indianapolis, May 7, 1968.

Kennedy rides with Gary mayor Richard G. Hatcher (left) and East Chicago mayor John B. Nicosia (right) on a campaign swing through northwest Indiana on April 29, 1968. *Calumet Regional Archives, Indiana University Northwest.*

Editorial cartoon "Guests in the House!" that appeared on the front page of the April 24, 1968, edition of the *Indianapolis Star* depicting Kennedy and McCarthy as unwelcome visitors attempting to woo Indiana voters. Governor Branigin is depicted warily watching the two interlopers. *Indianapolis Star.*

Hoosier reporter and author John Bartlow Martin played a key advisory role to the Kennedy campaign during the Indiana primary. *Gary Yohler/Frederick Vollrath, Indianapolis Times Collection.*

hope for the start of peace negotiations, the war faded as a chief topic of concern. According to Larner, without Johnson and Vietnam as issues, there existed for McCarthy "no ready-made backdrop to throw into relief his qualities of thoughtfulness, caution, and responsibility." McCarthy believed that the campaign had transformed itself into merely a personality contest between himself and Kennedy. "You see, once he came in it was old politics, pretty much," McCarthy later said. "It wasn't really the challenge to the Johnson position, it got into the question of what's your record on civil rights, and why is your [Senate] attendance record bad? And all these other side issues that Bobby introduced." McCarthy became particularly upset about a pamphlet circulated during the Indiana campaign by the Citizens for Kennedy office in New York (McCarthy blamed Salinger as the person behind the effort). The document cited McCarthy's less-than-liberal voting record on such issues as Medicare, Social Security, and rent supplements. McCarthy said that the pamphlet included distortions and "positively false statements" about his voting record, and said that if any such material had been issued with his name he would have "repudiated it at once and set the record straight." Dr. Martin Shepard, chairman of the Citizens for Kennedy group, defended the brochure's accuracy and accused McCarthy of attempting to get "a Kennedy backlash going in Indiana." Kennedy later disavowed the statements made in the brochure and indicated his national campaign headquarters had nothing to do with its release. "I have never seen the material on Senator McCarthy's voting record," said Kennedy. "But if that material contains erroneous or misleading representations, I would urge that its distribution be halted and that those responsible for its publication apologize to Senator McCarthy forthwith." Stephen Smith, Kennedy's brother-in-law and overall campaign coordinator, noted that if the attack had come from the Kennedy campaign, it would "have done a better job."[28]

During his first visits to Indiana, McCarthy observed good omens for his campaign among Hoosiers. The candidate appeared impressed that people in Indiana did not cut down lilac bushes as people did in other states, and that farmers left large trees standing in their plowed fields. McCarthy remembered with fondness an appearance he made in Crawfordsville, where a Wabash College quartet consisting of a harpsichord, cello, violin, and flute had performed Vivaldi's *Four Seasons*. "This was the first time, I believe," McCarthy wrote in his memoirs of the 1968 campaign, "that a candidate for the presidency had been accompanied by a harpsichord." Gans had put together a "rural strategy" for the Indiana primary, concentrating on sending McCarthy on to rural areas and smaller communities. "My schedulers seemed preoccupied with having me appear in every courthouse square in the state of Indiana," McCarthy remembered. The strategy failed, however, because of unpredictable sched-uling. With little advance notice, there existed no time to attract large crowds to McCarthy events. The candidate did not help matters by some-times skipping planned appearances with no warning; once he disappointed a crowd that had been patiently waiting for him because he stopped his mo-torcade for an impromptu picnic and baseball game. "He was overscheduled, underscheduled, lost, driven impossibly long distances, and later estimated that he wasted eighty percent of his time," noted Arthur Herzog, a McCar-thy volunteer.[29]

By the time the McCarthy campaign reached Indiana, Larner had grown "disenchanted" with his candidate, who seemed "amused" by his young speechwriter because he differed from the "same style of guys who worked for him in his Senate office, but I wasn't quite the kind who would work for Bobby either." Late at night and into the early hours of morning Larner's hotel room became filled with "lost souls" who had expended great effort on McCarthy's behalf during the day but were unsure "if they really wanted or if they had any business being there." During the day, however, Larner and the other staff acted as if they were "in the service of a wise and calm daddy, crudely attacked by a renegade brother who stirred up crowds with his long hair, squeaky baby talk, and unfair money," Larner said. Although they were critical of Kennedy's method of politics, according to Larner, they were unaware that for McCarthy the "new politics" being practiced by his campaign of dedicated volunteers really meant for him "personal freedom from commitments to anyone." A few years after the campaign ended, Larner believed that McCarthy had not put forth his best effort to win the Indiana primary. "He's a terrible snob and he de-cided early that the Indiana people just weren't his kind," Larner told a colum-nist for the *Indianapolis Star*. "All he did was go to the rituals where all the people present already agreed with him."[30]

One member of McCarthy's team who proved to be an effective cam-paigner in Indiana was actor Paul Newman. The star of such films as *Hud* and *Cool Hand Luke* made a number of appearances on the Minnesota senator's behalf in such cities as Indianapolis, Lafayette, and Crawfordsville, where a crowd of more than a thousand people jammed downtown streets to catch a glimpse of the matinee idol's famous blue eyes. "I feel I'm a better man—win, lose, or draw—for having been a part of this campaign," Newman said during an appearance at a McCarthy storefront headquarters in Indianapolis. "I wear this button with considerable pride and, for the first time, with a great deal of hope." Newman's passionate embrace of McCarthy's cause attracted the sup-port of a normally Republican voter, who told a McCarthy volunteer she and her husband had decided to work on the senator's behalf. Newman also impressed local African American leaders Charles Hendricks and Ben Bell in his meeting with them. "I tell you what," Hendricks said to Newman. "You sell him better than he sells himself. You've done more for McCarthy in these few minutes than he did for himself."[31]

The chance to meet Hollywood celebrities proved to be an effective method of attracting a crowd to attend McCarthy events, including a few members of the enemy camp. Louie Mahern, who had been a vital part of the petition drive to place Kennedy on the ballot in Indiana, heard that one of his favorite actresses, Myrna Loy, one of the stars of the famous *Thin Man* film series, had been scheduled to appear at a McCarthy event at the Claypool Hotel. "I'm for Bobby Kennedy," said Mahern, "but I wanted to see Myrna Loy, and I met her that night." Hoping to avoid the prying eyes of McCarthy staff members, Mahern, when asked his name and ward and precinct upon entering the hotel, had given them the name of one of his Democratic friends, Bud Myers, who worked with Congressman Andy Jacobs Jr. and who also supported Kennedy, and filled out a name tag with his new pseudonym. After grabbing a free drink, Mahern made his way through the crowded room only to see Myers coming his way wearing a name tag that read "Louie Mahern."[32]

McCarthy later admitted that he probably should never have entered the Indiana primary, but that once he did, his time would have best been spent playing baseball instead of campaigning. While John Bartlow Martin had urged Robert Kennedy to identify with Hoosier legends, McCarthy placed little faith in such connections. Richard Stout, a reporter covering the campaign for *Newsweek* magazine, came from Indiana and had become a fan of James Whitcomb Riley's poetry. One evening at a hotel bar in Indiana, Stout recited Riley's poem "Joney" to an audience that included McCarthy. By the time Stout came to the poem's final line, "Purty is as purty does," the candidate had long since left the room.[33] McCarthy's feelings about Indiana were best expressed in three poems he wrote about the state under the overall title "Three Bad Signs." Inspired by a sign indicating that peddlers were not allowed, McCarthy wrote:

The first Bad Sign is this:
"Green River Ordinance Enforced Here.
Peddlers Not Allowed."

This is a clean, safe town.
No one can just come round
With ribbons and bright threads
Or new books to be read.
This is an established place.

We have accepted patterns in lace,
And ban itinerant vendors of new forms
    and whirls,
All things that turn the heads of girls.
We are not narrow, but we live with care.
Gypsies, hawkers and minstrels are right
    for a fair.
But transient peddlers, nuisances, we say
From Green River must be kept away.
Traveling preachers, actors with a play,
Can pass through, but may not stay.
Phoenicians, Jews, men of Venice—
Know that this is the home of Kiwanis.

All of you who have been round the world
    to find
Beauty in small things: read our sign
And move on.[34]

With McCarthy's campaign floundering to get its bearings in alien territory, Kennedy supporters tried to ignore the Minnesota senator. Instead, they acted as if the biggest threat in the race was Governor Branigin. Kennedy believed it would be a mistake to attack Branigin, that doing so would only hurt his own standing with Indiana voters. "My advantage is he's not a serious candidate," Kennedy told a reporter, "but that's all I can afford to say about him." Instead, the senator's staff attempted to convince reporters that in the Indiana primary the Kennedy forces were fighting an uphill battle against Branigin. In a background briefing, Pierre Salinger, the former press secretary to John Kennedy, suggested that Robert Kennedy was in for a "tough time in Indiana." Most of the reporters were quite skeptical, noting that Salinger had made similar claims during the 1960 presidential campaign. "But I meant it; I was serious about it," Salinger emphasized. "I thought we were going to have a tough time winning that one." Martin too spent time telling reporters why Kennedy might do poorly in the state, pointing out the positive role the powerful Democratic machine would play for Branigin. Martin believed he could do a better job of talking to the press than Salinger or Frank Mankiewicz because he knew Indiana so well, had been a reporter himself, and believed what he was saying. "I told the reporters where to check what I was saying," said Martin, noting that one *Time* magazine reporter returned from a trip to Kokomo with a briefcase full of literature from the Ku Klux Klan.[35]

The Kennedy campaign's attempts to cover itself against the possibility of a setback were quickly attacked by the Branigin camp as "poor-mouthing." Gordon St. Angelo, the Democratic state chairman and manager of Branigin's favorite-son effort, pointed out to the media covering the race that no Kennedy had ever lost a political battle. "They don't run to lose," St. Angelo said. "They obviously have polls showing them doing very well or they wouldn't have come." In a point he would hammer on again and again during the primary, St. Angelo charged that Kennedy would use his family's comfortable financial resources to buy the election; he estimated that the Kennedy and McCarthy campaigns would spend $2 million each in the state, in contrast to the Branigin campaign's budget of approximately $150,000. "I have no illusions about what we're up against. I've worked with the Kennedys before—but always on the other side of the bulldozer," St. Angelo noted. "I tell you, it's a lot more fun following that bulldozer." Branigin followed St. Angelo's lead in lamenting the amount of money to be spent by his opponents. "I think it's a question of whether emotionalism and a crash program and the expenditure of large sums can purchase the election," Branigin commented to reporters. "This points up a real problem in the country today. Could a very talented man, such as Abraham Lincoln, compete?" To emphasize the theme, the Branigin campaign slyly distributed flyers featuring a non-negotiable check for $3 million made out to a "Presidential Campaign Slush Fund" signed by "Robert Ruthless."[36]

Both the McCarthy and Kennedy campaigns disputed St. Angelo's estimates of the money they were spending in the state. When McCarthy heard of the Indiana Democrat's $2 million figure, he had a one-word reply: "Nonsense." Speaking for the Kennedy campaign, Salinger said he admired St. Angelo's political abilities, but not his mathematical skills. According to a report of campaign spending in Indiana by the *Los Angeles Times–Washington Post* news service, managers of the Kennedy campaign asserted that the senator would spend between $600,000 to $650,000 in the state, which included a media budget of between $200,000 and $225,000. While critics had put Kennedy's media costs at $750,000, such a sum, the news service reported, would buy five hundred hours of broadcast time on Indiana's largest television station (WFBM-TV in Indianapolis), instead of the ten and a half hours the Kennedy organization had purchased as of the final days of the primary campaign at a cost of approximately $15,000. "The rest of the $200,000 radio-TV budget is going into spot commercials of both the one-minute and five-minute variety," according to the report. Rose Kennedy, the candidate's mother, candidly assessed the issue in an interview with *Women's Wear Daily*: "It's our own money," she said, "and we're free to spend it any way we please. It's part of this campaign business. If you have money, you spend it to win."[37]

A number of Hoosier politicians from both parties and reporters in the state believed that Branigin had a good chance of capturing control of Indiana's delegation by winning the primary; out-of-state media predicted that Kennedy, with his national reputation and deep pocketbook, would win. Branigin made a strong effort to sway voters to his cause, traveling to nearly every county to repeat his call for the state to have a strong voice at the upcoming national convention. "This is not time to debate the national issues," the governor said. "The issue in Indiana today is who is going to represent Indiana at Chicago. Well, I can tell you—I am!" Radio jingles for the governor urged voters: "Count us for Branigin / Count us American and stamp out fear and doubt / Branigin knows what counts / We Hoosiers know what counts / He counts for wisdom, faith and unity." In stops before small crowds at county courthouses, barbershops, and schools, the governor talked about his opponents as if they were merely tourists in the state. "We don't mind them having a fight here," Branigin said of Kennedy and McCarthy, "but we don't want them to carry away the arena." The governor hinted that if he did win the primary in his home state, he might consider entering the Nebraska, Oregon, and Florida primaries as a write-in candidate. Branigin compared his favorite-son candidacy in Indiana to "entering a horse in a race." If a horse did well, he told reporters, an owner might be inclined to enter him in other contests. Vice President Hubert Humphrey's announcement on April 27 that he had entered the competition for the nomination did not deter Branigin from pushing his campaign with Hoosier voters. The governor later acknowledged to James Farmer, his press aide, that Johnson's decision to withdraw had left him in the difficult position of trying to explain why he remained in the contest, as the average voter did not really understand the role of a favorite son. The media and his opponents "wanted to embarrass me by saying I was carrying Humphrey's bucket of water," Branigin told Farmer. "Well, I wasn't. I'd made no commitment to Humphrey."[38]

Humphrey's late entrance into the presidential race cast a large shadow over the fight between Kennedy and McCarthy, as the vice president enjoyed the wholehearted support of Democratic Party regulars and organized labor. He named two young U.S. senators, Fred Harris of Oklahoma and Walter Mondale of Minnesota, to head his campaign organization, United Democrats for Humphrey. Although the vice president had decided to run within days of Johnson's withdrawal from the contest, he had delayed making any formal announcement of his intentions so as not to "appear too eager, too self-seeking, overly ambitious." But by waiting until late April to make his declaration,

Humphrey had been able to avoid entering any primaries. Instead, he was content to gather the delegates needed for the nomination from party caucuses and state conventions. (Reforms enacted by the Democratic Party in the early 1970s made such a tactic impossible for future candidates, who need to enter and win nearly every primary to get the nomination.) As Democratic national chairman John Bailey pointed out, even if McCarthy had won every delegate available in every primary he entered, only 15 percent of the convention vote would have been committed to him. "This nomination will not be decided by the primaries, even though primaries are important psychologically," Humphrey confidently said in *U.S. News and World Report*. "The nomination will be decided by the convention delegates, and better than three fourths of those delegates are selected in non-primary states."[39]

Announcing his candidacy in Washington, D.C., Humphrey had described his campaign for president as "the way politics ought to be in America, the politics of happiness, the politics of purpose, the politics of joy." The phrase "politics of joy" struck a discordant note with most political observers, who wondered how much joy the American public could find in a year that had already seen U.S. forces fighting desperate battles for their lives in the Tet Offensive and Martin Luther King Jr. gunned down in Memphis. Just four days earlier, Americans had sat stunned in front of their television sets watching students at Columbia University in New York take over the main building on their campus to protest the war and the building of a new gymnasium. On April 30 thousands of police evicted the students, carting five hundred off to jail. Humphrey later said that the "politics of joy" statement haunted him throughout the campaign, and he had to constantly explain that he was not "unaware of the misery in our land and our world." He added that by using the phrase he simply meant to point out that "the right to participate in democratic processes was, in part, 'the pursuit of happiness' of which our founding fathers spoke."[40]

In the Indiana primary, Governor Branigin seemed to enjoy home-field advantage. There were cracks, however, in the Branigin machine. Although as governor he controlled patronage in the Democratic Party, his single four-year term was coming to an end, making him a lame duck and leaving other party leaders battling to replace him. While St. Angelo supported the gubernatorial candidacy of Richard Bodine of Mishawaka, former governor Matthew Welsh and his allies were supporting Lieutenant Governor Robert Rock of Anderson. And although county chairmen were lining up publicly to back Branigin against Kennedy and McCarthy, some of that support was given only halfheartedly. Branigin did not have the same level of rapport with county chairmen that his predecessor, Welsh, had enjoyed. Veteran political reporter Gordon Englehart of the *Louisville Courier-Journal* predicted that the governor might very well win the Indiana primary, but he had neglected his responsibilities to the party during his governorship. Instead of courting county chairmen in their home counties, Branigin, according to Englehart, preferred to rule "in virtual seclusion from the big red chair in the governor's office." An unnamed county chairman from Indiana's Fourth District had bitterly commented: "In three years he has made 'politician' a dirty word in Indiana." The Kennedy campaign took advantage of these weaknesses. In telephone conversations and face-to-face discussions, John Bartlow Martin had discovered "soft spots in the Branigin machine," including politicians and Democratic Party workers who were secretly upset with the governor and who offered clandestine assistance to Kennedy whenever they could.[41]

As his opponents struggled, Kennedy was hitting his stride with Hoosier voters. Martin believed the campaign effort turned the corner with Kennedy's visits to the Hoosier historic sites in southern Indiana on Monday, April 22, and the backlash factory cities in the central part of the state on Tuesday, April 23. "Before then it had lacked direction, had been all razzle dazzle and high pressure, had not been in tune with the Hoosier voters," Martin recalled. "On those days, and thereafter, he got on the same wave length with the Indiana voters, he felt at home with them, and they with him." Kennedy seemed relaxed and in good spirits during his visit to such sites as the George Rogers Clark Memorial; Grouseland, the home of William Henry Harrison; and the grave of Nancy Hanks Lincoln. The candidate received a warm reception in Vincennes, where he said he had come to the state's oldest city because he "believed deeply that the seeds of national greatness lie in the greatness of the past." The stop was not uneventful, however. When Kennedy and his wife, Ethel, visited Vincennes's Old Cathedral Catholic Church, their springer spaniel, Freckles, caused some excitement when he bounded into the church, ran up to the wooden altar, and started sniffing around in preparation for relieving himself. Dutton caught the dog before he could do any damage and eased him out of the house of worship.[42]

The visit to southern Indiana ended on a sour note for the Kennedy entourage: the candidate drew only fifteen hundred people for an early evening speech at Roberts Municipal Stadium in Evansville. During his remarks, Kennedy criticized the Johnson administration for letting inflation run out of control and called on the "enthusiastic if small audience," most of whom had been waiting for nearly an hour and a half for the candidate's speech, to not waste their votes come primary election day. According to Joe Dolan, who scheduled the event, he had confused one of the advance men with a person in whom he had confidence and "took his judgment that we could go in and fill a hall of fourteen thousand people at 6:30 in the evening when everybody in Evansville eats, apparently." In addition, the local Democratic Party backed Branigin and had not been as forthcoming as they could have with information.

After the Kennedy group returned to Indianapolis for the evening, Kennedy met with Dolan and Jerry Bruno, his main advance man, to discuss the fiasco, which Kennedy later called "the worst public appearance he'd ever made in his life." Although Bruno tried to take some of the blame, Dolan refused to let him, telling Kennedy it had been entirely his fault. "It was the worst time he ever read me out," Dolan remembered, "but he was tired, and it was a ghastly mistake. But we had taken chance after chance, and we won, you know. And you get so you don't look at it as carefully."[43]

The unpleasant memory of the Evansville event, however, soon faded away. On April 23 the Kennedy campaign embarked on a highly successful one-day whistle-stop railroad trip on the old Wabash Cannonball (made famous by a song sung by baseball pitcher Dizzy Dean in the 1940s) to Logansport, Peru, Wabash, Huntington, and Fort Wayne. Originally put into service in the 1880s, the Cannonball ran from Saint Louis to Omaha. Discontinued in 1900, the train rose to life again in the early 1950s and altered its route to pass through Indiana. In 1954 the Wabash Railroad merged with the Norfolk and Western Railway. Railroads had been the transportation of choice for American politicians for many years, reaching their peak of popularity in Harry Truman's 1948 reelection efforts against Republican Thomas Dewey. Since then, aircraft had replaced railroads in importance, but many in the media had fond memories of the old days—something the Kennedy staff capitalized on for its campaign. Dolan noted that travel by railroad offered several advantages for a candidate. "He doesn't have to get in or out of the car. And on the plane everybody has access to him," said Dolan. Local political officials could also ride the train with the candidate and chat with him in relative comfort until the next stop, when a new set would climb on board. And as the train traveled from town to town, Kennedy could confer with his staff about his next speech or other matters. The candidate "has greater freedom of movement than you do on an airplane," Dolan said. "So that was the best thing we did in Indiana." Later, as his campaign moved on to other states, Kennedy looked back with great fondness to the railroad trip in Indiana. "After that," remembered Dolan, "all he did was complain and ask, 'Can't you think of something new? Why don't you think of something like the Wabash Cannonball?'"[44]

At each stop the five-car train made, two Indiana University musicians, Robert Waller and Wayne Schuman, entertained the crowds with renditions of "The Wabash Cannonball" and "This Man Is Your Man," a campaign ditty written by Sorenson and sung to the tune of Woody Guthrie's "This Land Is Your Land." Martin described the crowds as "huge and friendly and enthusiastic." Even some local Republicans were swept up by the excitement. A group of Peru Democrats who had ridden with the candidate from Logansport to Peru noticed that the train's conductor was Dale Dawalt, a onetime candidate for GOP chairman of Miami County. Dawalt pulled back his coat to reveal that he wore a Kennedy button and told everyone "to keep it quiet." Kennedy seemed at ease as he greeted the crowds who trooped to the local Northwest and Norfolk railroad depots to meet the famous candidate and his wife (a woman in Wabash declared that she had come to "see what a woman who's had 10 kids looks like"). Kennedy had been well briefed by Martin on the history and legends of each city. At Peru, Kennedy received a copy of an elephant book made by former circus man Ollie Miller and presented by his wife, Midge, before two thousand spectators, a number of them schoolchildren who had been dismissed from class to witness Kennedy's visit. "I may not get to use this until next November," Kennedy joked about the book. In Wabash the city's mayor, W. D. Bryant, a Republican, wore a Nixon for President button as he presented Kennedy a key to the city. "I had thought maybe you would introduce me as the next president of the United States," Kennedy told Bryant, before reminding the crowd that Indiana had the chance to decide who the next president would be. "I personally have my own choice," he added, "which won't come as a surprise to you." Playing off Wabash's fame as the first electrically lighted city in the world, signs supporting Kennedy read "Socket to 'em Bobby" and "Bobby Turns Me On." Before a crowd of three thousand in Huntington, Kennedy received a box of petunias—as the community was known as the City of Petunias—and said he hoped to plant some petunias in the White House garden. He also praised the community's national champion YMCA swimming team. "I thought if some of their success could rub off on me, I could be the next President of the United States," Kennedy said. Turning to national issues, he called for aiding the elderly in the country by raising Social Security payments to a minimum of $150 for couples and $100 for individuals "so that the promise of Social Security would not be a hollow one."[45]

Even the members of the national media were affected by the good mood generated by the trip. Several members of the press—Warren Rogers, David Broder, David Halberstam, Jack Germond, and David Breasted—gathered in the train's club car to write their own version of "The Wabash Cannonball." Breasted, who had brought along a guitar, serenaded Kennedy and his wife with the following verses:

Oh listen to the speeches that baffle, beef and bore
As he waffles through the woodlands, and slides along the shore.
He's the politician who's touched by one and all.
He's the demon driver of The Ruthless Cannonball.

He came down to Logansport one sunny April day.
As he pulled on through the depot you could hear the Hoosiers say,
He's the heir apparent, full of chutzpah, full of gall.
I'll bet he wants our helpin' hand on The Ruthless Cannonball.

His Eastern states are dandy, so all the people say,
From Boston to Virginny, and New York by the way.
The Blacks in Gary love him, the Poles will fill his hall
There are no ethnic problems on The Ruthless Cannonball.

There goes Roger Branigin, the Hoosier's favorite son.
He doesn't want the office, he only wants to run.
His highballin' days are over, he's riding for a fall.
They're noted for long memories on The Ruthless Cannonball.

Now good clean Gene McCarthy came down the other track.
A thousand Radcliffe dropouts all massed for the attack,
But Bobby's bought the right-of-way from here back to St. Paul,
'Cause money is no object on The Ruthless Cannonball.

Old Hubert's got Big Business, Big Labor and Big Mouth,
Aboard the Maddox Special, a'comin' from the South.
Lyndon's got him preachin', so ecu-meni-call,
But soon he'll be a'heavin' coal on The Ruthless Cannonball.

So here's to Ruthless Robert, may his name forever stand,
To be feared and genuflected at by pols across the land.
Old Ho Chi Minh is cheering, and though it may appall,
He's whizzing to the White House on The Ruthless Cannonball.

Kennedy gave as good as he got upon the song's conclusion, telling the gathered reporters: "As George Bernard Shaw once said—The same to you, sideways." He did ask for a copy of the song, and when handed one by a reporter who had helped write it was told to forget where it had come from. "Oh, no, I won't," Kennedy responded, before adding, "See, it [his supposed ruthlessness] keeps slipping out all the time."[46]

The Wabash Cannonball ended its run for the day in Fort Wayne, where Kennedy spoke to more than three thousand people in the gym of Concordia Senior College. In his speech he stressed the importance of education and the need for the federal government to do something about the rising costs of higher education, which threatened to put it out of reach for poor and middle-class citizens. "It would be a national tragedy if college once again became the haven for a privileged few. It must not be allowed to happen, and I'm not going to let it happen if I am elected President of the United States," said Kennedy. He also reiterated his call for Hoosiers not to waste their votes on primary election day May 7. During Kennedy's remarks, a baby in the audience started crying, causing the candidate to glance its way. The parents of the infant took it out of the building despite Kennedy's pleas to remain. Martin remembered Kennedy making a face and saying to the audience: "You see how ruthless I am—I've just thrown a baby out of the hall." He recovered, however, during a half-hour question-and-answer session that ranged from student deferments for the Vietnam War to jobs. After announcing he would take one last question, Kennedy answered it and the crowd, believing the event over, as did Martin, stood and clapped. Kennedy then asked for silence and said: "Camus once said there will always be suffering children in this world but perhaps we can make it a little less suffering and if you and I don't help them, who will." Kennedy added, "Help us," and walked off the stage. "It was . . . one of the most moving political moments of my life," said Martin.[47]

Even when surrounded by crowds, Kennedy always seemed alone, particularly traveling around the state in motorcades and standing up by himself on the trunk of his convertible, Martin said. The candidate did not chop the air with his hands, as his brother John Kennedy had done when speaking. "Instead," Martin said, "he had a little gesture with his right hand, the fist closed, the thumb sticking up a little, and he would jab with it to make a point." If his remarks earned applause from the crowd, he did not smile or look pleased, but looked down at the ground or at his speech and waited until the crowd had finished before going on with his talk. "He could take a bland generality and deliver it with such depth of feeling that it cut like a knife," Martin noted. "Everything he said had an edge to it." This "edge" may have contributed to Kennedy arousing both "wild enthusiasm and love and equally wild hate," Martin mused. Nobody seemed to hate McCarthy or Humphrey, he added, but a number of people in the country hated the Kennedys.[48]

Robert Kennedy knew there were many people in the United States hostile both to his effort to capture the presidency and to him personally. Talking about the phenomenon with journalist Jack Newfield of the *Village Voice*, Kennedy said he could understand the feelings of the student activists who were upset with him for deciding to hold back early on from a direct challenge to President Johnson. Because of his decision, Kennedy said it was perfectly natural for the students to have turned their support to McCarthy, and he admired and respected them for their loyalty to their candidate. "I feel now that I made a mistake in not going into New Hampshire," said Kennedy, "but that's past." The candidate seemed genuinely puzzled, however, at the blind and personal hostility some showed toward him, including a man holding a sign that read "You Punk" and another who grabbed his hand and tried to squeeze it as hard as he could. "Frankly, I don't understand it. I see people out there call me names, and say they want to actually hit me, and I just don't know what to say." He did, however, have tough words for what he called "New York liberals," those who had pleaded with him to speak against the war in Vietnam and today were supporting Humphrey, who continued to support President Johnson's conduct of the war. "I personally prefer many of the poor white people I've met here in Indiana," Kennedy told Newfield. "They are tough, and honest, and if you help them, they remember it, like the people who live in the poorer sections of West Virginia. They're not fickle."[49]

When faced with skeptical audiences, Kennedy always managed to find the right words, rising above the usual campaign rhetoric. On April 26 he appeared before an audience of 450 medical and nursing students at the Indiana University Medical Center's Emerson Hall. Kennedy used the occasion to discuss the need for reforms in the country's health-care system to make "medical care available to all," including allowing non-professional staff to treat minor cases and creating additional neighborhood clinics. From the outset, the crowd seemed set to challenge the candidate. After Kennedy arrived about a half hour behind schedule, someone in the audience shouted, "We want Bobby." A larger group responded, "No we don't." One student held a blue Reagan balloon. Kennedy made a point of acknowledging the audience's less than enthusiastic greeting, noting that his campaign had been trying to "form a doctor's committee in Indiana—and they're still trying." In his twenty minutes of prepared remarks, the candidate used statistics to show how America's health-care system had failed its citizens, including the fact that fifteen other nations had higher ratios of hospital beds to patients, twelve had higher life expectancies, and the cost of medical care had been rising seven times faster than the standard of living. This litany of failures failed to elicit any cheers from his audience.[50]

Opening the floor to the audience, Kennedy faced a barrage of pointed questions. When the student holding the Reagan balloon asked where the money would come from for any new programs, Kennedy said it would have to be supplied by the federal government. When the student said such money implied a loss of local control, the candidate, in a response that had the audience roaring, responded: "Barry Goldwater lost that struggle in 1964." When Kennedy received another question about where the money would come from, he had a simple answer: "From you." He went on:

"Let me say something about the tone of these questions. I look around this room and I don't see many black faces who will become doctors. . . . Part of civilized society is to let people go to medical school who come from ghettos. You don't see many people coming out of the ghettos or off the Indian reservations to medical school. You are the privileged ones here. It's easy to sit back and say it's the fault of the federal government, but it's our responsibility too. It's our society, not just our government, that spends twice as much on pets as on the poverty program. It's the poor who carry the major burden of the struggle in Vietnam. You sit here as white medical students, while black people carry the burden of fighting in Vietnam."

Students interrupted Kennedy's remarks with shouts of "We're going. We're going." The senator responded: "Yes, but you're here now and they're over there. The war might be settled by the time you go." Kennedy ignored hisses and boos from the crowd to repeat his assertion that there were not many African American faces in the audience, then one black student cried, "Hey, don't forget me." Kennedy replied: "I can see you, but you sure stand out." Later, when someone asked if he was in favor of ending medical school draft deferments, Kennedy answered: "The way things are going here today, probably yes." The candidate's firmness under pressure impressed the students, who applauded him as the event ended. The encounter, however, had shaken Kennedy, who later asked reporters with him on his campaign plane about the medical students: "They were so comfortable, so comfortable. Didn't you think they were comfortable?"[51]

During a speech to more than three thousand students at Valparaiso University's gymnasium on April 29, Kennedy ignored catcalls from McCarthy supporters to focus on a just-released study that indicated millions of men, women, and children in America were slowly starving to death, with more than fourteen million going to bed every night without enough nourishment to keep them healthy. "Starvation in the land of enormous wealth is nothing short of indecent," Kennedy said, calling for changes in the government's food stamp program. When queried during a question-and-answer session about the federal government's role in delivering such services, the candidate challenged those in attendance to use their talents to help others. "How many of you spend time over the summer, or on vacation, working in a black ghetto, or in Eastern Kentucky, or on Indian reservations?" Kennedy asked. "Instead of asking what the Federal Government is doing about starving children, I say what is your responsibility, what are you going to do about it? I think you people should organize yourselves right here, and try to do something about it."[52]

According to Joe Dolan, the Kennedy campaign deliberately placed its candidate before antagonistic audiences. "He was at his best before a polite but hostile audience on a Q and A," said Dolan. "That was where he was best as a campaigner, and that was the best kind of crowd to give him." Such confrontations made better stories, and thus focused more attention on Kennedy's reform proposals, than visits to senior citizens' homes. "Then the story would have been, 'Robert Kennedy told the old folks what they wanted to hear,'" Dolan said. "He rose to the occasion there and got a little feisty and got a lot of stories out of it." Two years later, Dolan met a businessman on an airplane who told him he had begun to admire Kennedy after reading about the exchange with the medical students because he had the courage of his convictions. "People that really didn't know him . . . didn't know that he would do that sort of thing," Dolan added.[53]

The confrontation between Kennedy and the medical students showcased what had become the sometimes schizophrenic coverage of his campaign in Eugene Pulliam's *Indianapolis Star*. Throughout the early days of the Indiana primary, the *Star*, on Pulliam's orders, had actively promoted Branigin's cause on its front page, relegating coverage of the other contenders to the inside pages. The paper's editors seemed at a loss as to how to proceed as the campaign progressed. Kennedy's verbal battle with medical students in Indiana received a respectful, dispassionate treatment by *Star* reporter Jep Cadou Jr. one day, then a few days later the newspaper ran a page-one article quoting Frank M. McHale, former Democratic national committeeman from Indiana, accusing the Kennedy campaign of injecting "racism and religion into Hoosier politics." McHale's charge of racism had been prompted by Kennedy's remarks to the Indiana University medical students about blacks carrying a disproportionate share of the fighting in Vietnam. The religion aspect, McHale asserted, came from Ethel Kennedy's statement that she had been "invited" by Archbishop Paul Schulte to appear before the Indiana Province meeting of the National Council of Catholic Women when instead Schulte had simply allowed her to appear. By claiming to have been invited, McHale said, Ethel Kennedy had made a "deliberate attempt to make Hoosier Catholics think that Bobby has official sanction." The *Star* ran an article by nationally syndicated columnist Joseph Kraft calling Indiana "one of the last backwaters in the country" and criticizing the state's isolation from the mainstream of American life, but appended an editors' note that Kraft was a friend of the Kennedy family and his work was "typical of the propaganda being turned out by pro-Kennedy writers to push the candidacy of Senator Robert F. Kennedy." The *Star* also blasted Kraft's column in an editorial.[54]

Governor Branigin received a boost to his campaign when the *Star* ran a page-one article quoting anonymous sources that he had a strong chance of becoming Humphrey's vice presidential running mate. An article by Ben Cole of the newspaper's Washington, D.C., bureau noted that a spokesman for Humphrey had indicated Branigin's name was being frequently mentioned, along with three or four others, as a candidate for vice president if he could capture the Indiana primary. As for Kennedy and McCarthy, the *Star* treated them as unwelcome outsiders. One infamous cartoon on the front page of the *Star*'s April 24 issue under the title "Guests in the House!" had McCarthy and Kennedy wooing a worried woman labeled "Mrs. Indiana" as Branigin looked balefully down at them from behind his glasses. In the drawing, McCarthy tickles the woman under the chin while Kennedy's hand appears to be fondling her breast. The *Star* also gave continued coverage to charges from St. Angelo and Branigin that Kennedy was out to buy the election with his family fortune. Editorial cartoons blasting Kennedy for using his money to buy Indiana votes appeared on its news pages. It ran on its front page an editorial from the *New York Times* titled "Is Indiana for Sale?" The editorial noted that the Kennedy campaign had estimated they would spend $500,000 in the state, but nobody would be "surprised at an expenditure by them twice or three times as great." Because Indiana had no effective law requiring reports on campaign expenditures, the *Times* editorial said no one would ever know the real amount. In reprinting the editorial, however, the *Star* edited out a mention that the Branigin campaign could draw for financial support upon what the *Times* called "the ancient and disreputable practice" of collecting 2 percent from patronage employees' paychecks.[55]

When Pierre Salinger picked up a copy of the *Star* the morning after Kennedy's now-famous speech in Indianapolis following Martin Luther King Jr.'s death, he had a hard time finding any mention of the event: it was buried in an article on the formation of a statewide youth group on Branigin's behalf. Salinger met with Pulliam's son, Gene, to discuss what Salinger perceived as the *Star*'s unfair treatment of the Kennedy campaign, and left on what he thought were cordial terms that might translate into more balanced coverage. "Of course, I mean that was one of the most wasted calls of all time because we were really killed by the newspaper," he said, noting that the *Star* continued to savage Kennedy in both its editorial and news pages. By the end of the campaign, Salinger had called on the American Society of Newspaper Editors's Freedom of Information Committee to investigate the Pulliam newspapers for what he called "outrageous and callous disregard for fairness." Eugene C. Pulliam fired back at Kennedy, comparing him to a spoiled child. "When he doesn't get what he wants, he bellyaches about it," Pulliam said in a statement. "The facts are Kennedy and his entourage received more space in the *Indianapolis Star* and *Indianapolis News* than any other candidate, largely for the reason he brought his whole family, including his mother, to Indianapolis and they made news and we printed the news and the pictures."[56]

The Kennedy campaign attempted to counter the influence of the Pulliam newspapers by going over their heads and concentrating on television and radio advertising. In general, however, as press secretary Frank Mankiewicz noted, there was not much Kennedy could do about what he saw as biased political coverage. One new technique employed by the campaign to circumvent the Indianapolis newspapers came from Jim Dunn, who had worked on Democrat Pat Brown's gubernatorial contests in California. Dunn set up a recording machine in Kennedy headquarters with a phone line and notified every radio station in the state that they could call twice a day to obtain a live feed of Kennedy's speeches to use in their news reports and programs. Dunn recorded and edited every Kennedy speech and also provided commentary on the size of the crowd and the location of the speech. "It was a good device," Mankiewicz recalled. "We got a lot of good radio publicity that way."[57]

The candidate attempted to joke about the rough coverage he received in the *Star*. During a visit to Indianapolis on May 1, Kennedy made brief remarks to an enormous crowd of approximately three thousand people that pressed around his car as it traveled on Monument Circle. Lacking the proper permit to make a speech, the senator said he did not want to say too much and risk spending the last few days of the campaign reading the *Indianapolis Star* while incarcerated. In a talk at the Christian Theological Seminary later in the day, Kennedy turned serious, noting he had always considered the *Manchester Union Leader*, run by arch-conservative New Hampshire publisher William Loeb, as the country's nastiest newspaper. "I think, really, the *Indianapolis Star* must run it neck and neck," he said. "I've been here two weeks, and I've never seen a worse newspaper. . . . It's certainly the most distorted, I think, one of the most warped." He went on to say, in a dig at Pulliam, that it must be a great thing to "have a toy like that." The *Indianapolis Star* reporter who covered the event at the seminary failed to include Kennedy's remarks about the newspaper, noting only that the candidate digressed from his remarks to indicate "his displeasure with some of the news coverage he encounters in Indiana."[58]

By the time the campaign entered its homestretch, Gene Pulliam had convinced his father to give equal space to all campaigns by running news briefs about their efforts along the bottom of the front page. Branigin, however, continued to be the newspaper's main focus. The front page of the *Star* on primary election day, May 7, had a large headline above the fold reading: "Branigin Predicts Victory." Later that fall, in a meeting with Indianapolis executives, William Dyer, the *Star*'s general manager, tried to convince Eugene Pulliam that such slanted news coverage should never be allowed to happen again in the newspaper. After taking time to puff on his cigar, Pulliam finally said: "Well, I guess we did go a little too far."[59]

1 · 2 3 4 5 **6** 7

The Voters Speak

On a spring day in 1968, residents of northwest Indiana were treated to a rare sight. In a caravan of automobiles that swept along city streets could be seen icons of the past and the present. One was a boxer, the son of Polish immigrants from Gary, Indiana, who had risen to become middleweight champion of the world, earning for himself the nickname "The Man of Steel" both for the place of his birth and his ability to take the punishment handed out by his opponents in the ring. The other man had also traveled a hard road to success, winning a place in the state's history as its first African American mayor. From their very different backgrounds, Tony Zale, the boxer, and Richard G. Hatcher, the mayor of Gary, were brought together by Robert F. Kennedy's campaign to win the Indiana primary. The two heroes of the region joined Kennedy in a motorcade through the streets of Gary on May 6, the day before Hoosier voters trooped to the polls. They represented Kennedy's attempt to bridge the gap between whites and African Americans and bring both into a coalition that could win elections for the Democratic Party. "We have to write off the unions and the South now," Kennedy told a reporter, "and replace them with Negroes, blue-collar whites, and the kids. If we can do that, we've got a chance to do something."[1]

The motorcade in Gary was part of a final whirlwind effort by Kennedy. The candidate's family, including his mother, Rose, and his sister-in-law, Joan, traveled around the state to promote his candidacy. Prince Stanislaw Radziwill, Jacqueline Kennedy's brother-in-law and an opponent of the Communist government in Poland, proved to be a highly effective campaigner with Polish groups in Lake County. At one speech a Polish American worker asked Radziwill about problems between Poles and African Americans. "Better to be in America living next to a thousand blacks," Radziwill said, drawing applause, "than in Poland living next to one commissar."

But despite all the resources at his disposal—his fortune; a large, dedicated staff devoted to ensuring his success; and the mystique of his family's name—Kennedy worked harder than anyone to capture the hearts and minds of Hoosier voters. David Hackett, a friend of Kennedy's since childhood, noted that whenever he happened to see him during those days "he was so tired he could hardly move." John Douglas observed that probably no national candidate in modern times worked as hard as Kennedy did. "He came across as authentic, direct, and straightforward—a person in whom people could have confidence," Douglas remembered. "And that's what, I think, brought Indiana around." John Bartlow Martin noted that Kennedy had aged more than he should have since the death of John Kennedy and the process continued at a heightened pace during the hectic campaign. "He was worn-out," said Martin. Every day Ethel Kennedy doled out a score of vitamins to help her husband's frayed voice. Crowds in communities throughout the state pressed close to shake Kennedy's hand and in doing so tore at him and his clothes. During a stop in Mishawaka, an eager supporter held on to the candidate's hand too long and pulled him out of the car and onto the pavement, chipping Kennedy's tooth in the process. "The crowds were savage," remembered Martin. "They pulled his cufflinks off, tore his clothes, tore ours. In bigger towns, with bigger crowds, it was frightening." The campaign could be a ferocious spectacle, but it was exhilarating as well, especially when victory appeared imminent. "We were beating the terrible local press, the suspicious national press, the sanctimonious McCarthy, the dull governor, the skeptical parochial narrow-minded Hoosiers themselves," Martin said. "We were beating them all. Or, rather, Bob Kennedy was."[2]

Kennedy's staff attempted to match the great effort shown by the candidate. They used every bit of the knowledge honed in countless winning campaigns to secure victory in Indiana. "We've got a hell of a lot at stake here," a top Kennedy adviser told reporters. "We've got to impress in Indiana." Lawrence F. O'Brien, the former postmaster general in President Lyndon Johnson's administration, had turned down an offer from Vice President Hubert Humphrey to manage his campaign. O'Brien said he made his decision to work for Kennedy instead based on his roots in Massachusetts, the memories of his days working for President John F. Kennedy, and his longtime affection for the Kennedy family. "It was a personal decision, not a political one," he noted in his memoirs. "I had to go with Bob." Once he had made his choice, O'Brien joined the Kennedy staff in the Hoosier State on Good Friday, April 12. He knew Indiana well, having spent much time in the state organizing get-out-the-vote drives for John Kennedy's 1960 campaign, a task he performed again eight years later. "I did the job the best I could," O'Brien recalled, "but it was a job, not the adventure it once had been."[3]

For assistance in Indiana, O'Brien turned to an old friend, Matt Reese, whom he had known since the 1960 West Virginia primary. Reese had become an expert in using telephone banks for political campaigns. O'Brien's goal was to assemble several thousand volunteers around the state for the May 7 primary. These volunteers would be tasked with "ringing doorbells in key areas throughout the state to ensure maximum voting among potential Kennedy supporters," O'Brien said. Block captains recruited by Reese through his telephone bank would be the backbone of the operation, augmented by student volunteers. Reese managed to organize fifteen thousand block captains in such major cities as Indianapolis, Gary, South Bend, Fort Wayne, and Evansville. On the first day of the telephone canvassing, Reese's phone effort successfully recruited 1,872 block captains—904 in Gary, 455 in South Bend, 216 in Fort Wayne, and 297 in Evansville.[4]

To test the motivation of the block captains, O'Brien had the Kennedy campaign mail them invitations to a thank-you reception. "What we conceived was if we could get these people in groups, fairly good-sized groups, prior to the effort, thank them in advance, it brought us face to face with them," O'Brien recalled. "It tested whether or not they were truly motivated." He wanted to make some effort at encouraging personal contacts instead of relying entirely on brief telephone calls, which were the usual way of communicating during a campaign. Ten receptions were scheduled throughout the state by the central headquarters; others were organized by local Kennedy offices. "Then we had to distribute the family—Bobby, Teddy, their sisters or whoever—so there would be some presence at every one of these meetings," O'Brien said. The day before the election, the telephone crew also called everyone who had not attended a reception to ask if the Kennedy campaign could still rely on his or her assistance. "If you have fifteen thousand people say yes and that means you have five thousand people combined with the youth volunteers then you've got a fairly good operation going," O'Brien noted. "It was all emphasis on grass roots." Gerard Doherty had been skeptical about the telephone bank at first, believing it was not the best use of resources, but later he acknowledged that it "worked fantastically." On the weekend before the election, Doherty, in Indianapolis, was surprised to see people popping up on the streets wearing Kennedy badges. "At that time I thought we were in pretty good shape," he recalled. Kennedy's opponents took notice of his ability to secure workers for his cause. Virginia Crume, secretary to Governor Roger Branigin, informed her boss that a party loyalist had been in her office with a report about Kennedy forces "not leaving a stone unturned in Lake County. Says they are knocking on every door and ringing everyone's phone and spending money that he thought had just been made."[5]

While organizing the block captains, the Kennedy campaign flooded the state with thousands of tabloids, bumper stickers, posters, and flyers. Approximately six hundred thousand tabloids promoting Kennedy's campaigns were distributed in such cities as Indianapolis, East Chicago, Michigan City, South Bend, Fort Wayne, Terre Haute, Evansville, Columbus, and Muncie. Kennedy staff also organized a variety of citizens' organizations to promote his candidacy among such groups as lawyers, clergy, elementary school teachers, professors, senior citizens, farmers, and conservationists. Nearly a week before the election, Kennedy aide Nick Zumas reported to Ted Kennedy that mailings had been sent out to fifty thousand teachers and six thousand farmers seeking their support. "Our teacher sources indicated that we could have the public support of over 10,000 teachers," wrote Zumas. Efforts to attract leaders for the senior citizens' group, however, had not been successful. "If nothing else," he said, "we hope to surface a Senior Citizens for Kennedy . . . by May 3 or 4." The most difficult groups were the doctors and the businessmen. Of the 130 doctors in the Indianapolis area called by the Kennedy campaign, only two offered to endorse the candidate. "Whatever impact will be made on the doctors," Zumas said, "it will come from [Kennedy's] Indiana University Medical School confrontation on April 24." As for the businessmen, none of any prominence could be found to join the Kennedy team.[6]

To help prepare for election day, Doherty made plans to produce for African American precincts "throw-away cards" with Kennedy's name, photograph, and position on the ballot. These cards would be handed out in such cities as Indianapolis, Gary, Evansville, Terre Haute, Hammond, and East Chicago. "It appears that McCarthy will have a great number of poll workers," Doherty reported to Ted Kennedy, "and for public relations, we should too.

Certainly, in the ghetto areas we should have them passing the above described cards." Doherty also recommended that in organizing to transport people to the polls the highest priority should be given to African American areas in the state. He suggested traveling down city streets in caravans from 4:00 PM to 6:30 PM on election day. (The polling places in the state's 4,361 precincts in the state were open from 6:00 AM to 7:00 PM.) "Three or four cars in a row with four people in each car getting out to knock on doors," said Doherty. He stressed that volunteers should be sure to call voters to see if they needed a ride to the polls, especially in black, Irish Catholic, and blue-collar precincts that could produce reliable votes for Kennedy.[7]

Making sure voters were able to get to their polling places and were able to mark their ballots involved cash payments for various precinct committeemen throughout the state. This kind of incentive was nothing new in Marion County. During the first election Michael Riley ever worked in the county, his job consisted of picking up bushel baskets full of alcohol to deliver to various precincts. Voters who lined up for the proper candidate were rewarded with a drink for their efforts. Instead of alcohol, the Kennedy staff used cash. About ten days before the primary, Steve Smith, Kennedy's brother-in-law and the overall campaign coordinator, came to Indianapolis to meet with the leaders of the eleven congressional districts, whom Doherty had recruited mainly from out-of-state. On a table in a suite at the Indianapolis Athletic Club was a large table loaded down with bundles of currency in tens, twenties, fifties, and hundreds. "Where they got the cash, I don't know," said Riley, who attended the meeting as the coordinator for Marion County. The coordinators for each of Indiana's congressional districts lined up, indicated how much they needed for their districts, and left with paper sacks bulging with cash. Riley estimated that he dispensed approximately $100,000 in "walking-around money" to ward chairmen in his county. "This was how it was done," Riley said. In those days there was no Federal Election Commission to ban such payments. "We were not buying votes," he added, "but paying to get people to the polls, for poll watchers, people to knock on doors, people to drag people to the precincts."[8]

The Kennedy campaign faced another challenge as the primary campaign hit the homestretch when Governor Branigin, hoping to find some way to offset Kennedy's financial advantage, called upon Hoosier Republican voters to cross party lines and vote for him in the primary. "I welcome all of you, regardless of party, to support me," Branigin said to a crowd of approximately four hundred people on the lawn at the Putnam County Courthouse in Greencastle. Branigin also told reporters during a stop in Lafayette that such crossover voting was legal in Indiana. The governor confided in his diary that he and Gordon St. Angelo had discussed his campaign problems. Although his volunteers had been working hard, his campaign had a tough fight ahead to entice votes from the state's African Americans and Catholics. "Whether we can prevail, I don't know—crossovers can help but how many will occur. No one can say," Branigin wrote. Eugene Pulliam's newspapers did all they could to promote the idea of Republicans crossing party lines to cast ballots for the governor. A front-page editorial in the *Indianapolis Star* on May 5 called upon members of the GOP to "uphold the honor of Indiana and prove to the world that Indiana can't be bought by crossing over in the primary to vote for Branigin. Republican poll watchers can't challenge them; we don't think Democrats will."[9]

The governor's attempt to attract Republican crossover votes did concern key members of Kennedy's staff. In a memo to Ted Kennedy, Doherty noted that there had been a similar effort in the state during the 1964 presidential primary when Republicans threatened to cross party lines and vote for insurgent candidate George Wallace in an attempt to embarrass President Lyndon Johnson. "Actually," reported Doherty, "this threat of cross over did not materialize, with the exception of Lake County." He noted that in order for a Republican to cast a vote in the Democratic primary, he or she would give up the right to vote in their primary, where Richard Nixon was running unopposed. Even if some did decide to cross over, they would have to sign an affidavit stating they would support the majority of Democratic candidates in the November election. "Any Republican who is hopeful of gaining patronage, party recognition or the like, is reluctant to do this," said Doherty. He advised that the campaign should be ready to have challengers available in some precincts, but it appeared to Doherty that there would not be a substantial number of crossover voters from the ranks of the GOP—a prediction that proved accurate on election day. Doherty surmised that the issue might even prove to be a boon for the Kennedy effort, as many Democrats had "indicated their displeasure with Branigin for seeking crossover voting."[10]

The danger of GOP crossovers proved worrisome enough to the Kennedy campaign that it even attempted to make an alliance with its old adversary Richard Nixon, who was now the leading candidate for the Republican Party's nomination. Although he was running unopposed in Indiana, Nixon wanted to stop Republicans from deserting the GOP primary for the Democratic side, as he sought to capture as many votes as possible to show his strength to a potential opponent, New York governor Nelson Rockefeller. The former vice president wanted to exceed the 408,000-vote total he had received in the 1960 Indiana primary, when he also ran unopposed. The Nixon campaign sponsored full-page advertisements in both the *Indianapolis Star* and the *Indianapolis News* warning that a "vote for Branigin is a vote for Humphrey," and also revised spots for radio and television emphasizing the importance of voting in the Republican primary. According to reporter Warren Weaver Jr. of the *New York Times*, the crossover threat (estimated at a possible sixty thousand voters by the Kennedy campaign and forty thousand by Nixon's staff) prompted an unnamed Kennedy aide to approach a Nixon assistant to suggest they work together to do something to stop crossover votes. "The Nixon agent, on the theory that nothing could make the former Vice President less popular here than an alliance with Senator Kennedy, declined," reported Weaver.[11]

Kennedy forces often resorted to direct action when it came to ensuring the proper counting of votes in areas key to their candidate's success, particularly in northwest Indiana. Six Kennedy volunteers, mostly college students, were sent out on Saturday, May 5, to carefully check voting machines in Gary's 132 polling places. William Levy, chairman of a Students for Kennedy organization at Roosevelt University in Chicago, and a young man accompanying him were arrested by Gary police in a church at Forty-sixth and Broadway streets at eight o'clock in the evening. The volunteers were later released, however, when police called Jerome Reppa, the Republican member of the three-person Lake County Election Board. Reppa noted there was no law on the books either permitting or barring persons checking polling places before precinct officials made their formal checks the day before the primary election. Police had received several calls complaining about the inspection. Thomas Farrell, the coordinator of Kennedy's headquarters in Gary, said the volunteers were checking the polling places to both familiarize the organization with the locations and to check to see if anyone had tampered with the voting machines. "Our problem was that these machines were delivered four days before the voting where anyone could have had access to them," Farrell told a reporter. "We wanted to record their serial numbers and find out where they were." In addition, the volunteers made sure to check the vote counters on the backs of the machines as long as they "didn't have to touch the machines to do so," Farrell said.[12]

Branigin attempted to match Kennedy's sizable array of paid staff and volunteers with loyal state patronage employees, who did all they could to promote the governor to Indiana voters. Margo Barnard of the state division of labor campaigned on Branigin's behalf at the Marcy Village Apartments, located just north of the Indiana State Fairgrounds in Indianapolis. She knocked on 187 apartment doors, visited six homes in the area, and also talked to employees of the Adams Drug Company. Although a large percentage of the apartment residents identified themselves as Republicans, Barnard reported they had nothing but kind words for the job the governor had been doing. "Win or lose," she wrote to Branigin in a letter, "I know it must be rewarding to you to know that so many people are proud of you and your record as Governor of our Great State. I, too, am proud to have served as an employee during your administration." In a note on the letter, the governor wrote: "Virginia, call her. Thanks!"[13]

As election day approached, McCarthy could once again count on the "children's crusade" that had been so effective for him in New Hampshire and Wisconsin; approximately six thousand student volunteers were expected to blanket the state during the weekend before the election. His volunteers worked to present McCarthy to Indiana voters as "the kind of man Hoosiers feel at home with." The weekend before voting began, for example, more than four hundred college and high school students—busloads from Loyola University and Boston University and colleges in Detroit—descended upon northern Indiana with plans to canvass every house in South Bend and Mishawaka. Working out of a warehouse on Ewing Avenue in South Bend, most of the students were veterans of McCarthy's earlier efforts. Bob Rothman of Toledo, Ohio, called the group "the drop-ins," as instead of "dropping out of society" they had chosen to drop in "to do something within the system." Jim Lagodeny, a sixteen-year-old Wisconsin high school student, had spent $20 out of his own pocket for a round-trip bus ticket for the weekend. "But I can't think of a better way to spend the money," Lagodeny said. Other students found cheaper ways to travel to aid McCarthy in Indiana. According to McCarthy campaign legend, entertainer Sammy Davis Jr. had promised free tickets for one of his performances to students who volunteered to canvass for Kennedy in Indiana. The busloads of students who traveled to Indianapolis thanked the Kennedy campaign for the free transportation, and then marched off to offer their services to McCarthy.[14]

Perhaps buoyed by the enthusiasm of his student volunteers, McCarthy began to place a new significance on the results in Indiana. For the first time, he told reporters that he considered the Hoosier primary to be critical for his presidential aspirations. Speaking in Vincennes at the George Rogers Clark Memorial, McCarthy indicated that the results from Indiana might well dictate "the way the Democratic party will go in Chicago. And the way that the Democratic party goes in Chicago, is the way the country will go next November." He advised voters that if they wished to select the next president of the United States, the best thing they could do would be to vote for him on May 7. McCarthy later backtracked a bit on his earlier statement, telling reporters during a campaign stop in Gary that if Kennedy won the Indiana primary, it did not necessarily mean that he would be the Democratic nominee for president. When he observed he had been trying to be "subtle" with his remarks in Vincennes, one reporter responded: "A little too subtle for your own good, maybe?" McCarthy replied: "Maybe too subtle for the press."[15]

The loss of the student support due to his late start in the campaign often gnawed at Kennedy. His aide Richard Goodwin remembered that late one night in Indianapolis the two men walked past McCarthy headquarters and saw a group of young volunteers sitting outside the building. Kennedy stopped and talked to the students. He said he knew why he was in Indiana—to run for office—but asked why they were. Many responded that they were working for McCarthy to end the war. When Kennedy interrupted to say that he, too, was against the war, one of the students noted: "I've been part of the peace movement for more than a year. McCarthy gave us a chance. I joined his campaign in New Hampshire to fight against the war because he was there. And you weren't there. And as long as he continues to fight I'll be with him." Kennedy said that while some of the students might view him as a usurper who had jumped in to spoil their victory, he praised their efforts and said that they made him "proud to be an American. You've done a wonderful thing. I'm only sorry we couldn't have done it together." As he walked away, Kennedy stopped, turned around, and waved farewell to the students, who waved back. As Kennedy and Goodwin returned to their hotel, the candidate remained lost in thought for a few minutes before lamenting the loss of what should have been his constituency. "Well, it can't be helped," Kennedy said. "If I blew it, I blew it."[16]

Without the dedicated support of students like the ones loyal to McCarthy, Kennedy had to rely on his own, as one of his aides described it, "sheer energy and personal drive." To promote the national media perception that the Kennedy campaign was a juggernaut that could not be stopped in Indiana, Joe Dolan, who handled the scheduling for the candidate, had devised a strategy whereby he tried to arrange events that promised the largest and most enthusiastic crowds for the final days before the election. "You generally go out into the weaker areas first and then try to build up so that you give the impression of building up even though you aren't," Dolan noted. With that in mind, Kennedy campaigned in key African American precincts in Indianapolis on May 4 accompanied by a group of black athletes that included Lamar Lundy of the Los Angeles Rams, Roosevelt Grier of the Rams, Timmy Brown of the Philadelphia Eagles, Herb Adderly of the Green Bay Packers, and Bobbie Mitchell of the Washington Redskins. White athletes also participated, including Jack Concannon of the Chicago Bears and Hoosier boxing champion Tony Zale. The crowd's biggest cheers were reserved for Indiana basketball great Oscar Robertson, former star of the state champion Crispus Attucks High School. "I am running as Oscar Robertson's vice president," Kennedy joked with an appreciative crowd during a stop at Thirty-ninth and Illinois streets. At other events he repeated his theme that the country could not tolerate lawlessness, but must also fight intolerance. He also urged African Americans to exercise their right to vote, telling a crowd at Blake Street and Indiana Avenue that many in the neighborhood "don't vote in elections and have not voted in past elections. I need your help on Tuesday."[17]

On Monday, May 6, Kennedy and his traveling press corps participated in what veteran journalist Jules Witcover called one of the most incredible final days of campaigning he had ever been a part of in his forty years of political reporting. Kennedy's long day began in Evansville, where the previous evening he attended a rally and reception at the Civic Center. Thousands of city residents had lined his route from Dress Memorial Airport to the center, where one young Kennedy supporter held up a sign reading: "Who Cares If His Hair IS a Silly Millimeter Longer." The hordes of fans impressed a reporter from the *New York Times*, who told a fellow member of the media that only a week before he had believed Branigin would win the primary, but now he thought Kennedy would carry the state. Among those waiting to greet Kennedy at the Civic Center was Vance Hartke, one of Indiana's U.S. senators and a former Evansville mayor, who appeared to be jumping on the bandwagon. "I hope you'll support me," Kennedy told the crowd of more than five hundred people. "I have to go home to those 10 little children of mine, and they'll ask, 'Dad, how did you do in Indiana?'" The rally's success prompted Kennedy to later say he would call Evansville mayor Frank McDonald to seek his last-minute support (McDonald had committed his organization to Branigin). Kennedy also admitted that early in the campaign his friends in Indiana had urged him not to enter the state's primary, but that he had known he could not win the Democratic Party's presidential nomination "without taking chances like these."[18]

From Evansville, Kennedy flew to Fort Wayne for a noontime downtown rally. Arriving at Baer Field, Kennedy countered charges from Branigin and his supporters that he had been attempting to buy the election. "If I were trying to buy the state I wouldn't be here," he said. The candidate called on radio and television executives to make free airtime available to all candidates as a method that would decrease the expense of campaigning by 80 percent; he also favored making campaign contributions of $25 or $50 tax-deductible to encourage voters to give money to the candidate of their choice. As he worked his way through the crowd waiting to greet him at the airport in balmy, sunny weather, Kennedy said he had received fair coverage from most of Indiana's media, but singled out the *Indianapolis Star* as "a very biased and prejudiced newspaper." Kennedy returned to familiar campaign themes during his remarks at the Allen County Courthouse, recommending tax credits for businesses willing to invest in poor rural and urban areas; urging more local control over decisions then being made in Washington, D.C.; and speaking against violence and rioting but urging that changes be made "so everyone has an equal opportunity no matter where they live." He added that the problem was not one of race, as more whites lived in poverty than African Americans. Refusing to disparage either of his opponents in the Democratic primary, Kennedy did question Republican presidential candidate Nixon's plans to achieve peace in Vietnam. "All he said on Vietnam is that everybody should keep quiet," Kennedy charged. "That's a good suggestion by somebody who doesn't have anything to suggest."[19]

Before leaving Fort Wayne for South Bend, Kennedy and the media covering his campaign stopped for an entertaining lunch at Zoli's Café Continental on Broadway Street, an establishment owned by a former Hungarian freedom fighter named Zoltan Herman. According to Fort Wayne newspapers, Kennedy enjoyed a submarine sandwich and a beer, while his wife, Ethel, ate pizza and drank a Coke. Reporters joined the Kennedys in partaking of the establishment's fare, pizza, apple strudel, and especially beer, which caused a delay in the day's carefully prepared schedule. Inspired by Kennedy's visit, Herman produced a bottle of wine he had been saving for a special occasion and the candidate proposed a toast in honor of the Hungarian freedom fighters. Witcover noted that Herman refilled their glasses and the following scene ensued: "Now it was the proprietor's turn. But he said nothing. 'Who shall we toast now?' Kennedy asked hopefully. No answer. 'Does any particular name come to mind?' he asked. None did, although the bartender was drinking with a candidate for President of the United States." Breaking up the impromptu party, Kennedy stood on the seat of an empty booth, raised his wineglass, and said: "As George Bernard Shaw once said . . . ," prompting the reporters and broadcasters to clamber back aboard the waiting press bus.[20]

Kennedy remained in high spirits as he continued to press his case in South Bend and then in LaPorte. Although he arrived in LaPorte almost an hour and a half behind schedule, more than two thousand people were still on hand to cheer at a courthouse rally. Pleased by the enthusiasm shown by the young people in the crowd, Kennedy, in his fifteen-minute speech, wondered if people "can vote in Indiana at the age of seven." He joked that when he had announced his candidacy for the presidency, his wife had asked him if he planned on running in the Indiana primary. When he told her he had not yet decided, she had pointed out, "If you enter the primary in Indiana, you will be able to visit LaPorte." Said Kennedy, "That convinced me, and here I am." In addition to laying out his program for America, the candidate made sure to take note of a LaPorte native son with the traveling press, Dan Blackburn, a 1957 graduate of LaPorte High School, who worked as a congressional correspondent for Metromedia News. "He was a friendly and conscientious young man to whom Kennedy took a liking," noted Witcover. Kennedy pointed out that the community "obviously has produced many successful people," as Blackburn had recently been named as an outstanding young man by the National Jaycees.[21]

The festive mood was dampened for a bit as Kennedy prepared for a nine-hour motorcade from LaPorte through Gary, Hammond, and Whiting. The senator learned that the Indiana Department of the American Legion had secured a court order to block the planned telecast that evening of a half-hour paid program from the Kennedy campaign. Judge John L. Niblack of the Marion County Circuit Court issued the order barring the showing. The Legion objected because its emblem could be seen on the caps of Legion members who appeared in the film asking questions of Kennedy, a Legion member, about his stands on the issues of the day. Although the Legion members only appeared for approximately fifty seconds in the film, the Legion noted that its constitution forbid any unauthorized use of its emblem in such a partisan political activity. Donald Wilson, who worked on media for Kennedy, noted that the Legion was angry because the campaign had been able to arrange the use of a Legion hall (Post Number 34) for the shoot and had included Legion members. "Oh, we'd gotten releases from all of them," said Wilson. "But on the technicality that the Legion emblem showed and therefore involved the Legion in politics—which of course, it's up to the top of its head in Indiana, and anti-Kennedy—caused them to issue an injunction." Late in the evening, the Indiana Supreme Court lifted the injunction, but too late for any prime-time broadcast. Another film had to be used in its place.[22]

The masses of people along the motorcade route through northwest Indiana soon pushed the problems with the American Legion into the background. A reporter for the *Hammond Times* estimated that anywhere from fifteen thousand to twenty thousand people patiently jammed together along the route from Hammond to Whiting. "In Lake County," Witcover wrote, "there was no telling where one city ended and the next began. Sometimes there were so many reaching well-wishers that Kennedy simply put his arm out, letting it run along through the outstretched hands like Tom Sawyer scraping a stick along a picket fence." The day was scheduled to end with a speech in Hammond at 6:30 PM. Kennedy didn't arrive till 9:40. Speaking from the steps of the Whiting City Hall, the candidate blamed his lateness on his motorcade having to travel over "railroad tracks as 16 different trains came by." He promised that his first task if elected president would be to "put an overpass over all of Lake County!" As the crowd erupted in cheers, Kennedy added that he had taken about thirty deep breaths of air and that his second step as president "will be to do something about air pollution." Actually, unscheduled stops to accept a bouquet of flowers from a young girl, to autograph the cast on the arm of a young boy, and to chat for ten minutes with Monsignor Stanley Zjawinski slowed the motorcade's progress more than any trains. "We've had a fair hearing from everybody all across the state and now it's in the hands of the people," Kennedy said before leaving for Chicago's Midway Airport and a flight to Indianapolis to await the next day's results.[23]

Kennedy arrived in Indianapolis too late for a scheduled reception, but still exhilarated by the day's events. He later told Gerard Doherty it had been the best day of campaigning he had ever experienced. The Kennedy campaign had come a long way from its early days in Indiana, when Doherty had warned the candidate not to visit Lake County, as the organization had yet to establish itself there. Ignoring Doherty's warning, Kennedy made a visit there to meet with local party leaders. He returned aghast at remarks from a county Democratic official who prophesied the senator stood no chance against Governor Branigin. When he returned to Indianapolis, he asked to see Doherty and confronted him about the problem. Just minutes before, a volunteer who had been in northwest Indiana had given Doherty a flyer being circulated supporting Branigin and signed by the same county official who had talked so pessimistically to Kennedy. Doherty gave the circular to Kennedy and said, "If you want to listen to people on the other side, I guess you're not as smart as you think you are." Weeks later, the tide had turned and the Kennedy organization had delivered a day to remember.[24]

Exhausted from the marathon day of campaigning, tired reporters checked into the Airport Holiday Inn to sleep for a few hours before the polls started opening around the state. Some of the media adjourned to the hotel's bar for a nightcap, including Witcover and his friend Jack Germond. In a rare occurrence, Kennedy walked over to where the two men were sitting at a small table. Declining their invitation to sit down, the candidate remained standing as he contemplated what had happened that day. "Well, I've done all I could do," said Kennedy. "Maybe it's just not my time. But I've learned something from Indiana. The country is changing." Witcover said Kennedy continued to talk about the need for the Democratic Party to look to new coalitions of voters that included whites and blacks in the North. He also could not keep from thinking about one of the few negative aspects of the day: a young man holding a sign denigrating Kennedy and then running beside his car, grabbing his hand, and squeezing it so hard he thought he was trying to break it.[25]

Kennedy continued his reflective mood during an early morning meal he shared with reporters and friends at about 1:30 AM at Sam's Attic, a restaurant near the Marott Hotel. Among those in attendance were Jack Newfield of the *Village Voice*, David Halberstam of *Harper's* magazine, Loudon Wainwright of

Life magazine, and John Douglas from the senator's campaign staff. "He was in a good mood," Douglas said of Kennedy. "He was satisfied that he'd done all that he could." Newfield recalled that Kennedy looked the way boxer Zale must have looked like following his epic bouts with Rocky Graziano: the candidate's hands were "red and swollen and cut" by the thousands of people who had grabbed for them during the day, and he looked worn-out. In a nostalgic mood, Kennedy reflected on his experiences in the state and concluded that Hoosier voters, for the most part, had treated him with fairness. "They listened to me. I could see this face, way back in the crowd, and he was listening, really listening to me," Kennedy recalled. "The people here are not so neurotic and hypocritical as in Washington or New York. They're more direct. I like rural people, who work hard with their hands. There is something healthy about them." He did complain about how he had been treated recently in the *New York Times*; he said he would rather be reported on by the *Indianapolis Star* because with it at least he knew where he stood—as did its readers.[26]

Douglas said Kennedy seemed pleased by the vast numbers who had come out to see him, but he talked about a few episodes that stuck in his mind. One involved a woman who had come up to him and asked if he could come over to see her mother, a victim of a stroke. "The older woman had been wrapped up in a shawl and had been sitting on her lawn for a long time," said Douglas. "Bob had gone up and had a nice chat with her." He had also enjoyed seeing again a young man he had noticed on a previous visit to Gary, who was carrying a sibling on his back as he ran to meet the Kennedy motorcade. Kennedy asked him to ride along in the car with him for a while. In addition to reflecting on the campaign, Kennedy also talked about his love for his family—his brothers, sisters, and mother. "He talked again about something which he apparently referred to quite a bit," said Douglas, "about how the faces of many of the black youngsters in their early years were very animated, and how as the youngsters got older their faces turned into kind of lifeless masks as a result of the prejudice and hostility and difficulties which they encountered." The contemplative mood was shattered when a man who had been drinking wandered over and said some harsh things about the candidate. Kennedy refused to respond. When the man finally left, the candidate said: "You get so tired sometimes. You have to restrain yourself."[27]

On primary election day, Tuesday, May 7, Kennedy relaxed by playing touch football on the lawn of the Airport Holiday Inn, where he, some of his staff, and reporters planned to watch the election returns. Kennedy's opponents were both sanguine about their chances with voters. A confident Governor Branigin, who the day before had received an endorsement from the Indiana Conference of Teamsters, told the *Indianapolis Star* in a page-one article: "I think I'll win. I think the large number of undecided voters shown by the polls is a good sign." The Teamsters, the union Kennedy had investigated for corruption during his days as chief counsel for a U.S. Senate subcommittee, sent out a sound truck to Indianapolis, sponsored by Local 135, to blast out an anti-Kennedy message. "We just feel this primary is serious enough not only for the people of Indiana but for the nation as a whole that we have to do all we can to support Governor Branigin and stop Kennedy," said Loran W. Robbins, the local's president. "Kennedy is a most dangerous man in our opinion." McCarthy, who the day before had embarked on a three-and-a-half-mile hike through central Indianapolis, said his polling indicated that it should be "quite close," as only five percentage points separated the three contenders. A last-minute surge of optimism had spread among McCarthy's supporters. Larner, who used his experiences in a political campaign to write the Oscar-winning screenplay for the Robert Redford film *The Candidate*, remembered that on election day one of McCarthy's aides raced around the hotel exclaiming that the feeling hit him today: McCarthy would win Indiana. "They touch off a small swirl of ecstasy," said Larner. "Lost souls hug and kiss cheeks in the corridor."[28]

Because of the importance of the Indiana primary to Kennedy's presidential hopes, his campaign staff made ready to pass along any good news to the waiting media. The campaign selected twenty-five representative precincts in the state and placed staff members in those areas on election night to obtain early results and phone them into headquarters. "We'd brief the press ahead of time on what those precincts were," explained press secretary Frank Mankiewicz. "Then we'd get those results early so that an hour or two after the polls were closed we'd be able to give them fifteen or twenty of those sample precincts. And those stories were used by almost everybody." In fact, the technique proved so successful in Indiana that the Kennedy campaign used it again in the Nebraska, Oregon, and California primaries.[29]

For most reporters, the place to be on election night as the results were announced was with Kennedy in his private suite at the Airport Holiday Inn. Kennedy had invited two of his favorite reporters, Jack Newfield and Jimmy Breslin, a columnist for *Newsday*, to his room to watch the returns come in. At the door, however, the two reporters were barred for a brief moment by another writer, Theodore H. White, the author of the highly successful *The Making of the President* series. White did not want to lose his exclusive access to the candidate, but Newfield barged into the room, screaming an expletive at White as he entered, an effort that impressed Kennedy, who had just finished taking a shower. The first returns reported to Kennedy by Lawrence O'Brien were almost too good to be true. A Polish precinct in South Bend had Kennedy garnering 241 votes, McCarthy 86, and Branigin 62. A majority black district in Indianapolis gave Kennedy 341 votes to only 14 for Branigin and 11 for McCarthy. In one African American precinct in Gary, Kennedy had received 697 votes; McCarthy, 52; and Branigin, 16. Hearing the news, an exultant Ethel Kennedy asked, "Don't you just wish that everyone was black?" Meanwhile, in the District of Columbia primary, Kennedy's slate of convention delegates appeared to be on its way to winning a landslide victory over two slates pledged to Humphrey.[30]

Before leaving his room for a victory celebration at the Sheraton-Lincoln Hotel, Kennedy noticed that his vote total had fallen from 54 percent to 48 percent. "He made a child's face, said 'eecch,' and left for downtown," Newfield reported. Later, as he watched a television correspondent report that Kennedy was not doing as well as expected, the candidate replied: "Not as well as *you* expected." The final returns had Kennedy winning with 42.3 percent of the 776,000 votes cast. Governor Branigin finished second with 30.7 percent of the vote, and McCarthy trailed the field at 27 percent. In winning nine of eleven of Indiana's eleven congressional districts (losing only the fifth and sixth districts to Branigin), Kennedy captured fifty-six of the state's sixty-three delegates to the Democratic National Convention, with Branigin winning the remaining seven. Kennedy swept fifty-seven of the state's ninety-two counties, and also captured most of Indiana's largest urban centers, including Indianapolis, Gary, Hammond, South Bend, Kokomo, Muncie, Fort Wayne, Terre Haute, and East Chicago. In African American precincts, Kennedy destroyed his opponents, winning them with better than 85 percent of the vote. Kennedy defeated Branigin in the governor's home county (Tippecanoe), his home city (Lafayette), and even his home precinct. The Hoosier Democratic machine, however, did its work for Branigin in Evansville, where the governor captured Vanderburgh County with 11,616 votes to Kennedy's 10,801, and students from Indiana University helped McCarthy take Bloomington. Hoping to persuade Democratic Party leaders of Kennedy's ability to draw white as well as African American voters, the Kennedy campaign also pointed out that he carried the seven largest counties in Indiana where George Wallace had secured his greatest support in the 1964 primary—Lake, Delaware, Howard, Grant, Madison, Allen, and Marion. "I've proved I can really be a leader of a broad spectrum," Kennedy observed to O'Brien. "I can be a bridge between blacks and whites without stepping back from my positions."[31]

Kennedy's ability in Indiana to achieve his goal of attracting white as well as African American voters came under close scrutiny in the years following the primary. A column by political reporters Roland Evans and Robert Novak immediately following the election titled "Kennedy's Indiana Victory Proves

His Appeal Defused Backlash Voting" credited Kennedy with winning 90 percent of the vote in Gary's black precincts and running nearly two to one ahead of his opponents in some Polish precincts—figures touted by the Kennedy camp. In a later examination of the voting for a biography of Kennedy, two of his aides, William vanden Heuvel and Milton Gwirtzman, found that in fact Kennedy only achieved such positive results in two Polish precincts and had lost fifty-nine of the seventy white precincts in Gary. "The lesson of Lake County, then, was that the more personally involved the white voters were with the racial struggle, the more they identified Kennedy with the black side of it, and turned to his opponents as an outlet for their protest," vanden Heuvel and Gwirtzman concluded. Approximately sixty miles away in South Bend, however, Kennedy had been able to amass large pluralities in a number of Polish precincts "where there had been some threat of a 'backlash' vote against him," noted *South Bend Tribune* political writer Jack Colwell. At a polling place at the West Side Democratic and Civic Club, a spot Kennedy had visited with Prince Radziwill, the New York senator won 201 votes to 84 for Branigin and 78 for McCarthy. In one west side Polish American precinct, the polling location, Saint Adalbert's Parish Hall, gave Kennedy 224 votes to just 90 for McCarthy and 83 for Branigin. In the only precinct in Saint Joseph County carried by Wallace in 1964—a west side neighborhood with a polling place at Benjamin Harrison School—Kennedy won with 190 votes to 95 for McCarthy and 55 for Branigin.[32]

Before Hoosiers went to the polls, Kennedy strategists had expected their candidate to attract between 40 and 45 percent of the vote. They had also told the *New York Times* that if Kennedy garnered 40 percent or more of the vote and ran ahead of his nearest rival by at least 10 percentage points—a goal he achieved—they would consider Indiana "a significant victory that should have an important psychological impact in the remaining primaries and on the delegates to the Democratic national convention." Television analysts, however, interpreted the results very differently: they called Kennedy's victory inconclusive. An irate Fred Dutton complained to one network correspondent that McCarthy had won 42 percent of the vote in New Hampshire against a single write-in opponent (President Lyndon Johnson) and newsmen had called it an heroic victory. "Kennedy gets 42 percent here against two active candidates," Dutton pointed out, "one the Governor of the state, and you say it's really meaningless." As Kennedy watched the campaign coverage on a television at the Sheraton-Lincoln, McCarthy told interviewers it did not matter who finished first, second, or third. "That's not what my father told me," Kennedy responded. "I always thought it was better to win. I learned that when I was about two."[33]

The candidate himself also battled the press. Before speaking to the cheering supporters gathered in the Cole Porter Ballroom at the Sheraton-Lincoln Hotel, Kennedy gave interviews to the various television networks covering the campaign. Asked by one interviewer if he would accept McCarthy's challenge to debate him on the issues, Kennedy expressed willingness to debate, but said he would also like to see Vice President Humphrey participate. "I would also like to see him also participate for the popular vote," Kennedy added in a dig at Humphrey's failure to run in any of the primaries. CBS anchorman Walter Cronkite questioned Kennedy about the large amount of money spent on the campaign. Kennedy decided to turn the issue against Cronkite and the people he worked for, pointing out that candidates would not need so much money if the networks made free airtime available to all candidates on an equal basis. "The only thing I wish I had thought to ask Cronkite," Kennedy said later, "was what his annual salary was."[34]

Kennedy appeared at the victory celebration with his wife, Ethel, and two of the men who had made his victory in Indiana possible—Gerard Doherty and Michael Riley. According to Doherty, Kennedy had come up to him on election night and expressed his gratitude for what he had done in the Hoosier State and asked Doherty to accompany him to the ballroom. "I said, 'What? Hey, you know, you brought it up. My obligation is to your brother. If he's happy, I'm happy,'" Doherty recalled. The two men also agreed that it would be appropriate to have someone from Indiana with them, and immediately thought of Riley. The moment was doubly sweet for Riley, because it gave him an opportunity to settle an old score with U.S. Senator Vance Hartke. Prior to being elected president of the Marion County Young Democrats, Riley had participated in a Democratic meeting in French Lick where Hartke posed for photographs with fellow party regulars. Although somewhat in awe of the senator, Riley apparently did something to annoy Hartke, who chastised him by saying, "You've got a long way to go boy." When Kennedy asked Riley to join him, Ethel, and Doherty on stage at the victory celebration, Hartke had come up and also volunteered to join the party. Kennedy declined the offer, and Hartke asked Riley to convince Kennedy to let him onstage. Riley turned to Hartke and said: "You've got a long way to go, senator. I guess you just can't be up there with him." Riley never thought Hartke would make the connection between the two conversations, but a number of years later, after he had left the Senate, Hartke told Riley that he had given him his comeuppance that evening.[35]

In his remarks to his supporters, Kennedy thanked all the volunteers who had come from such states as Massachusetts, New York, Pennsylvania, Florida, and Illinois to help with the Indiana campaign. He also gave special thanks to his mother, Rose, who had been "campaigning since McKinley was President and who has been going about the state telling people I'm not as bad as the newspapers say I am." The vote in Indiana had indicated a mood for change in the country. "I, at the moment, might be the personification of this change," said Kennedy. "You, the people, have decided that we can do better than we have in the past. You have decided that we cannot just heal the divisions, but face what the divisions mean." In a final jab at the Indianapolis newspapers, Kennedy concluded his remarks by saying: "I want to quote the Greek poet Aeschylus—I will sleep better tonight knowing Eugene Pulliam won't."[36]

Another member of the Kennedy team slept well that night. Returning with his wife, Fran, to his mother's home on Kessler Boulevard after the long day, John Bartlow Martin felt relief at finally being on the winning side again. For the first time since John Kennedy's death in 1963, Martin felt hope for the nation's future because of what Robert Kennedy represented. "Somehow, with him, you really felt it didn't all have to be race riots at home and war in Southeast Asia and crap from the White House and the rest of the government," said Martin. "The United States could become again what it ought to be, a great nation able to live with itself and with the rest of the world."[37]

Kennedy's victory had not been large enough to knock McCarthy out of the race. Instead of a West Virginia, the Indiana primary had been more like John F. Kennedy's inconclusive victory in the 1960 Wisconsin primary. There, Kennedy had defeated Humphrey by winning all the districts in the state dominated by Roman Catholic voters; to solidify his position with Democratic Party leaders, he was forced to enter the West Virginia primary to show he could attract support from Protestant voters as well. But at a press conference after the victory celebration with his supporters, Robert Kennedy indicated his pleasure at the outcome in the Hoosier State. He noted he had decided to enter the Indiana primary despite warnings from political professionals in the state who said he could never expect to defeat Governor Branigin. "To come in here under those circumstances . . . to be able to do this well is very encouraging," said Kennedy. "It's very encouraging." He pointed out, however, that he would be "less than candid" if he failed to note that there was still a long way to go before the Democratic convention in August. "Vice President Humphrey says he's the front runner, Senator McCarthy says he's the front runner," said Kennedy, who now prepared to do it all over again for the May 14 Nebraska primary. "I'm not making any predictions where I am because the only way I can do well is to take my campaign to the people." Reporters also noted that following its victory the Kennedy camp immediately attempted to mend fences with the state's Democratic leaders: Lawrence O'Brien paid a personal visit to the party's state headquarters to talk with chairman Gordon St. Angelo.

As for Branigin, he heard the bad news while attending a testimonial dinner for a friend in Chicago. "I never conceded," he joked, "I just got whipped." The governor added that he wrote his own speeches and drove his own car during the campaign, but "you can't beat $2 million."[38]

Coming after such triumphant campaigns as the ones in New Hampshire and Wisconsin, the loss failed to discourage McCarthy's supporters. As a band played the campaign's theme song, "The Saints Come Marching In," the volunteers cheered wildly for their candidate when he appeared before them at the James Whitcomb Riley Room in the Claypool Hotel. Jeremy Larner called the scene "miraculous," as the defeated McCarthy, whose face had been "dead and gray" when he left the hotel for the rally, began to come alive when faced with his adoring young volunteers. "I want you to know I'm not here to dismiss the troops," McCarthy declared. He promised to carry on the fight in primaries to come and predicted success in the future after this first confrontation with Kennedy. "We have tested the enemy and we know his techniques, and we also know his weaknesses," said McCarthy. Earlier, the Minnesota senator had said in spite of his defeat he was still the "strongest potential candidate" for the Democratic nomination and the general election in November. McCarthy's supporters believed he would have won the Indiana primary in a head-to-head battle with Kennedy; they claimed he would have been able to capture 80 to 90 percent of the votes taken by Branigin. "We had Governor Branigin between us all the way," said McCarthy. "I think the direct confrontation that was denied us in Indiana will be given us in Nebraska."[39]

Reviewing the McCarthy effort in Indiana, the senator's top aides lamented the lack of organization, believing a more efficient effort would have pushed McCarthy's vote total well above the 27 percent he received. "We're still in business," one of his advisers said, "but we will have to do a lot of things in Oregon and California that we didn't do here." The chief weakness came in two areas the Kennedy campaign proved to be superb at—scheduling and advancing. "No one knew the state," according to an aide, pointing out that McCarthy had been sent to Notre Dame to address a seminar of 125 people when he could have drawn a much larger crowd. McCarthy did himself no favors in the state, canceling meetings and failing to connect with African American voters. "They turned him off as they might a white school teacher who didn't understand them," said a McCarthy aide. "They listened to Bobby because he shakes them up."[40]

Late on election night, Kennedy left downtown Indianapolis to eat dinner at a restaurant at Weir Cook Airport on the city's west side. As Kennedy and his small group, including reporter Newfield, walked through the airport they came across two college-age students, a woman and a man. The woman wore a McCarthy campaign hat and the man had attached to his jacket his campaign identification badge. They were using their luggage to sit on as they waited for an early-morning flight. The woman was Pat Sylvester, a student at the University of Massachusetts, and the man was Taylor Branch of the University of North Carolina (who would go on to win the Pulitzer Prize for his history of the civil rights movement).

Sylvester expressed disbelief that Kennedy had won, given the poor quality of his canvassers as compared to the volunteers working for McCarthy. Asked by Kennedy how they felt about the results in Indiana, Sylvester firmly declared they would both stick with the man from Minnesota. When Branch lamented his inability to reach African American voters in the state, Kennedy wondered why McCarthy had been ineffective in those areas. Sylvester said the answer came down to one simple fact—the fame associated with Kennedy's name. "Look, I agree I have a tremendous advantage with my last name," Kennedy admitted to the McCarthy supporters. "But let me ask you, why can't McCarthy go into a ghetto? Why can't he go into a poor neighborhood? Can you tell me that he's been involved in those areas? Why did he vote against the minimum wage for farm workers? Why did he vote against a large proportion of people from the Minimum Wage Act?" Kennedy's reasoning, however, failed to sway Sylvester's and Branch's allegiance to McCarthy. "You're dedicated to what you believe," Kennedy told them, "and I think that's terrific." Looking back on the conversation, Branch said Kennedy had managed to reach him with his words. "I still worked for McCarthy," said Branch, "but I was drawn to Kennedy because of his flair and passion for the black people."[41]

The next morning Kennedy left Indiana for his home in New York before returning to the campaign trail in Nebraska. The senator's breakfast of champagne and scrambled eggs was ruined, however, by coverage of the Indiana election results in the *New York Times*. Kennedy objected strongly to a comment in an analysis prepared by journalist Tom Wicker stating that in the Hoosier State primary McCarthy had proven he was "a serious contender" for president and had "done the most to advance his cause." That statement caused Kennedy to exclaim to Newfield: "He [McCarthy] finished last!" Kennedy furnished his own interpretation of his victory in Indiana for Newfield, saying it meant he had a chance, a small one at that, "to organize a new coalition of Negroes, and working-class people, against the union and party Establishments."[42]

1 2 3 4 5 6 **7**

The Train

The call came to the home of Anthony M. Boysa, a fireman for the Penn Central Railroad, at eight o'clock the morning of Friday, June 8, 1968, from a crew dispatcher in Newark, New Jersey. Boysa had been assigned to a twenty-one-car train pulled by two black electric locomotives scheduled to leave New York on Saturday from Pennsylvania Station for a 226-mile journey to Union Station in Washington, D.C. "They told us when they called us up to dress special—but I didn't stay clean long," Boysa said. "When you walk through the aisles in the engine, you brush past all the motor casings." He remembered that the train's engineer came to work that day in a suit with a white shirt and tie. "That was unusual," said Boysa. Supervisors and laborers worked most of the day Friday at the Sunnyside Yards loading the train with provisions for its trip, including steaks, hamburgers, and cheesecake. The train, with an observation car at the rear draped in black bunting, finally left Pennsylvania Station at 1:02 PM Saturday. Onboard were nearly a thousand people—the family and friends of U.S. Senator Robert F. Kennedy, who had died two days earlier, another victim that violent year of an assassin's bullets.[1]

When Senator Kennedy stepped off the stage at the ballroom of the Ambassador Hotel in Los Angeles early the morning of June 5, he had just declared victory over Eugene McCarthy in the crucial California primary. "We are a great country, an unselfish country, and a compassionate country," Kennedy told his cheering supporters. "I intend to make that the basis for running." Much had happened in the race for the Democratic presidential nomination since Kennedy had won his first primary, Indiana, nearly two months earlier. In Nebraska, the contest immediately following his triumph in the Hoosier State, Kennedy had an easy time. McCarthy campaigned in Nebraska for only four days. Instead, he concentrated his efforts on the May 28 Oregon primary. "Although I hoped that I would not do too badly in Nebraska," said McCarthy, "I had no real reason to expect that I would run very well." His assessment proved accurate. Kennedy continued to connect with rural audiences as he had done in Indiana. At one campaign stop a gust of wind blew a single piece of paper from his hands, prompting the candidate to joke, "Give me that back. That's my farm program." In another community, he told the farmers gathered to hear him that he represented the best friend they had in the campaign. "I'm already doing more for the farmer than any of them, and if you don't believe me, just look down at my breakfast table," Kennedy said. "We are consuming more milk and more bread and more eggs, doing more for farm consumption—than the family of any other candidate." The farmers, according to Kennedy aide Peter Edelman, represented "his kind of people." On May 14 Kennedy won with 51.5 percent of the vote to 31 percent for McCarthy. The combined figures for the two antiwar candidates showed that the country stood ready to move in a new direction, Kennedy told reporters. In a direct swipe at the candidacy of Vice President Hubert Humphrey, Kennedy said, "We can't have the politics of happiness and joy when we have so many problems in our own country."[2]

With two primary victories in a row under its belt, the Kennedy campaign appeared poised to sweep the McCarthy threat aside once and for all in Oregon. The northwestern state, however, proved to be inhospitable territory for Kennedy. McCarthy had been able to establish a solid presence in the state over the past six months. "In Oregon we had a better organization than we had in any other state," said McCarthy. "It was also the best financed of our efforts because we had money well enough in advance to plan the spending effectively." Meanwhile, Kennedy's campaign in the state floundered under the direction of Oregon congresswoman Edith Green. Just a month before the May 28 primary, Kennedy's headquarters had just three people and only two desks. The mostly middle-class, suburban, well-educated, prosperous citizens of the state responded favorably to candidate McCarthy. Strategists for Kennedy knew their campaign was in trouble when during one meeting they asked Green if the ghettos had been organized and she responded, "There are no ghettos in Oregon." As Kennedy candidly admitted to a reporter for the *National Observer*: "Let's face it. I appeal best to people who have problems." He also did his campaign no favor when he told another reporter a week before the election that if he happened to be defeated "in any primary, I am not a very viable candidate." The people of Oregon seemed to be problem-free, and gave McCarthy 44.7 percent of the vote, as compared to 38.8 percent for Kennedy. It marked the first time in twenty-seven elections that a Kennedy had gone down to defeat. Kennedy responded by sending a congratulatory telegram to McCarthy, something the Minnesota senator had failed to do following his losses in Indiana and Nebraska. "He took it very hard," said John Bartlow Martin of Kennedy's Oregon loss. "It really flattened him to lose."[3]

With its 174 delegates, California stood as a crucial test for Kennedy following the debacle in Oregon. Since the Indiana primary, McCarthy had been calling on Kennedy to debate him. In California he finally accepted the challenge. "I'm not the same candidate I was before Oregon, and I can't claim that I am," he said. The debate was set for June 1 in San Francisco. The two candidates prepared in different ways. Kennedy ensconced himself with his advisers and briefing books at the Fairmont Hotel, but the sunny weather seemed to distract him from his task. "There was no sense stuffing the candidate's head full of facts from speeches he had already given," said Martin. "There is always danger in over-briefing." Thomas Finney, who ran McCarthy's California effort, attempted without success to hide his candidate at a Hilton hotel in San Francisco from the members of his entourage that his campaign staff called the "astrologers." Noted McCarthy aide Andreas Teuber: "We tried to keep [poet] Robert Lowell from McCarthy at crucial times, because we thought he always took the edge off. Every time Lowell and McCarthy would get together, Lowell . . . would convince McCarthy that really, he was above all this." Lowell found McCarthy and on the way to the debate the two men sat in the back of a limousine and tried to create a modern version of "Ode for St. Cecilia's Day."[4]

To Teuber, it appeared that neither candidate wanted to be at the debate, with Kennedy trying hard "not to be ruthless, and McCarthy trying not to be there" as they were questioned by three ABC reporters, Robert Clark, William

Lawrence, and Frank Reynolds, who served as moderator. Most observers believed the debate had been a draw. "It was a conversation rather than a debate," according to the *New York Times*, "and it demonstrated that the two rivals are in substantial agreement on every major issue." But with expectations high that McCarthy, known for his caustic wit and intellectual vigor, would easily defeat his opponent in such a setting, Kennedy gained most from the encounter. Jeremy Larner noted that Kennedy's performance made it clear to everybody that he "could take McCarthy head-on with no fear of his magic powers. If McCarthy had something new and different in American politics, it did not show in open competition with Kennedy." As he left the studio, Kennedy told his aide Fred Dutton that McCarthy had not done his homework. In a poll conducted by the *Los Angeles Times*, viewers watching on television had voted two and a half to one that Kennedy had won the debate. Martin believed Kennedy's performance finally "put out the McCarthy fire which had been ignited by his Oregon victory and Kennedy's bad reaction to that victory."[5]

On Tuesday, June 4, California voters went to the polls. A nervous Martin feared that during the last week McCarthy had caught up to Kennedy. "I thought the debate had dampened him down a little but was afraid he might catch us on Sunday, Monday, and election day," Martin remembered. His fears were almost realized, but Kennedy held on to win the primary, capturing 46.4 percent of the vote to 41.8 percent for McCarthy. Trying to relax at his suite at the Ambassador Hotel, Kennedy received good news from South Dakota, whose primary was also being held that day. He had accomplished a smashing victory in Humphrey's native state, winning 59 percent of the vote to just 20 percent for McCarthy (other votes went to a slate pledged to President Lyndon Johnson and Humphrey). "I feel now for the first time that I've shaken off the shadow of my brother," Kennedy said to family friend Kenneth O'Donnell. "I feel I made it on my own." With his victory, Kennedy hoped to convince McCarthy supporters that he now stood as the only antiwar candidate with the chance to beat Humphrey at the Democratic convention in August. Talking privately with Richard Goodwin, Kennedy said while he and McCarthy were battling one another, Humphrey had been picking up delegate after delegate around the country. Kennedy did not want to have to spend his time the next few weeks campaigning on every street corner in New York in hopes of winning the primary there. "I've got to spend that time going to the states, talking to delegates before it's too late," Kennedy stressed to Goodwin. "My only chance is to chase Hubert's ass all over the country. Maybe he'll fold."[6]

A few days before the California vote, Martin had prepared a memo outlining suggestions for the Kennedy campaign in the months leading to the convention. For the next primary, New York, Martin urged the candidate to attack McCarthy; the Minnesota senator, he said, was not an ally but an enemy. "There is no hope he will throw to you at the convention," Martin said. "Counterattack him earlier than you did in California." Once the New York primary had been decided, Martin wanted Kennedy to buy time on national television in order to speak out when events warranted, for example, if the peace talks between the United States and North Vietnam broke down. Using tactics that had worked in Indiana and California, he also suggested a transcontinental whistle-stop railroad tour from the East Coast to the Midwest, then by airplane to the West Coast. "Make it a 'whistle-and-listen' trip—announce you are traveling to listen to the people's views as well as to present your own," Martin advised. Mayor Richard Daley of Chicago could be the key to Kennedy's success or failure at the convention, and Martin urged Kennedy to visit with him after the California primary, give a few speeches while in the city, and plan a motorcade through African American or Polish neighborhoods. "Daley probably would not approve heavy motorcading," said Martin. "But a show of strength in Negro and backlash wards would impress him and people he sees." Above all, stressed Martin, Daley wanted to be able to support a Democratic candidate who could win in the November general election.[7]

Shortly after midnight on the evening of the California primary, Kennedy went down to the hotel's Embassy Ballroom to address his happy group of supporters that had been singing "This Land Is Your Land" and chanting "We want Kennedy." Standing behind a lectern decorated with one of his bumper stickers, Kennedy first expressed his regard for the work of Los Angeles Dodgers' pitcher Don Drysdale, who had pitched his sixth straight shutout that day, adding that he hoped his campaign would have such good fortune in the future. Emphasizing once again his campaign's main themes, Kennedy told the crowd: "I think we can end the divisions in the United States. What I think is quite clear is that we can work together in the last analysis. And that is what has been going on within the United States over a period of the last three years—the division, the violence, the disenchantment with our society, the division, whether it's between blacks and whites, between the poor and the more affluent, between the age groups or in the war on Vietnam—that we can start to work together." Larner considered Kennedy's remarks the best speech of the entire campaign.

Ending his speech, the candidate thanked his supporters, flashed a "V" sign with his fingers, and said it was "on to Chicago and let's win there." While walking through the hotel's kitchen on his way to attend a press conference in the hotel's Colonial Room, Kennedy was hit in the head and neck by bullets from a .22 caliber Iver Johnson revolver fired by Sirhan Sirhan.

Those who had gathered in the hotel ballroom for Kennedy's victory cele-bration reacted with shock and fury when they learned of the shooting. Young women wearing campaign paraphernalia dropped to their knees to pray for Kennedy's well-being. One reporter saw a large African American man pound-ing on the wall and screaming, "Why, God, why? Why again? Why another Kennedy?" Martin had been viewing the victory celebration on television in a crowded room adjoining Kennedy's suite and quit watching for a moment to go into the hall for some air. All of a sudden, Jeff Greenfield ran by saying some-thing that Martin thought sounded like "shot." Greenfield told him that there was a rumor that Kennedy had been shot. Martin returned to the room where he had been and watched the events unfold on television. "We kept watching the horror. Then the announcer said that it was said that Kennedy had been shot in the head," Martin remembered. "Every one of us said, 'Oh no.'"

Although Kennedy underwent three hours of surgery at Good Samaritan Hospital, he never regained consciousness. Early in the morning of June 6, Frank Mankiewicz, the senator's press secretary, stepped before gathered news-men at a gymnasium serving as press headquarters and said: "I have a short an-nouncement to read which I will read at this time. Senator Robert Francis Kennedy died at 1:44 AM today, June 6, 1968. With Senator Kennedy at the time of his death was his wife, Ethel, his sisters, Mrs. Patricia Lawford, and Mrs. Stephen Smith, his brother-in-law, Stephen Smith, and his sister-in-law, Mrs. John F. Kennedy. He was 42 years old."[8]

Martin was devastated by his friend's death. "Now I feel nothing but bleak despair," Martin wrote later that month. "The last five years have been bad, but always there was the thought, 'Well, there's always Bob.' Now there isn't. There's nothing. The last hurrah, all right. Now nothing, no hope, nothing. . . . This time the bastards have finally beaten me." Other supporters shared Martin's grief. Carla Verdina, a twenty-one-year-old volunteer from New Jersey, said she might agree with McCarthy on the issues, but could not see herself working on his behalf. "Nobody takes Senator Kennedy's place," said Verdina.[9]

More than two thousand people, including President Johnson, gathered at Saint Patrick's Cathedral in New York City for a high requiem mass held in Kennedy's honor. "My brother need not be idealized or enlarged in death be-yond what he was in life," Senator Edward M. Kennedy said, "to be remem-bered simply as a good and decent man, who saw wrong and tried to right it, saw suffering and tried to heal it, and saw war and tried to stop it. Those of us who loved him and who take him to his rest today pray that what he was to us and what he wished for others will someday come to pass for all the world." Ted Kennedy ended his eulogy with the George Bernard Shaw quotation often used by his brother to end his speeches on the campaign trail: "Some men see things as they are and ask why. I dream things that never were and say, why not." After the one-hour-and-forty-minute ceremony, performed by Archbishop Terence J. Cooke of New York, Kennedy's coffin was taken by hearse to the train at Pennsylvania Station for what was supposed to be a four-hour journey to its final destination—a gravesite at Arlington National Cemetery. Robert Kennedy's final resting place was located just a few feet from the grave of his elder brother, John F. Kennedy.[10]

From New York, the Penn Central train carrying Robert Kennedy's coffin traveled slowly through Newark and Trenton, New Jersey; Philadelphia, Pennsylvania; and Baltimore, Maryland. When the train cleared the tunnel on the Jersey side, Boysa expressed surprise at what he saw. "The people were standing along the tracks and on the factory roofs," he recalled. "I didn't know what they were doing there at first." All along the route people stood silently, paying tribute to Kennedy, whose coffin rested on top of chairs in the last car. Along the railroad right-of-way people held signs, many saying merely "Good-bye Bobby," while in New Brunswick, New Jersey, a bugler on a station platform played "Taps" as the train passed through. "When you looked outside and saw the emotions of the people standing beside the tracks," said Milton Gwirtzman, who was on the train, "you got very drawn to the tragedy of the occasion; so you would leave that and turn back to the people in the car and almost forget the nature of the occasion." John Bartlow Martin called his time on Kennedy's funeral train as both "terrible and great." He added that it was fitting that his friend's last trip came on a train, as he had loved whistle-stop campaigning. In addition, railroads ran through poorer neighborhoods, the homes of African Americans and factory workers. "They were his people," said Martin. "The disadvantaged."[11]

Because of the throngs of people lining the tracks to pay their respects, the journey from New York to Washington took more than eight hours. Upon the train's arrival at Union Station, more people lined city streets along the approximately five-mile route from the station to Arlington Cemetery. Elvin Smith, a fifty-year-old African American from Los Angeles, had flown in especially for the funeral and had to return for work the following day. "He was the only one who would represent all the people," Smith said of Kennedy, "and if he could give his life, the least I could do was to come and pay my respects." After stopping at the Lincoln Memorial, where the U.S. Marine Corps Band played "The Battle Hymn of the Republic," the motorcade arrived at the

cemetery at 10:30 PM. Due to the late hour, Arlington officials placed floodlights around the open grave and distributed fifteen hundred candles to
mourners. A young soldier witnessing the scene commented that Kennedy had
been a good man, and that the good died young. At the end of the brief service, astronaut John Glenn presented a folded flag to Kennedy's wife, Ethel,
and his son, Joe.[12]

Kennedy's death left McCarthy as the only true candidate against the war
still in the running for the Democratic nomination. But the Minnesota senator squandered the opportunity, believing that with Kennedy's death, Humphrey had sewn up the nomination. "McCarthy did not resign his candidacy;
he left a lottery ticket in the big barrel to await the hand of God," Larner observed in his memoir of the 1968 campaign. "But he never again addressed
himself to the moment. He stood all summer passive and self-absorbed in the
wind-down of his campaign." (McCarthy later called Larner's book, *Nobody
Knows*, "a political *Portnoy's Complaint*," but did indicate his speechwriter's
views on his personality were "acceptable to me.") The long round of primaries had also taken its toll on McCarthy. "It's like someone gave you the football," he said to the *New York Times*, "and the field never ends. There's no goal
line. No opponent. You just run." He refused to take the necessary steps
needed to challenge Humphrey for the nomination, including calling or meeting with Democratic Party leaders. Peace advocates grew so frustrated with
McCarthy's antics that many rallied to Senator George McGovern when he
announced his candidacy on August 10. Others hoped Ted Kennedy might be
urged by his advisers to accept a draft for president—a hope that, after much
negotiation, never materialized.[13]

As Democrats gathered for their convention at the International Amphitheater in Chicago from August 26 to 29, they knew the person they would
face in the fall. Earlier that month, Republicans, at their convention at the Miami Beach Convention Center, had nominated as their presidential candidate
former vice president Richard Nixon, who had beaten back challenges from
Governor Nelson Rockefeller of New York and Governor Ronald Reagan of
California. The convention had gone off with few problems, and television
networks, with their equipment already in Miami, had called upon the Democratic Party to also hold its convention there. Under pressure from Mayor
Daley, however, the Democrats remained in Chicago. The choice proved to
be a poor one. A few thousand peace activists descended upon the convention
to protest the Vietnam War. Mayor Daley, however, had refused to grant the
protesters any permits to hold demonstrations or permission to camp in city
parks. "No thousands will come to our city and take over our streets, our city,
and our Convention," Daley declared, and he established an 11 PM curfew.

Opposing the dissidents were twelve thousand members of the Chicago police and six thousand members of the Illinois National Guard. Another six thousand regular army troops stood by if events warranted their use against the protesters. Agents from the Federal Bureau of Investigation and the Secret Service were also on duty. Fences and barbed wire ringed the amphitheater and vehicles were stopped and checked blocks away from the convention. Police and protesters clashed in the city's streets and parks and even in the hotels housing delegates and leading Democrats, including Humphrey and McCarthy. Demonstrators responded to the beatings by police and stinging tear-gas canisters with cries of "The whole world is watching." British reporters were aghast at what they witnessed, noting that the police "went, quite literally, berserk," beating not only protesters but newsmen and innocent bystanders as well. McGovern told reporters that the "Battle of Chicago," as it came to be known, made him "sick to his stomach" and that he had "seen nothing like it since the films of Nazi Germany." Watching the disturbance from the room on the twenty-third floor of the Conrad Hilton Hotel, McCarthy compared the skirmishing to the ancient battle of Dannae between Carthage and Rome. "A battle of purgatory," McCarthy added.[14]

As television viewers witnessed the carnage on Chicago's streets, Democratic delegates inside the amphitheater were aware of what was happening outside. Abraham Ribicoff, U.S. senator from Connecticut, during his speech nominating McGovern as the party's presidential candidate, declared that with McGovern as the nation's leader "we would not have to have such Gestapo tactics in the streets of Chicago." As a national television audience watched, an enraged Daley leapt to his feet to scream what seemed to be a series of expletives at his fellow Democrat. In response, Ribicoff said: "How hard it is to accept the truth." Another bruising battle occurred over adding a plank on the Vietnam War to the party's platform. Johnson's supporters were determined that his Vietnam policies would not be questioned at the convention, while a coalition of antiwar activists were equally determined to push a measure calling for a unilateral halt to American bombing and other measures to bring about a hoped-for peace. The Johnson measure passed by a vote of 1,567 to 1,041. In response to the defeat of the peace plank, delegates from such states as California, Colorado, New Hampshire, New York, Oregon, and Wisconsin donned black armbands and sang "We Shall Overcome." During the roll call for the presidential nomination, the Wisconsin delegation unsuccessfully attempted to adjourn the convention for two weeks and move the proceedings to another city. Martin, who shook off his grief at Kennedy's death and eventually went to work for Humphrey during the campaign, had admired President Johnson's commitment to socially progressive legislation, and considered Daley to be the best mayor the city of Chicago had ever had. These two stubborn old men, however, combined at the convention to "destroy any chance the Democratic party had to keep the unspeakable Richard Nixon out of the White House."[15]

In the chaos, Humphrey received his party's nomination on the first ballot, winning 1,761¾ votes to 601 for McCarthy and 146½ for McGovern. Indiana's delegation gave 49 of its 63 votes to Humphrey, with 11 going to McCarthy, 2 to McGovern, and 1 to Channing Phillips, an African American minister from Washington, D.C. Two members of Indiana's congressional delegation, John Brademas of South Bend and Andy Jacobs Jr. of Indianapolis, had cast their votes for McCarthy—a decision that irked Governor Roger Branigin. According to Jacobs, Branigin, who following Kennedy's death had released the seven delegates pledged to him, confronted him on the convention floor and sarcastically asked him, "Where's your McCarthy button? While I was staying with the President, you were off voting for Kennedy." The governor did add: "I stayed with him [Johnson], but for some reason people just don't seem to like him." Jacobs responded that it seemed as if he, and not the governor, had stayed with the people, whereupon Branigin predicted that the congressman would lose his reelection fight and be back among the people (Jacobs won his race).[16]

Humphrey had finally achieved the presidential nomination he had long sought, but his victory was tarnished by the horrible scenes on Chicago's streets. The violence at the convention, coupled with McCarthy's renegade campaign, the Tet Offensive, and the assassinations of Robert Kennedy and Martin Luther King Jr., all worked together to throw the Democratic Party into disarray as it attempted to take on Nixon and his running mate, Maryland governor Spiro T. Agnew. "It was like a mental breakdown for the American political community," Humphrey said. The Democratic candidate had to endure chants of "Dump the Hump" from protesters as he campaigned, and his party faced severe financial difficulties. Martin recalled that at one point in the campaign Larry O'Brien informed Humphrey that the Democratic National Committee had no money for television or radio advertisements, or even enough funds for bumper stickers or buttons. "All right. I see," said Humphrey. "Well, I can raise money." All that fall he did so without complaint. "His was a brave campaign," Martin added. Humphrey continued to battle, breaking away from his allegiance to Johnson's war policies and receiving at the last minute vital financial and logistical support from organized labor. It was too little, too late, as Nixon squeaked into office, winning 43.4 percent of the vote to 42.7 for Humphrey and 13.5 percent for Wallace. Nixon enjoyed a more substantial triumph in the Electoral College, with 301 electoral votes to 191 for Humphrey and 46 for Wallace.[17]

In the years since the traumatic events of 1968, arguments have persisted about what might have happened if Kennedy had not been gunned down in the Ambassador Hotel's kitchen on that June evening in Los Angeles. Kennedy aides had not been sanguine about their candidate's chances of capturing the Democratic nomination. Martin estimated that Kennedy had had "maybe a 3 to 5 shot for nomination," but that it might have been possible if Kennedy had gone into the convention with victories in California, New York, and one other large state. "I have no doubt at all that if nominated he would have been elected," said Martin. "And if elected a great President, maybe greater than his brother. But they would have killed him." Richard Goodwin said that Kennedy himself had estimated that his odds of winning the nomination were not better than even, as there were too many delegates available for Humphrey from party leaders. In addition, President Johnson still wielded some influence with Democrats. "I'm convinced that Johnson would have done anything in his power, which would not have been inconsiderable, to prevent Kennedy from being nominated," said Goodwin.[18]

The only hope of denying Humphrey's nomination, William vanden Heuvel and Milton Gwirtzman wrote in their study of Kennedy's final four years of life, depended upon a decision by McCarthy to withdraw from the race and throw his support to Kennedy—a highly unlikely occurrence given McCarthy's feelings. (They did give Kennedy an "excellent" chance of defeating Nixon if he had been the choice of the Democrats.) During his primary battles with Kennedy, McCarthy had developed a deep dislike for the senator and his campaign tactics, and his animus failed to diminish after Kennedy's death. In a private conversation with one of his key campaign advisers, McCarthy said of the assassination: "You know, he [Kennedy] kind of brought it on himself." The distaste McCarthy had for Robert Kennedy displayed itself in stark relief during the Democratic convention when Steve Smith, representing Ted Kennedy, met with McCarthy to discuss a growing movement to draft Ted Kennedy for the nomination. According to Smith, McCarthy said he did not believe he could win, but he did want to see his name placed in nomination. Once that had been accomplished, he would then withdraw and call on his supporters to switch their allegiance to Kennedy. "While I'm doing this for Teddy, I never could have done it for Bobby," McCarthy is reported to have said. According to a report from *Time* magazine, Smith had tears of gratitude upon hearing McCarthy's offer. Smith later told a journalist from *New York* magazine: "Somebody mistook it for all the spit in them."[19]

Some of those who reported on the 1968 campaign were skeptical that Kennedy could forge any kind of an electoral alliance between young college students opposed to the Vietnam War and old-time Democratic political bosses such as Mayor Daley. "The two are incompatible in the long run," said Tom Wicker, a columnist for the *New York Times*. He added that such a coalition had little chance of actually holding political power. Kennedy's death, however, did bring these unlikely forces together in grief. At Saint Patrick's Cathedral in New York for Kennedy's funeral, George McGovern saw Richard Daley sitting in a pew sobbing, while in the back student activist Tom Hayden, a green cap from Havana, Cuba, stuck in his back pocket, also openly wept. Witnessing the disparate groups of people who had come together to mourn one man, journalist Jack Newfield recalled a quote from French philosopher Blaise Pascal that essayist Albert Camus had used in one of his works: "A man does not show his greatness by being at one extremity, but rather by touching both at once."[20]

Kennedy's ability to bring people together had been one of the reasons his words of calm had struck such a chord with the crowd that heard him speak in Indianapolis following the death of Martin Luther King Jr. For many years, those who had witnessed Kennedy's exceptional talk, including longtime Hoosier Democrat and civic leader Larry Conrad, worked to memorialize the site in some manner. Conrad, a former Indiana secretary of state and unsuccessful Democratic nominee for governor, had been at the rally at Broadway and Seventeenth streets, as had Diane Meyer Simon, at that time a senior at Butler University who planned on attending graduate school. Simon skipped a Shakespeare class at the university and attended the rally with her then boyfriend. "After I heard the speech, I put everything aside to go to work for him," she recalled. "It literally became my immersion into the political process. It has stayed with me the rest of my life." Kennedy's call for love and compassion made Simon feel "as though God had touched everyone. At this moment of horror, it was glorious." She took a leave of absence from Butler and worked for the Kennedy campaign. "I was so moved that night," said Simon. "It sort of made sense out of my life. . . . I needed to work for a candidate who was doing God's work on Earth."[21]

Conrad's death in July 1990 slowed the progress toward a memorial to Kennedy and King, but through the efforts of various Indianapolis government and civic leaders, including the Indiana Pacers Foundation, ground was finally broken on Saturday, May 14, 1994, for a sculpture honoring the two victims of gun violence. Flanked by two large photos of King and Kennedy, and shielded from rainy weather by an umbrella held by then Indiana governor Evan Bayh, President Bill Clinton spoke at the ceremony at the Dr. Martin Luther King Jr. Park. Other dignitaries at the groundbreaking ceremony included Ethel Kennedy, Senator Ted Kennedy, and two of King's sons, Martin Luther King III and Dexter Scott King. Speeches like the one Robert Kennedy gave in Indianapolis helped to inspire Clinton to devote his life to public service, he said. "I believed that we could build a country where we would go forward instead of backward and where we would go forward together—where people would work with one another across the bounds of race and religion and income," Clinton went on, as children climbed nearby trees to see him speak. "What you saw in Robert Kennedy's speech that night was a miracle. . . . A miracle occurred here in Indianapolis." Among the estimated five thousand people who attended the rain-soaked event was a former worker for the Robert Kennedy campaign, Lloyd Milliken Jr., who brought with him an old poster from the campaign. Ted Kennedy autographed the poster for Milliken, writing: "Thanks for your loyalty." In his remarks at the ceremony, Kennedy said in all the years that had passed since his brother's speech in the city, the anguish that followed King's death remains. "It is still vivid in our memory," he said, "and the power of that memory sustains and encourages us as we carry on their work."[22]

Eight months after the groundbreaking, the day after the national holiday celebrating King's birthday, city officials announced the winner of a nationwide $50,000 competition for the memorial's design. A committee of community leaders and art professionals selected Greg Perry, a self-described "Kennedy-Catholic-Democrat," as the winner from the dozens of designs entered. The naming of the winning design had been delayed a day by a Ku Klux Klan rally held at the Indiana Statehouse on the same day as King's birthday. Rainy weather dampened attendance at the Klan gathering, something that pleased city officials. Mayor Stephen Goldsmith noted the Klan received no support for its "not very important and rather negative message."

When Perry first heard about the competition, he had his doubts about attempting to create a standard figurative memorial. "I thought, 'Oh, c'mon, do we need another bronze cast of some guy?'" he remembered. "But I couldn't get away from that sense of what it is that speaks across the decades in monuments. Sometimes it is a representation. Not wanting to give that away completely, I started playing with what happens when you mix the abstract and the figurative."[23]

Perry's work features two ten-foot curving walls of steel with King and Kennedy each emerging from one, each with an arm outstretched trying to reach the other. The gap that exists between the two men represents the breach that still remain between the two races. "The idea of emerging from the wall and reaching toward one another in an uncompleted handshake is sort of a representation of [the two men's] humanity," said Perry, "reaching toward one another despite the solid positions that had been defined for them through the years." The artist's favorite views of his creation come early in the morning and late in the evening. "Just as I had hoped, you get this big block of massive shadow on the ground and this illuminated, reaching figure," Perry noted. "It's almost as if there are shadows where the light is and, in their absence, we feel an energy. . . . The shadows are reaching away from one another in the light and I take that to mean they are reaching back to us."[24]

Since the memorial to the two men dedicated to nonviolence opened in the near northside park in 1995, complete with a plaque bearing the speech Kennedy gave on April 4, 1968, city officials have been trying to attract more visitors to the site. On April 2, 2005, the city held a rededication ceremony for the memorial that featured state representative William Crawford, who had attended the Kennedy rally in 1968, and Mayor Bart Peterson. "We commemorated Senator Kennedy's speech and the corresponding terrible tragedy of Dr. King's assassination in this city in 1994 when the president of the United States [Clinton] stood on this ground," said Peterson. "Then we promptly forgot about it." Crawford spoke of the site as "hallowed ground" and lamented the lack of reverence shown by many to the extraordinary event that had taken place there. Those associated with the memorial's creation, and those who still remember Kennedy's stirring words during a calamitous time in the country's history, hope that those who do visit the site will see what President Clinton saw as being possible at the Indianapolis park—a monument to peace "where all of us can live together."[25]

Appendix: Robert F. Kennedy's Speech in Indianapolis, April 4, 1968

Ladies and gentlemen, I'm only going to talk to you just for a minute or so this evening, because I have some very sad news for all of you. Could you lower those signs, please? I have some very sad news for all of you, and, I think, sad news for all of our fellow citizens, and people who love peace all over the world; and that is that Martin Luther King was shot and was killed tonight in Memphis, Tennessee.

Martin Luther King dedicated his life to love and to justice between fellow human beings. He died in the cause of that effort.

In this difficult day, in this difficult time for the United States, it's perhaps well to ask what kind of a nation we are and what direction we want to move in. For those of you who are black—considering the evidence evidently is that there were white people who were responsible—you can be filled with bitterness, and with hatred, and a desire for revenge.

We can move in that direction as a country, in greater polarization—black people amongst blacks, and white amongst whites, filled with hatred toward one another. Or we can make an effort, as Martin Luther King did, to understand, and to comprehend, and replace that violence, that stain of bloodshed that has spread across our land, with an effort to understand, compassion and love.

For those of you who are black and are tempted to fill with—be filled with hatred and mistrust of the injustice of such an act, against all white people, I would only say that I can also feel in my own heart the same kind of feeling. I had a member of my family killed, but he was killed by a white man.

But we have to make an effort in the United States. We have to make an effort to understand, to get beyond, or go beyond these rather difficult times. My favorite poem, my—my favorite poet was Aeschylus. And he once wrote:

> Even in our sleep, pain which cannot forget
> falls drop by drop upon the heart,
> until, in our own despair,
> against our will,
> comes wisdom
> through the awful grace of God.

What we need in the United States is not division; what we need in the United States is not hatred; what we need in the United States is not violence and lawlessness, but is love, and wisdom, and compassion toward one another, and a feeling of justice toward those who still suffer within our country, whether they be white or whether they be black. [Applause and cheers.]

So I ask you tonight to return home, to say a prayer for the family of Martin Luther King—yeah, it's true—but more importantly to say a prayer for our own country, which all of us love—a prayer for understanding and that compassion of which I spoke.

We can do well in this country. We will have difficult times. We've had difficult times in the past, but we—and we will have difficult times in the future. It is not the end of violence; it is not the end of lawlessness; and it's not the end of disorder.

But the vast majority of white people and the vast majority of black people in this country want to live together, want to improve the quality of our life, and want justice for all human beings that abide in our land. [Applause and cheers.]

And let's dedicate ourselves to what the Greeks wrote so many years ago: to tame the savageness of man and make gentle the life of this world. Let us dedicate ourselves to that, and say a prayer for our country and for our people. Thank you very much. [Applause and cheers.]

Notes

1. A Landmark for Peace

1. Park Facts, Indy Parks and Recreation website, http://www.indygov.org/eGov/City/DPR/Admin/Public/Indy+Parks+Facts.htm (accessed June 8, 2007).

2. Ronald Steel, *In Love with Night: The American Romance with Robert Kennedy* (New York: Simon and Schuster, 2000), 148.

3. Charles Kaiser, *1968 in America: Music, Politics, Chaos, Counterculture, and the Shaping of a Generation* (New York: Grove, 1988), 128.

4. Karl W. Anatol and John R. Bittner, "Kennedy on King: The Rhetoric of Control," *Today's Speech* 16, no. 3 (1968): 31.

5. Ibid., 32. See also Will Higgins, "A Tribute to Speech," *Indianapolis Star*, April 5, 2006, and Kathleen M. Johnston and Jon Schwantes, "Clinton Visit Spurs Memories," *Indianapolis News*, May 13, 1994.

6. Author interview with Michael Riley, April 18, 2006, and Evan Thomas, *Robert Kennedy: His Life* (New York: Simon and Schuster, 2000), 366.

7. Arthur Schlesinger Jr., *Robert Kennedy and His Times* (Boston: Houghton Mifflin Co., 1978), 874.

8. Ibid.

9. John Bartlow Martin, *It Seems like Only Yesterday: Memoirs of Writing, Presidential Politics, and the Diplomatic Life* (New York: William Morrow and Co., 1986), 283.

10. Tom Keating, *Indiana Faces and Other Places* (Indianapolis: Indiana Only Press, 1982), 148–49.

11. Jack Newfield, *Robert Kennedy: A Memoir* (New York: E. P. Dutton and Co., 1969), 247.

12. John Lewis with Michael D'Orso, *Walking with the Wind: A Memoir of the Movement* (New York: Simon and Schuster, 1998), 387.

13. Edwin O. Guthman and C. Richard Allen, eds., *RFK: Collected Speeches* (New York: Viking, 1993), 357.

14. RFK Notes, June 28, 1968, John Bartlow Martin Papers, Manuscript Division, Library of Congress, Washington, D.C.

15. Kaiser, *1968 in America,* 145.

16. Will Higgins, "A Tribute to Peace," *Indianapolis Star,* April 5, 2006.

17. Keating, *Indiana Faces and Other Places,* 148.

18. Martin, *It Seems like Only Yesterday,* 285–86.

19. For background on the Wallace effort in Indiana, see Matthew E. Welsh, *View from the State House: Recollections and Reflections, 1961–1965* (Indianapolis: Indiana Historical Bureau, 1981), 197–225. Welsh had decided to challenge Wallace because the Alabama governor's campaign "had obvious overtones of racial intolerance which I found most disturbing." Welsh feared a Wallace victory in Indiana might affect the state for years to come and "would revive and give credence to a racist philosophy my administration had worked very hard to defuse." Ibid., 197.

20. Jules Witcover, *85 Days: The Last Campaign of Robert Kennedy* (New York: Quill, 1988), 123.

21. Lester David and Irene David, *Bobby Kennedy: The Making of a Folk Hero* (New York: Dodd, Mead and Co., 1986), 300.

22. Witcover, *85 Days,* 124.

23. John Beasley, "Roger Branigin, Governor of Indiana: The View from Within" (Ph.D. diss., Ball State University, 1973), 247.

24. James E. Farmer, "The Individual Roger: Governor Branigin and the News Media," *Traces of Indiana and Midwestern History* 4 (Spring 1992): 31, and Ray E. Boomhower, "Roger D. Branigin," in Linda Gugin and James E. St. Clair, eds., *The Governors of Indiana* (Indianapolis: Indiana Historical Society Press, 2006), 346–51.

25. Witcover, *85 Days,* 125.

26. Memo from Gerry Doherty, March 22, 1968, Robert F. Kennedy 1968 Presidential Campaign Papers, John F. Kennedy Presidential Library, Boston, Mass.

27. Martin, *It Seems like Only Yesterday,* 277.

28. Walter Spencer, "Attucks' Cagers Inspired a Novel," *Indianapolis Observer and Courier,* January 28–February 4, 1966.

29. Jeremy Larner, *Nobody Knows: Reflections on the McCarthy Campaign of 1968* (New York: Macmillan, 1969), 76.

30. Ben Stavis, *We Were the Campaign: New Hampshire to Chicago for McCarthy* (Boston: Beacon, 1969), 56–57, and Arthur Herzog, *McCarthy for President* (New York: Viking, 1969), 128–29.

31. Eugene F. McCarthy, *The Year of the People* (Garden City, N.Y.: Doubleday and Co., 1969), 133.

32. Richard T. Stout, *People* (New York: Harper and Row, 1970), 227. Matters were so bad in Indiana that Stout, a *Newsweek* reporter, declined a trip with McCarthy on a small plane to a campaign stop in Bedford, Indiana. "I was convinced the plane would crash and did not want to be in it," said Stout. Ibid.

33. Undated memo from John Bartlow Martin to Robert F. Kennedy, Theodore Sorenson, and Indiana Schedulers, Writers, and Television Men, Martin Papers, Library of Congress.

34. Newfield, *Robert Kennedy,* 255.

35. Martin, *It Seems like Only Yesterday*, 296, and John Douglas Oral History Interview, by Larry J. Hackman, June 24, 1969, Washington, D.C., in Arthur M. Schlesinger Jr. Papers, John F. Kennedy Presidential Library, Boston, Mass.

36. Newfield, *Robert Kennedy*, 261.

2. The Decision

1. Gerard Doherty interview with Larry J. Hackman, February 3, 1972, Robert F. Kennedy Oral History Project, John F. Kennedy Presidential Library, Boston, Massachusetts, and author telephone interview with Doherty, July 13, 2006.

2. Tom Wicker, "Kennedy to Make 3 Primary Races; Attacks Johnson," *New York Times*, March 17, 1968.

3. Evan Thomas, *Robert Kennedy: His Life* (New York: Simon and Schuster, 2000), 348, 354; Michael Knox Beran, *The Last Patrician: Bobby Kennedy and the End of American Aristocracy* (New York: St. Martin's, 1998), 199; and Richard N. Goodwin, *Remembering America: A Voice from the Sixties* (Boston: Little, Brown and Co., 1988), 480.

4. William H. Chafe, *Never Stop Running: Allard Lowenstein and the Struggle to Save American Liberalism* (New York: Basic Books, 1993), 270–71, and Jean Stein and George Plimpton, *American Journey: The Times of Robert Kennedy* (New York: Harcourt Brace Jovanovich, 1970), 224.

5. Dominic Sandbrook, *Eugene McCarthy: The Rise and Fall of Postwar American Liberalism* (New York: Alfred A. Knopf, 2004), 167.

6. Arthur Herzog, *McCarthy for President* (New York: Viking, 1969), 30.

7. Tim Pugmire, "Eugene McCarthy, Who Galvanized a Generation of War Opponents, Dies," Minnesota Public Radio website, http://news.minnesota.publicradio.org/features/2005/06/15_olsond_genemccarthy/ (accessed June 8, 2007), and Sandbrook, *Eugene McCarthy*, 172.

8. Eugene McCarthy, *The Year of the People* (Garden City, N.Y.: Doubleday and Co., 1969), 18.

9. Herzog, *McCarthy for President*, 29, and McCarthy, *The Year of the People*, 23.

10. Albert Eisele, *Almost to the Presidency: A Biography of Two American Politicians* (Blue Earth, Minn.: Piper Co., 1972), 284, and Arthur M. Schlesinger Jr., *Robert Kennedy and His Times* (Boston: Houghton Mifflin Co., 1978), 831–32.

11. William vanden Heuvel and Milton Gwirtzman, *On His Own: Robert F. Kennedy, 1964–1968* (Garden City, N.Y.: Doubleday and Co., 1970), 300. Kennedy noted that if he ran in New Hampshire his reception would be quite different from what McCarthy faced. "The first day I go into a store or barber shop to shake hands, 60 reporters will be with me," he told friends at a dinner. "It can only be counter-productive. That's not the kind of campaign people in New Hampshire will go for." Ibid.

12. Dennis Wainstock, *The Turning Point: The 1968 United States Presidential Campaign* (Jefferson, N.C.: McFarland and Co., 1988), 15–17, and Richard T. Stout, *People* (New York: Harper and Row, 1970), 117–18.

13. Louie Mahern, Indy Pundit Blog, "Kelly Street VII" entry, August 20, 2004, http://www.indypundit.net/archives/000057.html.

14. Wainstock, *The Turning Point*, 22.

15. "Unforeseen Eugene," *Time*, March 22, 1968, 12, and Charles Kaiser, *1968 in America: Music, Politics, Chaos, Counterculture, and the Shaping of a Generation* (New York: Grove, 1988), 91.

16. Wainstock, *The Turning Point*, 20, 38–41, and Jeff Shesol, *Mutual Contempt: Lyndon Johnson, Robert Kennedy, and the Feud That Defined a Decade* (New York: W. W. Norton and Co., 1997), 412.

17. Don Oberdorfer, *Tet! The Turning Point in the Vietnam War* (Baltimore: Johns Hopkins University Press, 2001), 7–8.

18. Ibid., 158. See also Walter LaFeber, *The Deadly Bet: LBJ, Vietnam, and the 1968 Election* (Lanham, Md.: Rowman and Littlefield, 2005), 24.

19. Stanley Karnow, *Vietnam: A History* (New York: Viking, 1983), 542; Oberdorfer, *Tet!*, 164–70; and Kaiser, *1968 in America*, 68–69.

20. Joseph A. Califano Jr., *The Triumph and Tragedy of Lyndon Johnson* (New York: Simon and Schuster, 1991), 172–74.

21. Lewis L. Gould, *1968: The Election That Changed America* (Chicago: Ivan R. Dee, 1993), 37, and LaFeber, *The Deadly Bet*, 74–75.

22. LaFeber, *The Deadly Bet*, 28–29.

23. Califano, *The Triumph and Tragedy of Lyndon Johnson*, 257, and LaFeber, *The Deadly Bet*, 25–26.

24. Eisele, *Almost to the Presidency*, 288; Jeremy Larner, *Nobody Knows: Reflections on the McCarthy Campaign of 1968* (New York: Macmillan, 1969), 35–36; and McCarthy, *The Year of the People*, 60–61.

25. Wainstock, *The Turning Point*, 21–22.

26. McCarthy, *The Year of the People*, 70.

27. "Crusade of the Ballot Children," *Time*, March 22, 1968, 13.

28. Ben Stavis, *We Were the Campaign: New Hampshire to Chicago with McCarthy* (Boston: Beacon, 1969), 10.

29. Eisele, *Almost to the Presidency*, 295.

30. Stavis, *We Were the Campaign*, 14–15.

31. Goodwin, *Remembering America*, 481–95.

32. Eisele, *Almost to the Presidency*, 296; Lewis Chester, Godfrey Hodgson, and Bruce Page, *An American Melodrama: The Presidential Campaign of 1968* (New York: Viking, 1969), 96; and Kaiser, *1968 in America*, 90.

33. Herzog, *McCarthy for President*, 90, and Eisele, *Almost to the Presidency*, 296.

34. Stout, *People*, 169; Thomas Powers, *Vietnam: The War at Home; Vietnam and the American People, 1964–1968* (Boston: G. K. Hall and Co., 1984), 290; Goodwin, *Remembering America*, 505.

35. William P. McDonald and Jerry G. Smoke, *The Peasants' Revolt: McCarthy 1968* (Mount Vernon, Ohio: Noe-Bixby Publications, 1969), 39; Eisele, *Almost to the Presidency*, 298; and Kaiser, *1968 in America*, 104–105.

36. Joseph A. Palermo, *In His Own Right: The Political Odyssey of Senator Robert F. Kennedy* (New York: Columbia University Press, 2001), 133.

37. Goodwin, *Remembering America*, 512.

38. "Unforeseen Eugene," *Time*, 12.

39. Eisele, *Almost to the Presidency*, 300: Lawrence E. Davis, "Two New Yorkers on Oregon Ballot," *New York Times*, March 12, 1968; and John Herbers, "Kennedy Is

Ready to Run; Says Vote for McCarthy Discloses Split in Party," *New York Times*, March 14, 1968.

40. Goodwin, *Remembering America*, 508–509. As the results from the New Hampshire primary were being tallied, Goodwin received another phone call from Kennedy. Calling him back, Goodwin said the election results left Kennedy with two choices—either run himself or support McCarthy. If Kennedy threw his support to McCarthy, Goodwin believed McCarthy would be elected president. After hanging up the telephone, Kennedy turned to a friend and said: "I think I blew it." Ibid., 516–17.

41. McCarthy, *The Year of the People*, 88–89; Eisele, *Almost to the Presidency*, 300; and Herzog, *McCarthy for President*, 127.

42. Jack Newfield, *Robert Kennedy: A Memoir* (New York: E. P. Dutton and Co., 1969), 219.

43. Palermo, *In His Own Right*, 135–38; Shesol, *Mutual Contempt*, 419–20; and Jules Witcover, *The Year the Dream Died: Revisiting 1968 in America* (New York: Warner Books, 1997), 104. In his conversations with Sorenson and Kennedy about the Vietnam commission, Clifford warned Kennedy that he had no chance of defeating Johnson for the nomination and even if he did accomplish such a feat, he would so damage the Democratic Party that the GOP would win the election. See Clark Clifford with Richard Holbrooke, *Counsel to the President: A Memoir* (New York: Random House, 1991), 504.

44. Palermo, *In His Own Right*, 140.

45. McCarthy, *The Year of the People*, 92; Kaiser, *1968 in America*, 115–16; and Abigail McCarthy, *Private Faces/Public Places* (Garden City, N.Y.: Doubleday and Co., 1972), 372, 374.

46. "Kennedy's Statement and Excerpts from News Conference," *New York Times*, March 17, 1968.

47. Ibid. See also Arthur M. Schlesinger Jr., *Robert Kennedy and His Times* (Boston: Houghton Mifflin Co., 1978), 861.

48. Wicker, "Kennedy to Make 3 Primary Races"; Eisele, *Almost to the Presidency*, 302; Shesol, *Mutual Contempt*, 424; and "Crusade of the Ballot Children," *Time*, March 22, 1968, 13. Kennedy realized that his late entry into the race might adversely affect his relationship with young voters. "I'm going to lose them," Kennedy told an aide, "and I'm going to lose them forever." Schlesinger, *Robert Kennedy and His Times*, 844.

49. Doris Kearns, *Lyndon Johnson and the American Dream* (New York: Harper and Row, 1976), 339.

50. "Kennedy to Make 3 Primary Races," *New York Times*, and Kearns, *Lyndon Johnson and the American Dream*, 343.

3. The Governor

1. Ralph D. Gray, *Indiana's Favorite Sons: 1840–1940* (Indianapolis: Indiana Historical Society, 1988), 6, 9, and John Bartlow Martin, *Indiana: An Interpretation* (1947; Bloomington: Indiana University Press, 1992), 101.

2. Paul M. Doherty, "Governor Branigin to Be State's LBJ Stand-In," *Indianapolis Star*, March 17, 1968. See also John Beasley, "Roger Branigin, Governor of Indiana:

The View from Within," Ph.D. diss., Ball State University, 1972, 231–32, and author interview with Gordon St. Angelo, July 13, 2006, Indianapolis.

3. Ted Knap, "Roger Branigin Running Strong after Warming Up for 8 Years," *Indianapolis Times*, June 6, 1956, and author interview with St. Angelo. See also Ray E. Boomhower, "Roger D. Branigin," in Linda Gugin and James E. St. Clair, eds., *The Governors of Indiana* (Indianapolis: Indiana Historical Society Press, 2006), 346–51, and James E. Farmer, "The Individual Roger: Governor Branigin and the News Media," *Traces of Indiana and Midwestern History* 4 (Spring 1992): 27.

4. "Roger Branigin Rites Tomorrow at 2 Cities," *Indianapolis Star*, November 20, 1975.

5. Gerry LaFollette, "5 A.M. Risers See a Brief Inaugural," *Indianapolis News*, January 11, 1965.

6. "Roger Branigin Rites Tomorrow at 2 Cities," *Indianapolis Star*.

7. "Former Governor Never Missed the Humor in Public Situations," *Indianapolis Star*, November 20, 1975.

8. Beasley, "Roger Branigin, Governor of Indiana," 228.

9. Roger D. Branigin Oral History Interview, by Randall W. Jehs, October 19, 1971, Manuscript Division, Indiana State Library, Indianapolis.

10. Birch Bayh Oral History Interview I, by Paige E. Mulhollan, February 12, 1969, internet copy, http://www.lbjlib.utexas.edu/johnson/archives.hom/oralhistory.hom/Bayh-B/Bayh.pdf (accessed June 28, 2007), Lyndon Baines Johnson Library, Austin, Tex.

11. Beasley, "Roger Branigin, Governor of Indiana," 230, and James E. Farmer, "1968 Presidential Primary: Reluctant 'Favorite Son' Faces Kennedy and McCarthy," unpublished manuscript in author's collection.

12. Roger D. Branigin Daily Journal, March 15, 1968, Roger D. Branigin Papers, B. F. Hamilton Library, Franklin College, Franklin, Ind.

13. Branigin Journal, March 15 to 30, 1968, and Hubert Humphrey letter to Branigin, March 21, 1968, Branigin Papers; and author interview with St. Angelo.

14. "Governor Branigin to Be State's LBJ Stand-In," *Indianapolis Star*.

15. Gugin and St. Clair, *The Governors of Indiana*, 3, and Michael Stuart Devorkin, "Kennedy Campaigning in Primary States: Presidential Politics and Democratic Party Organizations and Leaders," master's thesis, Massachusetts Institute of Technology, June 1969, 42.

16. Ted Sorenson memo, March 19, 1968, Robert F. Kennedy 1968 Presidential Campaign Papers, John F. Kennedy Presidential Library, Boston, Massachusetts. In a conversation he had with Ted Kennedy about the situation in Indiana, Gordon St. Angelo warned against running in Indiana, and claimed the Kennedy campaign made its first mistake in obtaining help from Michael Riley. "I told him we will probably make a lot of other mistakes, but we have to work with outsiders," Kennedy said. Ted Kennedy memo, March 21, 1968, RFK 1968 Presidential Campaign Papers, Kennedy Library.

17. Author interview with Michael Riley, March 18, 2006, Rensselaer, Indiana.

18. Ibid., and Paul M. Doherty, "1st Steps to Get Bobby in State Primary Told," *Indianapolis Star*, March 22, 1968.

19. Author interview with Louie Mahern, November 14, 2005, Indianapolis.

20. Ibid.

21. Gerard Doherty Oral History Interview, by Larry J. Hackman, February 3, 1972, Kennedy Library. See also author telephone interview with Doherty, July 13, 2006.

22. Lewis Chester, Godfrey Hodgson, and Bruce Page, *An American Melodrama: The Presidential Campaign of 1968* (New York: Viking, 1969), 161; and author interview with Mahern, November 14, 2005; and Doherty memo to Ted Kennedy, March 25, 1968, Robert F. Kennedy 1968 Presidential Campaign Papers, Kennedy Library. Andy Jacobs Jr. noted that one of the judges who drew the new congressional districts in Indiana, Cale Holder, had once been chairman of the Indiana Republican Central Committee. "The new map of the Indianapolis congressional district came in the form of a gas chamber for me," Jacobs remembered, adding that his chances for reelection in 1968 "seemed slim." Andy Jacobs Jr., *Slander and Sweet Judgment: The Memoir of an Indiana Congressman* (Indianapolis: Guild Press of Indiana, 2000), 136–37.

23. Riley interview. See also Louie Mahern, Indy Pundit Blog, "Kelly Street VII" entry, August 20, 2004, http://www.indypundit.net/archives/000057.html.

24. Author interview with Michael Kendall, July 20, 2006, Carmel, Ind. See also "The Bobby-Sockers," *Notre Dame Scholastic*, March 29, 1968.

25. Author interview with Mahern; James B. Lane, *"City of the Century": A History of Gary, Indiana* (Bloomington: Indiana University Press, 1978), 265–67; and David Halberstam, *The Unfinished Odyssey of Robert Kennedy* (New York: Random House, 1968), 97. Halberstam noted that Dick Tuck became a hero to blacks in Gary for his efforts at ensuring a fair election during Richard Hatcher's mayoral campaign. When Tuck heard rumors of a plot to have all the voting machines in black wards break down at a vital point in the election, he recruited ten African American pinball machine repairmen from Chicago and trained them how to fix voting machines. "On election day, sure enough," wrote Halberstam, "when the machines started breaking down, always in black wards, Tuck's men fixed them in minutes instead of hours." Ibid.

26. Dr. Richard Wade Oral History Interview, by Roberta Greene, December 13, 1973, Kennedy Library.

27. Ibid.

28. Chester, Hodgson, and Page, *An American Melodrama*, 161–62, and Mahern, Indy Pundit Blog, "Kelly Street VII" entry.

29. Gerry Doherty memos, March 22, 1968, RFK 1968 Presidential Papers, Kennedy Library, and Robert P. Mooney, "Kennedy Will Visit City Tonight," *Indianapolis Star*, March 28, 1968.

30. Author telephone interview with Gerard Doherty, July 13, 2006.

31. Ibid.

32. Edward Ziegner, "Bobby Makes It a Three-Way Race," *Indianapolis News*, March 29, 1968; Earl Conn, "Reliving 'The Week'—Some Recent History," *Muncie Star*, March 23, 1969; and James Tolan Oral History Interview, by Roberta Green, June 16, 1969, Kennedy Library.

33. Ziegner, "Bobby Makes It a Three-Way Race," *Indianapolis News*.

34. Mahern interview, and Mahern, Indy Pundit Blog, "Kelly Street VII" entry.

35. Ziegner, "Bobby Makes It a Three-Way Race," *Indianapolis News*; Statement by Roger Branigin, March 29, 1968, Branigin Papers, B. F. Hamilton Library; Robert P. Mooney, "Bobby's Entry in Race Called 'Cutthroat' Act," *Indianapolis Star*, March 29, 1968.

36. Author telephone interview with Doherty, and Doherty Oral History Interview, Kennedy Library.

37. Doherty Oral History Interview, Kennedy Library.

38. Dennis Wainstock, *The Turning Point: The 1968 United States Presidential Campaign* (Jefferson, N.C.: McFarland and Co., 1988), 53; Lyndon Baines Johnson, *The Vantage Point: Perspectives of the Presidency, 1963–1969* (New York: Holt, Rinehart, and Winston, 1971), 428; and Clark Clifford with Richard Holbrooke, *Counsel to the President: A Memoir* (New York: Random House, 1991), 518.

39. Johnson, *The Vantage Point*, 425–26; Lawrence F. O'Brien, *No Final Victories: A Life in Politics—from John F. Kennedy to Watergate* (Garden City, N.Y.: Doubleday and Co., 1974), 228–29; and Joseph A. Califano Jr., *The Triumph and Tragedy of Lyndon Johnson: The White House Years* (New York: Simon and Schuster, 1991), 269.

40. Ben A. Franklin, "Wallace in Race; Will 'Run to Win,'" *New York Times*, February 9, 1968; Lewis L. Gould, *1968: The Election That Changed America* (Chicago: Ivan R. Dee, 1993), 66; and Walter LaFeber, *The Deadly Bet: LBJ, Vietnam, and the 1968 Election* (Lanham, Md.: Rowman and Littlefield, 2005), 137–38.

41. Randall B. Woods, *LBJ: Architect of American Ambition* (New York: Free Press, 2006), 834–35.

42. Clifford, *Counsel to the President*, 522.

43. Johnson, *The Vantage Point*, 427, 435.

44. Branigin Daily Journal, March 31, 1968, B. F. Hamilton Library, and Beasley, "Roger Branigin, Governor of Indiana," 237.

45. Arthur Herzog, *McCarthy for President* (New York: Viking, 1969), 118; Donald Janson, "Wisconsin Weighs Impact on Voting," *New York Times*, April 1, 1968; and Richard Goodwin, *Remembering America: A Voice from the Sixties* (Boston: Little, Brown and Co., 1988), 521.

46. Herzog, *McCarthy for President*, 118–19; Albert Eisele, *Almost to the Presidency: A Biography of Two American Politicians* (Blue Earth, Minn.: Piper Co., 1972), 307; and Ben Stavis, *We Were the Campaign: New Hampshire to Chicago for McCarthy* (Boston: Beacon, 1969), 47.

47. Jeremy Larner, *Nobody Knows: Reflections on the McCarthy Campaign of 1968* (New York: Macmillan, 1969), 59, 63–64. Reflecting on McCarthy's statement to Larner and Schell, Kennedy adviser and historian Arthur M. Schlesinger Jr., believed the Minnesota senator meant that with Johnson absent from the campaign, Kennedy would have to run against policies started during the administration of President John Kennedy. McCarthy's statement, "And I'm Jack," perhaps referred to his having "more of John Kennedy's qualities—maturity, intellectuality, urbanity, control—than Robert had. Perhaps he meant nothing at all." See Arthur M. Schlesinger Jr., *Robert Kennedy and His Times* (Boston: Houghton Mifflin Co., 1978), 870.

48. Eisele, *Almost to the Presidency*, 312.

49. Homer Bigart, "Kennedy, Told News on Plane, Sits in Silence amid the Hubbub," *New York Times*, April 1, 1968; Jeff Shesol, *Mutual Contempt: Lyndon Johnson, Robert Kennedy, and the Feud That Defined a Decade* (New York: W. W. Norton and Co., 1997), 436; and William vanden Heuvel and Milton Gwirtzman, *On His Own: Robert Kennedy, 1964–1968* (Garden City, N.Y.: Doubleday and Co., 1970), 332–33; and O'Brien, *No Final Victories*, 232.

50. Mahern, Indy Pundit Blog, "Kelly Street VII" entry, and author interview with Riley.

51. Mahern, Indy Pundit Blog, "Kelly Street VII" entry.

4. The Speech

1. Arthur M. Schlesinger Jr., *Robert Kennedy and His Times* (Boston: Houghton Mifflin Co., 1978), 864; Jean Stein and George Plimpton, *American Journey: The Times of Robert Kennedy* (New York: Harcourt Brace Jovanovich, 1970), 241; and William vanden Heuvel and Milton Gwirtzman, *On His Own: Robert F. Kennedy, 1964–1968* (Garden City, N.Y.: Doubleday and Co., 1970), 314–16.

2. Joe Caypo, "Indiana Vote Now Key in Gene-Bobby Race," *Chicago Daily News*, April 2, 1968.

3. Donald Janson, "Branigin to Stay in Race in Indiana," *New York Times*, April 2, 1968; John Beasley, "Roger Branigin, Governor of Indiana: The View from Within," Ph.D. diss., Ball State University, 1972), 245; Robert C. Kriebel, "Roger 'Serious' on Candidacy," *Lafayette Journal and Courier*, April 11, 1968; and Donald Janson, "Indiana Democrats Begin Drive for Governor as Favorite Son," *New York Times*, April 4, 1968.

4. April 3, 1968, telegrams, Roger Branigin Papers, B. F. Hamilton Library, Franklin College, Franklin, Ind.

5. Roger Branigin Daily Journal, April 7, 1968, Branigin Papers, B. F. Hamilton Library.

6. Russell B. Pulliam, *Publisher: Gene Pulliam, Last of the Newspaper Titans* (Ottawa, Ill.: Jameson Books, 1984), 6, 273, and Lawrence S. "Bo" Connor, *Star in the Hoosier Sky: The* Indianapolis Star *in the Years the City Came Alive, 1950–1990* (Carmel, Ind.: Hawthorne Publishing, 2006), 11.

7. Arthur Herzog, *McCarthy for President* (New York: Viking, 1969), 128; Jules Witcover, *The Year the Dream Died: Revisiting 1968 in America* (New York: Warner Books, 1997), 148; and Richard N. Goodwin, *Remembering America: A Voice from the Sixties* (Boston: Little, Brown and Co., 1988), 524.

8. Donald Janson, "Campaign Starts in Indiana Today," *New York Times*, April 3, 1968.

9. John Bartlow Martin, *It Seems like Only Yesterday: Memoirs of Writing, Presidential Politics, and the Diplomatic Life* (New York: William Morrow and Co., 1986), 281–82.

10. Robert F. Kennedy's Schedule for April 4, 1968, Robert F. Kennedy 1968 Presidential Campaign Papers, John F. Kennedy Presidential Library, Boston, Mass., and Jack Colwell, "Drive, Talk Planned by Kennedy," *South Bend Tribune*, April 4, 1968.

11. Jack Colwell, "RFK Revives 'Magic' in Visit Here," *South Bend Tribune*, April 5, 1968.

12. Ibid. See also Edwin O. Guthman and C. Richard Allen, eds., *RFK: Collected Speeches* (New York: Viking, 1993), 353, and Martin, *It Seems like Only Yesterday*, 282.

13. Thomas Jewell, "RFK Visits Elderly at County Home," *South Bend Tribune*, April 5, 1968.

14. Earl Conn, "Reliving 'The Week'—Some Recent History," *Muncie Star*, March 23, 1969; Author interview with Earl Conn, November 15, 2005; and Kim Medaris, "Remembering RFK," *Ball State Daily News*, June 3, 1993.

15. Conn, "Reliving 'The Week'—Some Recent History"; Author interview with Conn, November 15, 2005; "Enthusiasm Greets RFK at Airport," *Ball State News*, April 5, 1968; and Brian Usher, "Kennedy Gets Frenzied Greeting from Students," *Muncie Star*, April 5, 1968.

16. Robert F. Kennedy Speech, April 4, 1968, Kennedy Muncie Speech Collection, Archives and Special Collections, Ball State University Libraries, Muncie, Ind. Even the most liberal members of Kennedy's Senate staff sometimes wondered if he spent too much time in his speeches during the campaign on hunger in America. Jeff Greenfield noted that students on college campuses in the Midwest were "noticeably apathetic" about the issue and asked, "You sure you want to talk about hunger? I don't think they care. He said, 'If they don't care, the hell with them.'" Jeff Greenfield Oral History Interview, by Roberta Greene, December 10, 1969, New York, Kennedy Library.

17. Ibid.

18. Conn, "Reliving 'The Week'—Some Recent History."

19. Joan Turner Beifuss, *At the River I Stand: Memphis, the 1968 Strike, and Martin Luther King* (Brooklyn, N.Y.: Carlson Publishing, 1989), 280.

20. Ibid., 292. See also Witcover, *The Year the Dream Died*, 151–53; Earl Caldwell, "Martin Luther King Is Shot to Death in Memphis; White Suspect Is Hunted," *New York Times*, April 5, 1968; and Marshall Frady, *Martin Luther King, Jr.* (New York: Viking Penguin, 2002), 205.

21. Conn, "Reliving 'The Week'—Some Recent History," and Usher, "Kennedy Gets Frenzied Greeting from Students."

22. James Tolan Oral History Interview, by Roberta Greene, June 26, 1969, Kennedy Library; Arthur M. Schlesinger Jr., *Robert Kennedy and His Times* (Boston: Houghton Mifflin Co., 1978), 874; and Donald Janson, "Rivals in Indiana Woo Negro Vote," *New York Times*, April 5, 1968.

23. Janson, "Rivals in Indiana Woo Negro Vote."

24. Tolan Oral History Interview, Kennedy Library; Schlesinger, *Robert Kennedy and His Times*, 874; Jack Newfield, *Robert Kennedy: A Memoir* (New York: E. P. Dutton and Co., 1969), 57; and R. W. Apple Jr., "Kennedy Appeals for Nonviolence," *New York Times*, April 5, 1968.

25. Author telephone interview with Gerard Doherty, July 13, 2006, and author interview with Michael Riley, April 18, 2006.

26. Greenfield Oral History Interview, Kennedy Library, and Adam Walinsky Oral History Interview VI, by Roberta Greene, December 4, 1974, New York, Kennedy Library. Greenfield had few, if any, fond memories of his time in Indiana. "The idea of traveling down a godforsaken back road of a state which we never should have granted statehood to in the first place—it's a terrible state," he told an interviewer. Greenfield said the entire state, particularly Indianapolis, "was a depressing gray place to be." Greenfield Interview, Kennedy Library.

27. Stein and Plimpton, *American Journey*, 255, and Walinsky Oral History Interview VI, Kennedy Library.

28. John Lewis with Michael D'Orso, *Walking with the Wind: A Memoir of the Movement* (New York: Simon and Schuster, 1998), 386.

29. Karl W. Anatol and John R. Bittner, "Kennedy on King: The Rhetoric of Control," *Today's Speech* 16, no. 3 (1968): 31.

30. Author telephone interview with Mary Evans, June 21, 2006, and e-mail to author from Altha Cravey, January 8, 2007.

31. Anatol and Bittner, "Kennedy on King," 32; Author interview with Evans; Walinsky interview, Kennedy Library; and Cravey e-mail to author.

32. Greenfield interview, Kennedy Library; Schlesinger, *Robert Kennedy and His Times*, 618; and Lewis, *Walking with the Wind*, 388.

33. Guthman and Allen, *RFK: Collected Speeches*, 356–57; Jules Witcover, *85 Days: The Last Campaign of Robert Kennedy* (New York: Quill, 1988), 140–41; and Robert F. Kennedy on the Death of Martin Luther King, The History Place, Great Speech Collection, http://www.historyplace.com/speeches/rfk.htm (accessed June 9, 2007).

34. Tolan Oral History Interview, Kennedy Library; author interview with Riley; and Jack Newfield, *Somebody's Gotta Tell It: The Upbeat Memoir of a Working-Class Journalist* (New York: St. Martin's, 2002), 196.

35. Anatol and Bittner, "Kennedy on King," 32–33; "'To Tame the Savageness of Man': Robert Kennedy's Eulogy of Martin Luther King, Jr.," in Lloyd E. Rohler and Robin Cook, *Great Speeches for Criticism and Analysis* (Greenwood, Ind.: Alistair Press, 1988), 305; and author interview with Evans.

36. John Bartlow Martin, *It Seems like Only Yesterday: Memoirs of Writing, Presidential Politics, and the Diplomatic Life* (New York: William Morrow and Co., 1986), 284; Witcover, *85 Days*, 142; Coretta Scott King, *My Life with Martin Luther King, Jr.* (New York: Henry Holt and Co., 1993), 297; and Stein and Plimpton, *American Journey*, 257.

37. Author telephone interview with Gerard Doherty, July 13, 2006, and vanden Heuvel and Gwirtzman, *On His Own*, 338.

38. Homer Bigart, "Negroes Are Cool to McCarthy as He Opens Indiana Campaign," *New York Times*, April 19, 1968.

39. Greenfield interview, Kennedy Library.

5. The Campaign

1. Author interview with Bill Munn, March 28, 2006, Indianapolis.

2. Richard N. Goodwin, *Remembering America: A Voice from the Sixties* (Boston: Little, Brown and Co., 1988), 529–30. Goodwin would have liked to remain with the McCarthy campaign, but decided he could not work against Kennedy. If he remained with McCarthy, Goodwin believed he could help the Minnesota senator defeat Kennedy in Indiana. "And McCarthy had a chance to beat him in Indiana," Goodwin noted. "McCarthy was very tough and very smart . . . and Indiana was a pretty conservative state. So I just couldn't do it." Ibid., 527.

3. John Bartlow Martin, *It Seems like Only Yesterday: Memoirs of Writing, Presidential Politics, and the Diplomatic Life* (New York: William Morrow and Co., 1986), 17–18, 20, and Sherley Uhl, "John Martin, Former Reporter for *The Times*, Neck-Deep in New Book About Hoosier Land," *Indianapolis Times*, July 31, 1946. See also Ray E. Boomhower, "A Voice for Those from Below: John Bartlow Martin, Reporter," *Traces of Indiana and Midwestern History* 9 (Spring 1997): 5–6.

4. Memo on Memoirs, December 5, 1980, John Bartlow Martin Papers, Manuscript Division, Library of Congress, Washington, D.C.

5. Robert O. Boorstin, "John Bartlow Martin, 71, Author and Envoy, Dies," *New York Times*, January 5, 1987.

6. Martin, *It Seems like Only Yesterday*, 49; Arthur M. Schlesinger Jr., *Robert Kennedy and His Times* (Boston: Houghton Mifflin Co., 1978), 880; and Review of *Indiana and Interpretation* in *Indiana Magazine of History* 44 (September 1948): 308.

7. Boorstin, "John Bartlow Martin"; Robert G. Schultz, "Envoy Has Boss Now, His First in 25 Years," *Indianapolis Times*, March 4, 1962; and Memo on Memoirs, Martin Papers, Library of Congress.

8. Martin, *It Seems like Only Yesterday*, 174, and John Frederick Martin, "John Bartlow Martin," *The American Scholar* 59 (Winter 1990): 98.

9. Martin, *It Seems like Only Yesterday*, 173–74.

10. John Bartlow Martin, RFK Notes, June 29, 1968, Martin Papers, Library of Congress, and Martin, *It Seems like Only Yesterday*, 285–86.

11. Undated memo to Robert Kennedy and Ted Sorenson from John Bartlow Martin, Martin Papers, Library of Congress.

12. Martin, *It Seems like Only Yesterday*, 287.

13. William Haddad Oral History Interview, by Larry J. Hackman, February 27, 1969, New York, John F. Kennedy Presidential Library, Boston, Mass.

14. Hal Higdon, "Indiana: A Test for Bobby Kennedy," *New York Times*, May 5, 1968.

15. RFK Notes, Martin Papers, and "'Big Spending' Called 'Myth,'" *Evansville Courier*, May 6, 1968.

16. John Bartlow Martin letter to Ted Sorenson, April 14, 1968, Martin Papers, Library of Congress; RFK Notes, Martin Papers; John Douglas Oral History Interview, by Larry J. Hackman, June 24, 1969, Washington, D.C., in Arthur M. Schlesinger Jr. Papers, Kennedy Library; and RFK Notes, Martin Papers.

17. RFK Notes, Martin Papers, and Martin, *It Seems like Only Yesterday*, 288.

18. Martin, *It Seems like Only Yesterday*, 288–89; Milton Gwirtzman Oral History Interview, by Roberta Greene, Kennedy Library; and RFK Notes, Martin Papers.

19. Martin, *It Seems like Only Yesterday*, 292–93; Warren Weaver Jr., "Kennedy: Meet the Conservative," *New York Times*, April 28, 1968; Douglas Oral History Interview, Schlesinger Papers; and Jules Witcover, *The Year the Dream Died: Revisiting 1968 in America* (New York: Warner Books, 1997), 174.

20. RFK Notes, Martin Papers, Library of Congress, and Jules Witcover, *85 Days: The Last Campaign of Robert Kennedy* (New York: Quill, 1988), 161. Kennedy's use of the Shaw quote became a signal for newsmen that he had ended his remarks and they could return to the press bus. At one stop he failed to include the Shaw quote and a few members of the media were left behind. Those covering the Kennedy campaign appointed Warren Rogers of *Look* magazine to tell the candidate not to do something like that again. "The candidate laughed and agreed: from then on, there were few campaign speeches anywhere that didn't close with 'As George Bernard Shaw once said'—and with a mad scurrying for the train, or the press bus, or the airplane," wrote Witcover. Ibid., 161–62.

21. Douglas Oral History, Schlesinger Papers, Kennedy Library, and Gerard Doherty Oral History Interview, by Larry J. Hackman, February 3, 1972, Boston, Kennedy Library.

22. Jim Flug undated memo to Ted Kennedy, Gerard Doherty, John Douglas, and Richard Goodwin, David Hackett Papers, John F. Kennedy Presidential Library, Boston, Mass.

23. Ibid.

24. Author telephone interview with Gerard Doherty, July 13, 2006. The expert mentioned by Doherty may have been the same man who had briefly worked for the McCarthy campaign in New Hampshire. Ben Stavis, who headed McCarthy's canvassing efforts, noted that this "motivational analyst" had been helpful early on in the state but later attempted to take control of the effort in Manchester, New Hampshire, distributing literature, issuing press releases, and acquiring staff without proper authorization. Other staff members had to watch over him to see that he would not harm the campaign. "He showed up in Indiana working for Kennedy," Stavis said, "to the relief (and joy) of some of the staff." See Ben Stavis, We Were the Campaign: New Hampshire to Chicago for McCarthy (Boston: Beacon Press, 1969), 9.

25. Arthur Herzog, McCarthy for President (New York: Viking, 1969), 138–39; "'Big Spending' Called 'Myth,'" Evansville Courier, May 6, 1968; E. W. Kenworthy, "M'Carthy Themes Given New Stress," New York Times, May 5, 1968; Kenworthy, "McCarthy Staff Is Growing Professional as Campaign Widens," New York Times, April 25, 1968; and Stavis, We Were the Campaign, 56–57.

26. Richard T. Stout, People (New York: Harper and Row, 1970), 223–24, and Stavis, We Were the Campaign, 58.

27. Stout, People, 223; Jeremy Larner, Nobody Knows: Reflections on the McCarthy Campaign of 1968 (New York: Macmillan, 1969), 83, and Herzog, McCarthy for President, 133.

28. Larner, Nobody Knows, 77; Albert Eisele, Almost to the Presidency: A Biography of Two American Politicians (Blue Earth, Minn.: Piper Co., 1972), 312–13; E. W. Kenworthy, "M'Carthy Scores Kennedy Backers," New York Times, May 6, 1968; Emanuel Perlmutter, "Kennedy Backers Rebut M'Carthy," New York Times, May 7, 1968; Schlesinger, Robert Kennedy and His Times, 904.

29. Eugene McCarthy, The Year of the People (Garden City, N.Y.: Doubleday and Co., 1969), 136.

30. Jeremy Larner, Nobody Knows: Reflections on the McCarthy Campaign of 1968 (New York: Macmillan, 1969), 68–69, 72, 76; Author telephone interview with Larner, October 5, 2005; and Thomas Keating, "McCarthy a Snob, Says Author," Indianapolis Star, October 20, 1971.

31. E. W. Kenworthy, "Paul Newman Drawing Crowds in McCarthy Indiana Campaign," New York Times, April 22, 1968.

32. Author interview with Louie Mahern, November 14, 2005, Indianapolis, Ind. See also author interview with Andrew Jacobs Jr., October 18, 2005, Indianapolis, and Andrew Jacobs Jr., Slander and Sweet Judgment: The Memoirs of an Indiana Congressman (Indianapolis: Guild Press of Indiana, 2000), 139.

33. Lewis Chester, Godfrey Hodgson, and Bruce Page, An American Melodrama: The Presidential Campaign of 1968 (New York: Viking, 1969), 166, and Stout, People, 227.

34. McCarthy, The Year of the People, 139–40.

35. Witcover, 85 Days, 154; Pierre Salinger Oral History Interview, by Larry J. Hackman, April 18, 1970, Beverly Hills, Calif.; and Martin, It Seems like Only Yesterday, 293.

36. Douglas E. Kneeland, "Branigin Presses His Role in Presidential Race," *New York Times*, April 19, 1968; "Heavy Spending Charged," *New York Times*, April 20, 1968; "'Big Spending' Called 'Myth,'" *Evansville Courier;* and John Dreiske, "Indiana Primary: Branigin Fights the Gate-Crashers," *Chicago Sun-Times*, April 28, 1968.

37. "'Big Spending' Called 'Myth,'" *Evansville Courier*, and "Tarot Cards, Hoosier Style," *Time*, May 17, 1968, internet copy, http://www.time.com/time/magazine/article/0,9171,838342,00.html (accessed June 9, 2007).

38. Hal Higdon, "Indiana: A Test for Bobby Kennedy," *New York Times*, May 5, 1968; "The Hoosier Plank," *Time*, April 24, 1968; Frank Lynn, "Primary a Battle of Secondary Issues," *Newsweek*, April 25, 1968; "Governor Branigin Warns: 'Keep Delegation Intact for Voice in Convention'," *Fort Wayne News-Sentinel*, April 25, 1968; and James E. Farmer, "1968 Presidential Primary: Reluctant 'Favorite Son' Faces Kennedy and McCarthy," unpublished manuscript in author's collection.

39. Hubert H. Humphrey, *The Education of a Public Man: My Life and Politics* (Garden City, N.Y.: Doubleday and Co., 1976), 361, 369; Walter LaFeber, *The Deadly Bet: LBJ, Vietnam, and the 1968 Election* (Lanham, Md.: Rowman and Littlefield, 2005), 124; Albert Eisele, *Almost to the Presidency*, 330.

40. Lewis L. Gould, *1968: The Election That Changed America* (Chicago: Ivan R. Dee, 1993), 71, and Humphrey, *The Education of a Public Man*, 370.

41. John Beasley, "Roger Branigin, Governor of Indiana: The View from Within," Ph.D. diss., Ball State University, 1973; Gordon Englehart column, *Louisville Courier-Journal*, April 14, 1968, in Roger D. Branigin Papers, B. F. Hamilton Library, Franklin College, Franklin, Ind.; and RFK Notes, Martin Papers.

42. RFK Notes, Martin Papers; Dale Burgess, "Presidential Aspirant Draws Large Crowd," *Vincennes Sun-Commercial*, April 22, 1968; "Senator Kennedy Makes Sweep of Southern Indiana," *Evansville Courier*, April 23, 1968; and Witcover, *85 Days*, 155.

43. Art Hobbs, "Control of Inflation Urged by Kennedy," *Evansville Courier*, April 23, 1968, and Joseph Dolan Oral History Interview, Schlesinger Papers, Kennedy Library. The day after the Evansville debacle, media members traveling with Kennedy kidded Frank Mankiewicz, the campaign's press secretary, about the numerous empty seats the night before. As the motorcade traveled to Elwood, Mankiewicz took the microphone and told those on the press bus: "We are approaching the home of Wendell Willkie, the Republican candidate for President in 1940. It has been reported he had a crowd of 100,000 when he started his campaign here. Actually, it was badly advanced, because his speech was given in a stadium that held 300,000." Witcover, *85 Days*, 158.

44. Richard Witkin, "Kennedy Stumps Indiana in Train," *New York Times*, April 24, 1968; "RFK to Make Whistle-stop Speech Here," *Wabash Plain Dealer*, April 23, 1968; Dolan Oral History Interview, Schlesinger Papers; and Jean Stein and George Plimpton, *American Journey: The Times of Robert Kennedy* (New York: Harcourt Brace Jovanovich, 1970), 245.

45. RFK Notes, Martin Papers; Edith Needham, "Ten Local Demos Ride RFK Train," *Peru Daily Tribune*, April 23, 1968; Ken Weaver, "Bobby Turns 'em On . . . and Off," *Wabash Plain Dealer*, April 24, 1968; Jim Morrison, "Press Agents Ones Who Sweat on New RFK Cannonball," *Fort Wayne News-Sentinel*, April 24, 1968; "2,000 Greet Kennedy during Whistle Stop," *Peru Daily Tribune*, April 23,

1968; Paul Lehman, "RFK Hits Viet Policy in Talk Here," *Wabash Plain Dealer*, April 25, 1968; and "RFK Says Elderly in Need of Help," *Fort Wayne Journal-Gazette*, April 24, 1968.

46. Witcover, *85 Days*, 162–63.

47. Larry Allen, "Kennedy Tells Vast Needs of Education," *Fort Wayne Journal-Gazette*, April 24, 1968; Jerry Graff, "Votes for Branigin 'Wasted,' RFK Says," *Fort Wayne News-Sentinel*, April 24, 1968; and Martin, *It Seems like Only Yesterday*, 291.

48. RFK Notes, Martin Papers.

49. Jack Newfield, *Robert Kennedy: A Memoir* (New York: E. P. Dutton and Co., 1968), 257–58.

50. Jep Cadou Jr., "Kennedy, I.U. Medical Students Lock in Verbal Sparring Match," *Indianapolis Star*, April 27, 1968, and Chester, Hodgson, and Page, *An American Melodrama*, 163.

51. Cadou, "Kennedy, I.U. Medical Students Lock in Verbal Sparring Match"; Witcover, *85 Days*, 165–66; and David Halberstam, *The Unfinished Odyssey of Robert Kennedy* (New York: Random House, 1968), 121.

52. Karl D. Henrichs, "Kennedy at University: 'Starvation Indecent,'" *Valparaiso Vidette-Messenger*, April 30, 1968, and Newfield, *Robert Kennedy*, 256.

53. Dolan Oral History Interview, Schlesinger Papers, Kennedy Library.

54. Cadou, "Kennedy, I.U. Medical Students Lock in Verbal Sparring Match"; "McHale Raps Kennedy's Use of Racism, Religion," *Indianapolis Star*, April 30, 1968; Joseph Kraft, "Kennedy, McCarthy Seen Just like 'New' Hoosiers," *Indianapolis Star*, April 28, 1968; and "20th Century or Bust," *Indianapolis Star*, April 28, 1968.

55. "Guests in the House!" *Indianapolis Star*, April 24, 1968; Ben Cole, "State Primary Victory Seen Hiking Chances," *Indianapolis Star*, April 29, 1968; "Is Indiana for Sale?" *New York Times*, April 30, 1968; and "Is Indiana for Sale? Asks New York Times," *Indianapolis Star*, May 1, 1968.

56. "Young Hoosiers Back 'Favorite Son' Branigin," *Indianapolis Star*, April 5, 1968; Salinger Oral History Interview, Kennedy Library; and "Salinger Scores Papers in Indiana," *New York Times*, May 6, 1968.

57. Frank Mankiewicz Oral History Interview, by Larry J. Hackman, December 16, 1969, Bethesda, Md., Kennedy Library.

58. Witcover, *85 Days*, 170–71, and "Kennedy Shuns 'Poor' March," *Indianapolis Star*, May 1, 1968.

59. Russell Pulliam, *Publisher: Gene Pulliam, Last of the Newspaper Titans* (Ottawa, Ill.: Jameson Books, 1984), 277.

6. The Voters Speak

1. Jack Newfield, *Robert Kennedy: A Memoir* (New York: E. P. Dutton and Co., 1969), 253.

2. Richard N. Goodwin, *Remembering America: A Voice from the Sixties* (Boston: Little, Brown and Co., 1988), 529; David Hackett Oral History Interview, by John W. Douglas, July 22, 1970, Washington, D.C., John F. Kennedy Presidential Library, Boston, Mass.; Jack Colwell, "RFK Calls for End to Injustice, Violence," *South Bend Tribune*, May 3, 1968; John Douglas Oral History Interview, by Larry J. Hackman,

June 24, 1969, Washington, D.C., Arthur M. Schlesinger Papers, John F. Kennedy Presidential Library, Boston, Mass.; and John Bartlow Martin, RFK Notes, June 28, 1968, John Bartlow Martin Papers, Library of Congress, Washington, D.C.

3. Warren Weaver Jr., "Democratic Indiana Race Growing Tighter with Kennedy Given Edge," *New York Times*, May 5, 1968, and Lawrence F. O'Brien, *No Final Victories: A Life in Politics—from John F. Kennedy to Watergate* (Garden City, N.Y.: Doubleday and Co., 1974), 235, 237–38.

4. Transcript, Lawrence F. O'Brien Oral History Interview XXII, by Michael L. Gillette, June 19, 1987, Lyndon Baines Johnson Presidential Library, Austin, Tex., and Undated Report on Telephone Campaign, David Hackett Papers, Kennedy Library.

5. Ibid.; Author telephone interview with Gerard Doherty, July 13, 2006; and Memo from Virginia Crume to Governor Roger Branigin, April 24, 1968, Roger D. Branigin Papers, B. F. Hamilton Library, Franklin College, Franklin, Ind.

6. Distribution of campaign material report, and Memo from Nick Zumas to Ted Kennedy, April 27, 1968, Hackett Papers, Kennedy Library.

7. Memo from Gerard Doherty to Ted Kennedy, April 21, 1968, Hackett Papers, Kennedy Library, and E. W. Kenworthy, "McCarthy Scores Kennedy Backers," *New York Times*, May 5, 1968.

8. Author interview with Michael Riley, April 18, 2006.

9. Jep Cadou Jr., "Branigin Plea to GOP: Cross Over, Support Me," *Indianapolis Star*, April 20, 1968; Roger D. Branigin Daily Journal, April 22, 1968, Branigin Papers, B. F. Hamilton Library; and "Republicans Can Help Make Sure Indiana Is Not Marked 'For Sale,'" *Indianapolis Star*, May 5, 1968.

10. Memo to Ted Kennedy from Gerard Doherty, April 20, 1968, Hackett Papers, Kennedy Library.

11. Warren Weaver Jr., "G.O.P. Crossover a Key to Voting in Indiana Today," *New York Times*, May 7, 1968.

12. "Kennedy Forces Check Machines," *Hammond Times*, May 5, 1968.

13. Letter from Margo Barnard to Governor Roger D. Branigin, May 6, 1968, Branigin Papers, B. F. Hamilton Library.

14. Weaver, "Democratic Indiana Race Growing Tighter with Kennedy Given Edge," *New York Times*, May 5, 1968; Dolores Liebeler, "400 Students Arrive to Aid M'Carthy," *South Bend Tribune*, May 5, 1968, and Arthur Herzog, *McCarthy for President* (New York: Viking, 1969), 142.

15. E. W. Kenworthy, "McCarthy Calls Indiana Crucial," *New York Times*, May 3, 1968.

16. Richard N. Goodwin, *Remembering America: A Voice from the Sixties* (Boston: Little, Brown and Co., 1988), 530–31.

17. Goodwin, *Remembering America*, 532; Joseph Dolan Oral History Interview, Arthur M. Schlesinger Papers, John F. Kennedy Presidential Library, Boston, Mass., and "Pro Athletes Join Bobby in Daylong Tour of City," *Indianapolis Star*, May 5, 1968.

18. Jules Witcover, *85 Days: The Last Campaign of Robert Kennedy* (New York: Quill, 1988), 173; Jack Newfield, *Robert Kennedy: A Memoir* (New York: E. P. Dutton and Co., 1969), 260; Robert Flynn, "'Undecided' Vote May Decide Demo Primary's 3-Way Race," *Evansville Press*, May 6, 1968; and Robert Flynn, "Kennedy Admits Gambles," *Evansville Press*, May 6, 1968.

19. Larry Allen, "Kennedy Tells Voters 'All Eyes' on Indiana," *Fort Wayne Journal-Gazette*, May 7, 1968, and Jerry Graff, "Answers to Poverty, Crime Needed: RFK," *Fort Wayne News-Sentinel*, May 7, 1968.

20. "Kennedy's Lunch before Leaving," *Fort Wayne News-Sentinel*, May 7, 1968, and Witcover, *85 Days*, 174.

21. "Two Contrasting Campaign Styles" and "View of 'Big League' Politicking," *LaPorte Herald-Argus*, May 7, 1968, and Witcover, *The Year the Dream Died: Revisiting 1968 in America* (New York: Warner Books, 1997), 197.

22. "Court Blocks Kennedy Film," *Evansville Courier*, May 7, 1968; Donald M. Wilson Oral History Interview, by Roberta W. Greene, June 19, 1970, New York, N.Y., John F. Kennedy Presidential Library, Boston, Mass.; and Joseph A. Palermo, *In His Own Right: The Political Odyssey of Robert F. Kennedy* (New York: Columbia University Press, 2001), 204–205.

23. Witcover, *85 Days*, 175, and Donald R. Kenyon, "Tired, Eager RFK Jibes Crossings, Air Pollution," *Hammond Times*, May 7, 1968.

24. Author telephone interview with Gerard Doherty, July 13, 2006.

25. Witcover, *The Year the Dream Died*, 199.

26. Douglas Oral History Interview, Schlesinger Papers; Newfield, *Somebody's Gotta Tell It: The Upbeat Memoir of a Working-Class Journalist* (New York: St. Martin's, 2002), 199; and Newfield, *Robert Kennedy*, 261.

27. Douglas Oral History Interview, Schlesinger Papers, and Witcover, *The Year the Dream Died*, 200.

28. "Teamsters, Gary Negro Group Indorse [*sic*] Branigin," *Indianapolis Star*, May 7, 1968; Robert Mooney, "Governor Thinks Undecided Vote Is 'A Good Sign,'" *Indianapolis Star*, May 7, 1968; "McCarthy Hike Ends Campaign," *Indianapolis Star*, May 7, 1968; and Jeremy Larner, *Nobody Knows: Reflections on the McCarthy Campaign of 1968* (New York: Macmillan, 1969), 84.

29. Frank Mankiewicz Oral History Interview, by Larry J. Hackman, December 16, 1969, Bethesda, Md., John F. Kennedy Presidential Library, Boston, Mass.

30. Newfield, *Somebody's Gotta Tell It*, 200.

31. Newfield, *Robert Kennedy*, 263; Memo to Ted Sorenson, Tom Johnston, Dun Gifford from Pierre Salinger, May 8, 1968, Robert F. Kennedy 1968 Presidential Campaign Papers, Kennedy Library; and Witcover, *85 Days*, 180–81.

32. William vanden Heuvel and Milton Gwirtzman, *On His Own: Robert F. Kennedy, 1964–1968* (Garden City, N.Y.: Doubleday and Co., 1970), 348n., 349, and Jack Colwell, "McCarthy Hopes Are Kept Alive," *South Bend Tribune*, May 8, 1968. For a discussion of the issue, see also Ronald Steel, *In Love with Night: The American Romance with Robert Kennedy* (New York: Simon and Schuster, 2000), 175–76.

33. Newfield, *Robert Kennedy*, 263–64.

34. Witcover, *85 Days*, 179, and John Herbers, "'Vote for Change' Seen by Kennedy," *New York Times*, May 8, 1968.

35. Gerard Doherty Oral History Interview, by Larry J. Hackman, February 3, 1972, Boston, Mass., Kennedy Library, and author interview with Michael Riley, April 18, 2006.

36. Harrison J. Ullmann, "Kennedy Thanks All Who Helped," *Indianapolis Star*, May 8, 1968, and author interview with Riley.

37. RFK Notes, Martin Papers, Library of Congress.

38. "Kennedy Scores Solid Victory in Crucial Indiana Primary," *Evansville Courier*, May 8, 1968; Robert P. Mooney, "Kennedy Wins with 42 Percent," *Indianapolis Star*, May 8, 1968; and "Kennedy Surges to Clear Victory," *LaPorte Herald-Argus*, May 8, 1968.

39. Larner, *Nobody Knows*, 84–85; E. W. Kenworthy, "McCarthy Looking Ahead, Says He Won't 'Dismiss the Troops,'" *New York Times*, May 8, 1968; and Richard T. Stout, *People* (New York: Harper and Row, 1970), 236.

40. E. W. Kenworthy, "M'Carthy Aides Review Campaign," *New York Times*, May 9, 1968.

41. Newfield, *Robert Kennedy*, 264–65, and Stout, *People*, 237.

42. Tom Wicker, "The Impact of Indiana," *New York Times*, May 8, 1968; Newfield, *Somebody's Gotta Tell It*, 201, and Newfield, *Robert Kennedy*, 265. Kennedy had an often testy relationship with the *New York Times*. He complained to Newfield that when he had been named as John F. Kennedy's campaign manager in 1960, the newspaper said he was "too immature and inexperienced" for the job. When his brother appointed him as attorney general, the *Times* again said he was too inexperienced, although he had done a good job as campaign manager. They used the same reasoning, he said, when he ran for the U.S. Senate in New York against Republican Kenneth Keating. Now, in his race for the president, the newspaper criticized him on its editorial page while saying he had been a good senator. "They always admit I was effective in every job I've ever had," said Kennedy, "but that never affects their judgment, and each time they say I'm not qualified for the next job." When Kennedy had announced his decision to run against Keating, the *Times* had endorsed the GOP candidate, saying in an editorial that Kennedy inspired "an uneasiness that is no less real because it is elusive and difficult to define." Kennedy, in a takeoff on a series of ads run by the newspaper promoting its effectiveness in finding people jobs in its want ads, commented: "At least they can never say I got my job through the *New York Times*." See Newfield, *Somebody's Gotta Tell It*, 201–202, and Arthur M. Schlesinger Jr., *Robert Kennedy and His Times* (Boston: Houghton Mifflin Co., 1978), 669.

7. The Train

1. Jean Stein and George Plimpton, *American Journey: The Times of Robert Kennedy* (New York: Harcourt Brace Jovanovich, 1970), 5–6; Russell Baker, "They Line the Tracks to Say Good-by," *New York Times*, June 9, 1968; and J. Anthony Lukas, "Thousands in Last Tribune to Kennedy; Service at Arlington Is Held at Night," *New York Times*, June 9, 1968.

2. Arthur M. Schlesinger Jr., *Robert Kennedy and His Times* (Boston: Houghton Mifflin, 1978), 888–89, 914; Eugene McCarthy, *The Year of the People* (Garden City, N.Y.: Doubleday and Co., 1969), 143; Jules Witcover, *85 Days: The Last Campaign of Robert Kennedy* (New York: Quill, 1988), 198; and John Bartlow Martin, RFK Notes, June 29, 1968, Martin Papers, Library of Congress, Washington, D.C.

3. McCarthy, *The Year of the People*, 149; William vanden Heuvel and Milton Gwirtzman, *On His Own: Robert F. Kennedy, 1964–1968* (Garden City, N.Y.: Doubleday and Co., 1970), 367; Witcover, *85 Days*, 202, 206; Brian Dooley, *Robert Kennedy:*

The Final Years (New York: St. Martin's, 1996), 129; and Schlesinger, *Robert Kennedy and His Times*, 907.

4. Charles Kaiser, *1968 in America: Music, Politics, Chaos, Counterculture, and the Shaping of a Generation* (New York: Grove Press, 1988), 179; RFK Notes, Martin Papers; and Stein and Plimpton, *American Journey*, 311–12.

5. Stein and Plimpton, *American Journey*, 312, 314; Dennis Wainstock, *The Turning Point: The 1968 United States Presidential Campaign* (Jefferson, N.C.: McFarland and Co., 1988), 84; Jeremy Larner, *Nobody Knows: Reflections on the McCarthy Campaign of 1968* (New York: Macmillan, 1969), 117; Kaiser, *1968 in America*, 180; and RFK Notes, Martin Papers.

6. RFK Notes, Martin Papers; Wainstock, *The Turning Point*, 84–85; Lester David and Irene David, *Bobby Kennedy: The Making of a Folk Hero* (New York: Dodd, Mead and Co., 1986), 316; and Richard N. Goodwin, *Remembering America: A Voice from the Sixties* (Boston: Little, Brown and Co., 1988), 536–37.

7. Memo from John Bartlow Martin to Robert F. Kennedy, June 3, 1968, Martin Papers.

8. Jack Newfield, *Robert Kennedy: A Memoir* (New York: E. P. Dutton and Co., 1969), 297; Larner, *Nobody Knows*, 121; Wallace Turner, "The Shooting: A Victory Celebration That Ended with Shots, Screams and Curses," *New York Times*, June 6, 1968; Newfield, *Robert Kennedy*, 300; RFK Notes, Martin Papers; and Gladwin Hill, "Kennedy Is Dead, Victim of Assassin," *New York Times*, June 6, 1968.

9. RFK Notes, Martin Papers; and Donal Henahan, "Young Campaign Workers 'Lost,'" *New York Times*, June 7, 1968.

10. Lukas, "Thousands in Last Tribute to Kennedy," *New York Times*, and Senator Edward M. Kennedy, Eulogy, June 8, 1968, in Pierre Salinger, Edwin Guthman, Frank Mankiewicz, and John Seigenthaler, eds., *"An Honorable Profession": A Tribute to Robert F. Kennedy* (Garden City, N.Y.: Doubleday and Co., 1968), 3.

11. Stein and Plimpton, *American Journey*, 32; Baker, "They Line the Tracks to Say Good-by," *New York Times*; and Martin, *It Seems like Only Yesterday: Memoirs of Writing, Presidential Politics, and the Diplomatic Life* (New York: William Morrow and Co., 1986), 306.

12. John Herbers, "Many in Capital Throng Had Cheered Kennedy," *New York Times*, June 9, 1968, and "Robert F. Kennedy Memorial," Arlington National Cemetery website, http://www.arlingtoncemetery.org/visitor_information/Robert_F_Kennedy .html (accessed June 9, 2007).

13. Larner, *Nobody Knows*, 124, and Albert Eisele, *Almost to the Presidency: A Biography of Two American Politicians* (Blue Earth, Minn.: Piper Co., 1972), 338–41.

14. Lewis L. Gould, *1968: The Election That Changed America* (Chicago: Ivan R. Dee, 1993), 127–29; Lewis Chester, Godfrey Hodgson, and Bruce Page, *An American Melodrama: The Presidential Campaign of 1968* (New York: Viking, 1969), 521; Tom Wicker, "Humphrey Nominated on the First Ballot after His Plank on Vietnam Is Approved," *New York Times*, August 30, 1968; and Eisele, *Almost to the Presidency*, 357.

15. Kaiser, *1968 in America*, 241; Wicker, "Humphrey Nominated on the First Ballot after His Plank on Vietnam Is Approved," *New York Times*; "Delegates Protest 'Police Terror'; Tries to Get Convention Moved," *Indianapolis Star*, August 29, 1968; Chester, Hodgson, and Page, *An American Melodrama*, 581; and Martin, *It Seems like Only Yesterday*, 308.

16. Kaiser, *1968 in America*, 241; "Humphrey Given 49 Indiana Votes," *Indianapolis Star*, and Andy Jacobs Jr., *Slander and Sweet Judgment: The Memoir of an Indiana Congressman* (Indianapolis: Guild Press of Indiana, 2000), 142.

17. Eisele, *Almost to the Presidency*, 332–33, and Gould, *1968*, 161–62.

18. RFK Notes, Martin Papers, and Jules Witcover, *85 Days: The Last Campaign of Robert Kennedy* (New York: Quill, 1988), 341–42.

19. Vanden Heuvel and Gwirtzman, *On His Own*, 382–83; Kaiser, *1968 in America*, 216; and Chester, Hodgson, and Page, *An American Melodrama*, 573.

20. Stein and Plimpton, *American Journey*, 237; Schlesinger, *Robert Kennedy and His Times*, 915; and Jack Newfield, *Robert Kennedy: A Memoir* (New York: E. P. Dutton and Co., 1969), 303–304.

21. Mary Beth Schneider, "President Clinton's Visit Commemorates the Night Blacks, Whites Came Together to Rise above the Potential for Violence," *Indianapolis Star*, May 14, 1994, and Kathleen M. Johnston and Jon Schwantes, "Clinton Visit Spurs Memories," *Indianapolis News*, May 13, 1994.

22. Jon Schwantes and John Krull, "Clinton Issues Call for Change," *Indianapolis News*, May 14, 1994, and Kim L. Hooper, "Ceremony Awakens Memories of Tragedy and Triumph," *Indianapolis Star*, May 15, 1994.

23. Diana Penner, "King-RFK Sculpture Design Unveiled," *Indianapolis Star*, January 15, 1995, and David Hoppe, "Honoring the Peacemakers," *Nuvo Newsweekly*, January 10, 2007.

24. Hoppe, "Honoring the Peacemakers," *Nuvo Newsweekly*.

25. Rob Schneider, "Attention Promised for Peace Memorial," *Indianapolis Star*, April 3, 2005, and Hooper, "Ceremony Awakens Memories of Tragedy and Triumph," *Indianapolis Star*.

Selected Bibliography

Manuscript Collections

John F. Kennedy Presidential Library, Boston, Mass.
Peter Edelman Papers
K. Dun Gifford Papers
David Hackett Papers
William vanden Heuvel Papers
Kirby Jones Papers
Robert F. Kennedy 1968 Presidential Campaign Papers
Arthur M. Schlesinger Papers
Theodore White Papers

Manuscript Division, Library of Congress, Washington, D.C.
John Bartlow Martin Papers

Archives and Special Collections, Ball State University, Muncie, Ind.
Robert F. Kennedy Muncie Speech Collection

B. F. Hamilton Library, Franklin College, Franklin, Ind.
Roger D. Branigin Papers

Oral History Interviews

John F. Kennedy Presidential Library, Boston, Mass.
Doherty, Gerard. February 3, 1972

Douglas, John. June 24, 1969
Greenfield, Jeff. December 10, 1969
Haddad, William. February 27, 1969
Mankiewicz, Frank. December 16, 1969
Salinger, Pierre. April 18, 1970
Tolan, James. June 26, 1969
Wade, Dr. Richard. December 13, 1973
Walinsky, Adam. December 4, 1974
Wilson, Donald M. June 19, 1970

Lyndon Baines Johnson Presidential Library, Austin, Tex.

Bayh, Birch. February 12, 1969
O'Brien, Lawrence. June 19, 1987

Manuscript Division, Indiana State Library, Indianapolis

Branigin, Roger D. October 19, 1971

Author Interviews

Conn, Earl. November 15, 2005
Doherty, Gerard. July 13, 2006
Evans, Mary. June 21, 2006
Jacobs, Andrew, Jr. October 18, 2005
Kendall, Michael. July 20, 2006
Mahern, Louie. November 14, 2005
Munn, Bill. March 28, 2006
Riley, Michael. April 18, 2006
St. Angelo, Gordon. July 13, 2006

Newspapers

Ball State Daily News
Chicago Daily News
Chicago Sun-Times
Evansville Courier
Fort Wayne Journal-Gazette
Fort Wayne News-Sentinel
Indianapolis News
Indianapolis Star
Indianapolis Times
Lafayette Journal and Courier
LaPorte Herald-Argus
Louisville Courier-Journal
Muncie Star

New York Times
Nuvo Newsweekly
Peru Daily Tribune
South Bend Tribune
Valparaiso Vidette-Messenger
Wabash Plain Dealer

Books

Beifuss, Joan Turner. *At the River I Stand: Memphis, the 1968 Strike, and Martin Luther King.* Brooklyn, N.Y.: Carlson Publishing, 1989.

Beran, Michael Knox. *The Last Patrician: Bobby Kennedy and the End of American Aristocracy.* New York: St. Martin's, 1998.

Busby, Horace. *The Thirty-first of March: An Intimate Portrait of Lyndon Johnson's Final Days in Office.* New York: Farrar, Straus and Giroux, 2005.

Califano, Joseph A., Jr. *The Triumph and Tragedy of Lyndon Johnson.* New York: Simon and Schuster, 1991.

Chafe, William H. *Never Stop Running: Allard Lowenstein and the Struggle to Save American Liberalism.* New York: Basic Books, 1993.

Chester, Lewis, Godfrey Hodgson, and Bruce Page. *An American Melodrama: The Presidential Campaign of 1968.* New York: Viking, 1969.

Clifford, Clark, with Richard Holbrooke. *Counsel to the President: A Memoir.* New York: Random House, 1991.

Connor, Lawrence S. "Bo." *Star in the Hoosier Sky: The* Indianapolis Star *in the Years the City Came Alive, 1950–1990.* Carmel, Ind.: Hawthorne Publishing, 2006.

David, Lester, and Irene David. *Bobby Kennedy: The Making of a Folk Hero.* New York: Dodd, Mead and Co., 1986.

Dooley, Brian. *Robert Kennedy: The Final Years.* New York: St. Martin's, 1996.

Eisele, Albert. *Almost to the Presidency: A Biography of Two American Politicians.* Blue Earth, Minn.: Piper Co., 1972.

Goodwin, Richard N. *Remembering America: A Voice from the Sixties.* Boston: Little, Brown and Co., 1988.

Gould, Lewis L. *1968: The Election That Changed America.* Chicago: Ivan R. Dee, 1993.

Gray, Ralph D. *Indiana's Favorite Sons: 1840–1940.* Indianapolis: Indiana Historical Society, 1988.

Gugin, Linda, and James E. St. Clair, eds. *The Governors of Indiana.* Indianapolis: Indiana Historical Society Press, 2006.

Guthman, Edwin O., and C. Richard Allen, eds. *RFK: Collected Speeches.* New York: Viking, 1993.

Halberstam, David. *The Unfinished Odyssey of Robert Kennedy.* New York: Random House, 1968.

Heath, Jim F. *Decade of Disillusionment: The Kennedy-Johnson Years.* Bloomington: Indiana University Press, 1975.

Heuvel, William vanden, and Milton Gwirtzman. *On His Own: Robert F. Kennedy, 1964–1968.* Garden City, N.Y.: Doubleday and Co., 1970.

Herzog, Arthur. *McCarthy for President.* New York: Viking, 1969.

Humphrey, Hubert H. *The Education of a Public Man: My Life and Politics.* Garden City, N.Y.: Doubleday and Co., 1976.

Jacobs, Andy, Jr. *Slander and Sweet Judgment: The Memoirs of an Indiana Congressman.* Indianapolis: Guild Press of Indiana, 2000.

Johnson, Lyndon Baines. *The Vantage Point: Perspectives of the Presidency, 1963–1969.* New York: Holt, Rinehart, and Winston, 1971.

Kaiser, Charles. *1968 in America: Music, Politics, Chaos, Counterculture, and the Shaping of a Generation.* New York: Grove Press, 1988.

Karnow, Stanley. *Vietnam: A History.* New York: Viking, 1983.

Kearns, Doris. *Lyndon Johnson and the American Dream.* New York: Harper and Row, 1976.

Keating, Tom. *Indiana Faces and Other Places.* Indianapolis: Indiana Only Press, 1982.

King, Coretta Scott. *My Life with Martin Luther King, Jr.* New York: Henry Holt and Co., 1993.

LaFeber, Walter. *The Deadly Bet: LBJ, Vietnam, and the 1968 Election.* Lanham, Md.: Rowman and Littlefield, 2005.

Lane, James B. *"City of the Century": A History of Gary, Indiana.* Bloomington: Indiana University Press, 1978.

Larner, Jeremy. *Nobody Knows: Reflections on the McCarthy Campaign of 1968.* New York: Macmillan, 1969.

Lewis, John, with Michael D'Orso. *Walking with the Wind: A Memoir of the Movement.* New York: Simon and Schuster, 1998.

Martin, John Bartlow. *Indiana: An Interpretation.* 1947. Bloomington: Indiana University Press, 1992.

———. *It Seems like Only Yesterday: Memoirs of Writing, Presidential Politics, and the Diplomatic Life.* New York: William Morrow and Co., 1986.

McCarthy, Abigail. *Private Faces/Public Places.* Garden City, N.Y.: Doubleday and Co., 1972.

McCarthy, Eugene F. *The Year of the People.* Garden City, N.Y.: Doubleday and Co., 1969.

McDonald, William P., and Jerry G. Smoke. *The Peasants' Revolt: McCarthy 1968.* Mount Vernon, Ohio: Noe-Bixby Publications, 1969.

McQuaid, Kim. *The Anxious Years: America in the Vietnam-Watergate Era.* New York: Basic Books, 1989.

Newfield, Jack. *Robert Kennedy: A Memoir.* New York: E. P. Dutton and Co., 1969.

———. *Somebody's Gotta Tell It: The Upbeat Memoir of a Working-Class Journalist.* New York: St. Martin's, 2002.

Oberdorfer, Don. *Tet! The Turning Point in the Vietnam War.* Baltimore: Johns Hopkins University Press, 2001.

O'Brien, Lawrence F. *No Final Victories: A Life in Politics—from John F. Kennedy to Watergate.* Garden City, N.Y.: Doubleday and Co., 1974.

Palermo, Joseph A. *In His Own Right: The Political Odyssey of Senator Robert F. Kennedy.* New York: Columbia University Press, 2001.

Powers, Thomas. *Vietnam: The War at Home; Vietnam and the American People, 1964–1968.* Boston: G. K. Hall and Co., 1984.

Salinger, Pierre, Edwin Guthman, Frank Mankiewicz, and John Seigenthaler, eds. *"An Honorable Profession": A Tribune to Robert F. Kennedy*. Garden City, N.Y.: Doubleday and Co., 1968.

Sandbrook, Dominic. *Eugene McCarthy: The Rise and Fall of Postwar American Liberalism*. New York: Alfred A. Knopf, 2004.

Schlesinger, Arthur, Jr. *Robert Kennedy and His Times*. Boston: Houghton Mifflin Co., 1978.

Shesol, Jeff. *Mutual Contempt: Lyndon Johnson, Robert Kennedy, and the Feud That Defined a Decade*. New York: W. W. Norton and Co., 1997.

Stavis, Ben. *We Were the Campaign: New Hampshire to Chicago for McCarthy*. Boston: Beacon Press, 1969.

Steel, Ronald. *In Love with Night: The American Romance with Robert Kennedy*. New York: Simon and Schuster, 2000.

Stein, Jean, and George Plimpton. *American Journey: The Times of Robert Kennedy*. New York: Harcourt Brace Jovanovich, 1970.

Stout, Richard T. *People*. New York: Harper and Row, 1970.

Thomas, Evan. *Robert Kennedy: His Life*. New York: Simon and Schuster, 2000.

Wainstock, Dennis. *The Turning Point: The 1968 United States Presidential Campaign*. Jefferson, N.C.: McFarland and Co., 1988.

Welsh, Matthew E. *View from the State House: Recollections and Reflections, 1961–1965*. Indianapolis: Indiana Historical Bureau, 1981.

Witcover, Jules. *85 Days: The Last Campaign of Robert Kennedy*. New York: Quill, 1988.

———. *The Year the Dream Died: Revisiting 1968 in America*. New York: Warner Books, 1997.

Woods, Randall B. *LBJ: Architect of American Ambition*. New York: Free Press, 2006.

Articles and Dissertations

Anatol, Karl W., and John R. Bittner. "Kennedy on King: The Rhetoric of Control." *Today's Speech* 16, no. 3 (1968): 31–34.

Beasley, John. "Roger Branigin. Governor of Indiana: The View from Within" (Ph.D. diss., Ball State University, 1973.

Boomhower, Ray E. "A Landmark for Peace." *Traces of Indiana and Midwestern History* 11 (Winter 1999): 46–48.

———. "A Voice for Those from Below: John Bartlow Martin, Reporter." *Traces of Indiana and Midwestern History* 9 (Spring 1997): 4–13.

Devorkin, Michael Stuart. "Kennedy Campaigning in Primary States: Presidential Politics and Democratic Party Organizations and Leaders." Master's thesis, Massachusetts Institute of Technology, June 1969.

Farmer, James E. "The Individual Roger: Governor Branigin and the News Media." *Traces of Indiana and Midwestern History* 4 (Spring 1992): 24–33.

———. "1968 Presidential Primary: Reluctant 'Favorite Son' Faces Kennedy and McCarthy." Unpublished manuscript in author's collection.

Welsh, Matthew E. "Civil Rights and the Primary Election of 1964 in Indiana: The Wallace Challenge." *Indiana Magazine of History* 75 (March 1979): 1–27.

Index

Ray E. Boomhower is the author of numerous books and articles on Indiana history, including *Jacob Piatt Dunn, Jr.: A Life in History and Politics, 1855–1924* and *Destination Indiana: Travels through Hoosier History*. He is also the senior editor of *Traces of Indiana and Midwestern History*, the quarterly magazine of the Indiana Historical Society.